Immigration, Citizenship, and the Welfare State in Germany and the United States: Welfare Policies and Immigrants' Citizenship

INDUSTRIAL DEVELOPMENT AND THE SOCIAL FABRIC, VOLUME 14 (PART B)

editor: John P. McKay, Department of History
University of Illinois

Industrial Development
And The Social Fabric
An International Series of Historical Monographs

Edited by John P. McKay
Department of History
University of Illinois

Immigration, Citizenship, and the Welfare State in Germany and the United States: Welfare Policies and Immigrants' Citizenship

Edited by HERMANN KURTHEN

State University of New York, Stony Brook

JÜRGEN FIJALKOWSKI

Freie Universität Berlin

and GERT G. WAGNER

*German Institute for Economic Research, Berlin
and Viadrina European University, Frankfurt (Oder)*

 JAI PRESS INC.

Stamford, Connecticut   *London, England*

Library of Congress Cataloging-in-Publication Data

Immigration, citizenship, and the welfare state in Germany and the
    United States : immigrant incorporation / edited by Hermann Kurthen,
    Jürgen Fijalkowski, and Gert G. Wagner.

JAI PRESS LTD.
        p.   cm. — (Industrial development and the social fabric ; 14,

38 Tavistock Street
Covent Garden   graphical references and index.
London WC2E 7PB   467-7 (set). — ISBN 0-7623-0523-1 (pt. A). — ISBN
England   it. B)
            -Emigration and immigration—Government policy.
    2.   United States—Emigration and immigration—Government policy.
    3.   Immigrants—Government policy—Germany.   4.   Immigrants—
Government policy—United States.   5.   Social integration—Germany,
    6.   Social integration—United States.   7.   Social work with
immigrants—Germany.   8.   Social work with immigrants—United States.
    I.   Kurthen, Hermann.   II.   Fijalkowski, Jürgen.   III.   Wagner, Gert.
    IV.   Series.
JV8033.I56   1998
323.1'43—dc21   98-30666
                                                                    CIP

Copyright © 1998 JAI PRESS INC
100 Prospect Street
Stamford, Connecticut 06901-1640

Printed and bound by Antony Rowe Ltd, Eastbourne

Transferred to digital print on demand, 2005

ISBN: 0-7623-0524-X (Part B)
ISBN: 0-7623-0467-7 (Set)

Manufactured in the United States of America

CONTENTS

SECTION II.
CITIZENSHIP AND IMMIGRANT INCORPORATION

Contents   ix

PART A. IMMIGRANT INCORPORATION ACKNOWLEDGMENTS

SECTION I.
INCORPORATION INTO EDUCATION AND SCHOOL

SECTION II.
LABOR MARKET INTEGRATION AND ATTAINMENT

SECTION III.
ALLOCATION OF FISCAL BENEFITS AND CONTRIBUTIONS

LIST OF TABLES (PART B)

LIST OF FIGURES (PART B)

ACKNOWLEDGMENTS

Hermann Kurthen gratefully acknowledges the support of the German Marshall Fund of the United States (Grants #A-0243-01 and A-0371) for the conference he organized at which the research published herein was first reported. In addition, money from the German Institute for Economic Research Berlin (*Deutsches Institut für Wirtschaftsforschung*), and technical support from the Freie Universität Berlin were crucial to successfully complete the Berlin conference in December 1996 and cover costs for translation, proofreading, and indexing. The editors are also very grateful to Carol S. Lindquist at the State University of New York, Stony Brook, who helped prepare the index and proofread, and to Kay Losey, Writing Program director, State University of New York at Stony Brook, for her comments and support on various drafts of the introduction and summary. Jennifer Drolet's help in reading and correcting drafts at the Institute for Research in Social Science, University of North Carolina, was important to the timely completion of the first round of this project. Last but not least we appreciate the support of the staff of JAI Press.

INTRODUCTION

Hermann Kurthen, Jürgen Fijalkowski, and Gert G. Wagner

This is Part B of the volume *Immigration, Citizenship, and the Welfare State in Germany and the United States*, edited by Kurthen, Fijalkowski, and Wagner. Whereas the first part presented the most recent findings for both societies in three important areas of immigrant incorporation, that is, education, labor markets, and the welfare system, Part B investigates the importance of citizenship policies to fostering the inclusion of immigrants into their respective host country. Contributions in the first section, titled *Immigration Policy and Welfare Reform at the Crossroads*, concentrate on current efforts to reform the welfare system, particularly in the United States, and their relationship with or impact on immigrant policies, immigrant behavior, and the actual flow of migrants. In the final section, *Citizenship and Immigrant Incorporation*, of the two-part volume, the impact of new political environments, political cultures, institutionalized rules of citizenship, and prevailing ideologies on the current reformulation of the relationship between immigrants and native-born citizens, including the migrants' opportunities to promote their interests, will be analyzed. This part ends with concluding remarks by the editors about the present challenges of immigration policy and welfare reform in a comparative perspective.

Demleitner examines the problematic relation between immigration policy and welfare reform. She describes the drive to drastically restrict

1

welfare benefits even for permanent legal residents, starting with the passage of Proposition 187 in California and continuing with the "Personal Responsibility and Work Opportunity Reconciliation Act" of 1996. Both initiatives also seek the self-deportation of undocumented immigrants by denying them the welfare benefits that allegedly brought them to the United States and established a "culture of dependency." By comparing prevailing attitudes and the different strategies taken by the "border" states of Texas and California, *Demleitner* analyzes why immigrants lack the power to change the predominant views or resist the deprivation of their rights in the political arena. She concludes that the composition, political cohesiveness, participation in public affairs, and relative voting strength of immigrant communities has a strong impact on the outcome of current welfare reform. America could learn from Europe's policy of immigrant integration with regard to limited voting rights and comparatively extensive welfare rights for residents to avoid further erosion of immigrant rights.

Espenshade and *Huber* also examine the effects of the retrenchment in U.S. welfare legislation on immigrants and refugees. In addition to *Demleitner's* detailed description of political factors behind the full-blown national assault on all immigrants irrespective of their legal status, *Van Hook* and *Bean's* (Part A) disclosure of the American policymakers' intention to cut SSI means-tested benefits and to tighten eligibility criteria among noncitizens in favor of balanced budget objectives, and Kurthen's (Part A) warnings against the long-term effects of reforming public finances at the expense of the weakest members of society, Espenshade and Huber characterize current U.S. welfare reform policies as the result of a convergence of three trends: established anti-immigrant sentiments, the fiscal imperatives of balanced-budget conservatism, and the ascendancy of dependency politics to exclude the "undeserving" poor. Having little or no voice in the electorate and trapped by the forces of budgetary opportunism and political expediency, immigrants have increasingly become an attractive target for many policymakers seeking windfall gains for the federal treasury.

Parrillo's chapter compares and analyzes changes in public opinion about immigration and diversity in Germany and the United States over time. According to the author, immigrants' "alienness" in the eyes of the native born is a historical as well as transitory phenomenon, and the assumed homogeneity of host societies is a myth and an ethnogenetic phenomenon evolving over time. In Parrillo's view, past and present immigration has had an overall positive effect on both Germany and the United States. Immigrants bring considerable human, economic, social, and cultural capital which can benefit the host society and relations between the receiving country and the country of origin.

Hollifield and *Zuk* discuss the impact of noneconomic factors and normative political ideas about government intervention on the actual development of migrant flows. Since the late 1950s migration to the United States and Western Europe, which supposedly follows the business cycle to large degree, has substantially deviated from predictions. According to Hollifield and Zuk, factors such as the existence of a fragile coalition in Congress between left-liberal and human rights advocates and economic libertarian-conservatives who favor opening up international markets can explain the greater openness in U.S. immigration policy in past decades. Only recently has the so-called rights-market (trade) coalition dissolved, giving way to a new restrictionism. As the cold war waned—along with American hegemony—it became more difficult to sustain prior policies. It is now harder to sell free trade and admissionist immigration policies on the basis of rights (a more just and open world order) or markets (greater efficiency in labor markets). Politicians are now more sensitive to the distributional (as opposed to the allocational) consequences of immigration which has also led to new isolationist and protectionist tendencies in both domestic and foreign policy. Hollifield and Zuk argue that in other Western democracies similar processes and "rights-market" coalitions and breakups have taken place, marking a convergence of immigration policy among OECD countries with unclear global consequences for a possible revival of a new, liberal period of worldwide immigration.

In the next section concerning the significance of citizenship policies to immigrant incorporation, *Schmitter-Heisler* criticizes the current comparative literature on immigration and immigrant incorporation, because it suffers from the absence of a comprehensive comparative model that would allow more systematic comparisons of incorporation. She refers to a multidimensional U.S. model developed by Portes (1995), which identifies 12 different contexts of incorporation and three levels of reception: the level of government policy toward different immigrant groups (e.g., refugees, asylum seekers, and legal immigrants), the level of civic society and public opinion, and the characteristics of ethnic communities. Each level is seen to be relatively independent of the others. Whereas much of the existing literature focuses on the reception level of immigration policies, Schmitter-Heisler, in accordance with Portes, calls attention to the need to examine the independent effects of the levels of "civic society and public opinion" and "immigrant community" in both the United States and Germany. She concludes that greater state penetration in Germany creates more linkages between levels but fewer contexts for immigrant incorporation, thus restricting their range of opportunity structures to a greater extent than in the United States. The United States, on the other hand, proves to be less receptive than is often assumed, despite the relatively easy access to political citizenship. Because of lack of immigrant incorporation policies and the dominance of market forces, immigrants in America face social inequalities and economic risks unknown to foreigners in Germany.

Dittgen analyzes the significance of ideological conceptions for the formulation of immigrant policies and citizenship law. He focuses on the paradigms shaping debates in the United States and Germany and maintains that perceptions of national identity, collective memories, and expectations about diversity, unity, and liberties guide current debates and policies. Whereas conventional wisdom holds that the United States traditionally defines itself as a country of immigration and Germany as an ethnically defined nation, Dittgen asserts that in fact these trends have reversed. In the German immigration debate a strong Republican element has emerged in accordance with the *ius soli* principle and easier naturalization. In the United States the current debate is very much determined by a new nationalism. Intellectuals and journalists succeed with nativist arguments against immigration, construct an American identity as a *"Kulturnation,"* and argue for a need to protect American workers by proposing zero immigration. So far the liberal, republican strain in German political thinking has not been sufficiently translated into the legal system. On the other hand, American self-perception as a country of immigration is a myth: a non-exclusionary and nonracist liberal immigration policy has only materialized over the last 30 years but is now threatened again in times of crisis.

Kvistad deals with the question of whether expanded denizenship can compensate for a lack of political rights. He invokes T. H. Marshall's classic essay on "aspects" of citizenship to argue that full membership in a modern community cannot occur without political rights, that without political rights an individual's civil and social rights are vulnerable, and that full membership in a community is a product of political struggle and institutional reform and not bureaucratic largesse. Turning to Germany he argues that the nineteenth-century roots of the German welfare state had less to do with the extension of full community membership than with the effort of the state to control its subjects. Similarly, while generous welfare benefits are currently available to the Federal Republic's foreign residents, restrictive citizenship and naturalization laws (though recently reformed) have made the acquisition of political citizenship rare and frequently onerous for "ethnic non-Germans." This has prevented large numbers of people currently living in Germany from experiencing the democratic expansion of the "superstructure of legitimate expectations"—as German citizens have done in the past 30 years—that Marshall regards as part of the experience of full membership in a community.

Fijalkowski deals with the evaluation and the prospects of amendments to reform German citizenship regulations. He maintains that in modern nation-states political incorporation of individual migrants and resident aliens can follow different paths of in- or exclusion. This depends on a country's ability to deal with increasing ethnocultural diversity within the context of intensified transnational mobility. Two main types of incorporation can be distinguished: the individualist market approach and the communitarian state approach. Germany falls into the welfare state category with a strong communitarian orientation regarding citizenship and naturalization. The author argues that under circumstances where globalization of exchange and mobility is matched by decreased governing capabilities of the traditional nation-states, the real test for each of the incorporation models is in regaining governance capacities on a higher, supra-national level. Following the model of European integration, a traditional, "lesser," nation-state, incorporation model is distinguished from a post-national, "greater," integration path. In the latter all union member-state citizens ideally gain freedom of movement and access to common supra-national citizenship rights and comparable welfare entitlements. But this is only possible on condition of the development of a common political culture of pluralism and tolerance and only after successful, mutual adjustments of the public economies and national welfare systems.

The volume ends with concluding remarks about the compatibility of the welfare state and liberal immigration policies and the efficiency of immigrant incorporation policies and citizenship regimes. The editors summarize the common experiences, strategies, and challenges that the American and German societies face, or areas in which both nations could learn from each other. The answers that both societies give and the political solutions they find will determine the future of coming generations and the kind of societies and polities people will live in tomorrow.

REFERENCE

Portes, A. 1995. "Economic Sociology and the Sociology of Immigration: A Conceptual Overview." Pp. 1-41 in *The Economic Sociology of Immigration: Essays on Networks, Ethnicity and Entrepreneurship*, edited by A. Portes. New York: Russell Sage Foundation.

SECTION I

IMMIGRATION POLICY AND WELFARE REFORM AT THE CROSSROADS

POWER, PERCEPTIONS, AND THE POLITICS OF IMMIGRATION AND WELFARE

Nora V. Demleitner

Since the late 1980s increasing anti-immigrant sentiment has character-ized public discourse in the United States and Western Europe. In the United States the dominant perception of immigrants as nonworking beneficiaries, or even abusers, of a generous welfare system has over-shadowed any reasoned debate about immigration. The controversy about immigration has coalesced with a larger debate about the viability and purpose of existing welfare and social security systems in a time of perceived economic decline. As a consequence the anti-immigrant mood in the American population and in the state and federal legislatures has largely focused on depriving immigrants—documented and undocu-mented—of welfare rights. This development stands in stark contrast with the situation in European countries where the immigration debate has primarily emphasized restrictive admission policies, even though the welfare systems tend to be more extensive than in the United States. In Germany, for example, welfare rights for immigrants are an issue only with regard to asylum-seekers, while generally the focus has been on numbers of immigrants, naturalization requirements, and the methods by which citizenship can be acquired.

In 1996 the U.S. Congress fused the two issues—welfare and immigration—in the Personal Responsibility and Work Opportunity Reconciliation Act of 1996.[1] While this federal legislation further restricted already stringent benefits policies for all immigrants, so far Congress has not significantly altered the United States' comparatively liberal immigration and naturalization policies (Johnson 1995b, p. 1523).

The 1996 act was foreshadowed by the 1994 election of a Republican Congress that promised in its "Contract with America" to enact legislation that would "cut spending for welfare programs," because it viewed them as perpetuating a "culture of poverty" and welfare dependence. At the same time, by popular referendum, the citizens of California passed Proposition 187, which was designed to deprive undocumented immigrants of welfare and other public benefits.

The 1996 act indicates that welfare benefits to legal (and undocumented) immigrants are not secure, as long as immigrants do not share in political power. After all, the deprivation of social rights for a politically unrepresented group defeats the notion that citizenship is only slightly more valuable than permanent resident alien status (Schuck 1989).[2] Rather "the enfranchisement may be [needed] to protect alien residents from hostile government action..." (Neuman 1996, p. 144). However, even voting rights are no panacea, since they do not necessarily connote political clout, especially since ethnically or racially different immigrant groups might split their voting strength, because voter registration might remain low in light of high political apathy, and because an effective political organization will not be readily available. Despite the apparent importance of political power for an otherwise disenfranchised group, the European option of granting local voting rights to permanent residents does not appear even a possible subject for discussion in the current political climate in the United States.

The genesis of the 1996 federal legislation illuminates the import of (local) political power for immigrants. The impetus for depriving immigrants of welfare benefits originated in California and was not shared by all states and major cities with large immigrant populations. A comparison of Texas and California indicates that, even in the absence of voting rights, immigrants may be protected from anti-immigrant excesses by the existence of certain favorable demographic, economic, and political factors. Once those safeguards disintegrate, however, immigrants must be given the tools to protect themselves. One avenue is the European model of local enfranchisement. Alternatively, a further liberalization of the naturalization requirements, that is, a shorter residency period and quicker administrative processing, and bilateral agreements between the main countries of emigration and the United States recognizing dual citizenship would probably assure immigrants of similar protections.

RIGHTS OF CITIZENS—RIGHTS OF IMMIGRANTS

Throughout the nineteenth and the early twentieth centuries a number of U.S. states allowed noncitizen white male residents to vote. However, "[w]ith increasing levels of immigration from a variety of source countries, the political rights of 'foreigners' became more controversial" (Neuman 1996, p. 65). Today, the most dramatic, but not the only, distinction between long-term legal immigrants and citizens exists with regard to political rights and, especially, voting rights. The denial of voting rights to legally resident aliens limits their political influence as a group and as members of particular ethnic or national groups (Schuck 1989, p. 6). However, for permanent resident aliens ("PRAs") the disenfranchised status can be of relatively short duration, since they are entitled to petition for naturalization after five years (or three upon marriage to a U.S. citizen) in PRA status.

Even though voting rights have been limited to citizens, since World War II constitutional equal protection guarantees, due process rights, and welfare benefits have been extended to immigrants. While political rights are a remnant of the ideology of the nation-state, social rights are a construct of the modern welfare state. "Social rights are...more expandable, both in scope and content, and are less exclusive than political rights" (Soysal 1994, p. 131). The (social) rights granted to immigrants, however, do not encompass the whole panoply of rights to which citizens have access. In addition, even long-term permanent residents remain subject to deportation.

The protection awarded to PRAs has been more extensive than that granted to undocumented immigrants. Therefore, the specific nature of an immigrant's status has remained important, even though prior to the passage of the 1996 act, citizenship per se was not significant for the receipt of many benefits. Access to welfare services in Western Europe has been similarly delimited. Among the most important factors there that influence eligibility for benefits are the nature of the services sought and the legality, type (permanent or temporary), and length of residence.

In the United States emergency medical services and elementary and secondary public schooling are being provided to all residents. Even prior to 1996 undocumented immigrants were generally not eligible for federal or state welfare programs, with the exception of maternal and child health services, alcohol, drug abuse, and mental health services, immunizations against vaccine-preventable diseases, migrant health care, the Special Supplemental Nutritional Program for Women, Infants and Children ("WIC"), and school breakfast and lunch programs. The governments provided these benefits largely because they proved financially beneficial to society in the long run.

For legal immigrants the passage of time since their arrival in the United States has been crucial in determining their welfare eligibility. In *Mathews* v. *Diaz* the U.S. Supreme Court held that in bestowing Medicare benefits, Congress may not only legitimately distinguish between citizens and aliens but also *within* the category of aliens.[3] In addition, immigration legislation permits the government to use the receipt of welfare benefits by a legal immigrant within five years of his or her entry as a reason for deportation, unless the immigrant can prove that the causes of the dependency arose after entry.[4]

To sum up, prior to the mid-1990s four tiers of benefits and political participation had developed in the United States. First, citizens by birth and citizens by naturalization were treated equally; both were full participants in political and civil processes, with equal access to all benefits.[5] Second, citizens and PRAs had almost identical rights to public services, even though differences existed with regard to access to civil service and some other employment (Schuck 1989, p. 5). However, PRAs lack political rights and are subject to deportation. Third, the Immigration Reform and Control Act of 1986 drew a distinction between permanent and temporary resident aliens, with the latter being ineligible for some means-tested benefits for five years (Schuck 1989, p. 5, n.20). Finally, undocumented immigrants had only limited access to public benefits. A similar hierarchy of rights exists in many European countries. For example, in Germany social welfare rights are distributed differently between citizens who enjoy the most extensive benefits, *Aussiedler* (ethnic Germans) who occupy a status almost equal that of German nationals, successful asylees, foreign workers whose benefits are generally time limited, and asylum seekers who possess the fewest rights.

Because of the expansion of social benefits, it has been argued that "national citizenship is no longer an adequate concept upon which to base a perceptive narrative of membership in the postwar era" (Soysal 1994, p. 167). Undoubtedly, the extension of social rights to noncitizens made the modern welfare states, including the United States, more inclusive than the old nation-states. Within the last 36 months, however, limitations on benefits to legal and undocumented immigrants have widened the gap between immigrants and citizens in the United States. This turn of events could stall, if not reverse, the earlier inclusive trends, and eventually lead to "a narrowing conception of membership" (Aleinikoff 1995, p. 920). In addition, the rollback is indicative of the tenuousness of social rights, when they are not supported by political power on all levels of government.

CALIFORNIA'S PROPOSITION 187

As a consequence of the states' abuse of immigrants, since the late nineteenth century the federal government has exercised sole power and control over immigration (Neuman 1995, p. 1436). Ironically, in the 1990s attempts to limit immigration and, especially, illegal immigration, began in California, and from there moved to Washington, DC, the seat of the national government.

Proposition 187, a popular referendum, was designed to restrict benefits to undocumented immigrants. Despite the different categories of noncitizens established by federal immigration law, Proposition 187 distinguishes only three groups of individuals: citizens, PRAs, and aliens lawfully admitted for a temporary period of time. By default, everyone else is considered an "illegal alien" (Abriel 1995, pp. 1618-1619). With the exception of emergency medical care, Proposition 187 deprives those individuals of almost all public benefits, including elementary and secondary schooling.

Proposition 187 was not a product of legislative debate but rather "was born in suburban living rooms throughout California..." (Martinez and McDonnell 1994, p. A-1). The idea behind the Proposition was expressed in the first sentence on findings and declarations which states that "[t]he People of California...have suffered and are suffering economic hardship caused by the presence of illegal aliens in this state." Undeniably, animosity toward undocumented Mexican immigrants motivated most of the rhetoric surrounding Proposition 187 (Johnson 1995a).

With the help of Pete Wilson, the Republican Governor of California, who campaigned vigorously for Proposition 187, its advocates formed "a loose-knit, statewide coalition" (Martinez and McDonnell 1994, p. A-1). Eventually, Proposition 187 passed with a popular vote of 59 percent (Lesher 1997, p. A-1).

Wilson had used the issue of illegal immigration as his campaign mainstay and was reelected governor despite a weak California economy. Publicly, he portrayed Proposition 187 as partly symbolic, as one component in a larger effort to force the federal government to control the U.S.-Mexico border more effectively and to reimburse the states for expenses incurred because of the presence of undocumented immigrants. More importantly, Wilson argued that undocumented foreigners would "self-deport" once denied the welfare benefits that allegedly had drawn them to the United States in the first place. In these statements, he echoed the public perception that generous benefits attract new immigrants, while past immigration was dominated by hard-working individuals who were enticed by the equal opportunity to succeed.

Wilson disavowed any connection between the efforts to remove undocumented immigrants and legal immigration. However, in referring to the U.S.-born children of undocumented immigrants, Wilson used the term "the so-called citizen children" (Q&A 1994, p. G-5). This suggests that he views children born to undocumented immigrants as "illegal aliens" rather than as citizens, and that he would support limitations on the *ius soli* principle. Proposition 187 mirrors this view, since it makes the rights of children to attend public elementary and secondary schools dependent not only on their immigration/citizenship status but also requires their parents or guardians to prove their lawful presence.[6]

Upon passage of Proposition 187, some members of Congress from California began a national campaign to curtail welfare benefits to legal and illegal immigrants. With the focus on welfare benefits, anti-immigrant forces moved the battleground from race and ethnicity to economic analysis, which appears more neutral and objective.[7] Welfare restrictions on immigrants seemed defensible, because payments to all recipients were being reduced. In addition, a 1993 study asserted that legal and illegal immigrants cost the government more than they generate (Reich 1995, pp. 1581-1582). However, "the weakness of nativist claims in the face of contrary empirical evidence suggests that their motives arise from cultural and ethnic biases as much as from environmental concerns" (Reich 1995, pp. 1581-82). This is especially true for Proposition 187, since its enforcement would have likely been more expensive than the benefits paid to undocumented immigrants (Johnson 1995b, p. 1567).

SIMILAR BUT DIFFERENT:
CALIFORNIA AND TEXAS

Public, and even legal, discourse around immigration issues often portrays Texas and California as alike, because both are large southwestern states with sizable immigrant populations and long histories of discrimination against ethnic and racial minorities, especially Hispanics (Chia et al. 1996, p. 286). These states—along with Arizona, Florida, New Jersey, and New York—also unsuccessfully sued the federal government to recover the costs they incurred as a result of the influx of undocumented immigrants (Scaperlanda 1996, p. 710). Despite the similarities, in Texas the official political posture to immigrants has been diametrically opposed to that of California, even though attempts were made to make illegal immigration an important election issue in both states (Suro 1994, p. A-25). In 1993 the California legislature considered 21 immigration reform bills, 19 more than the year before. Proposals included the denial of education, public housing, prenatal care, driver's licenses, job training, and emergency care to undocumented immigrants (Brooks 1994, p. 152). When California passed Proposition 187, the Republican Governor of Texas, George W. Bush, on the other hand, warned his party to refrain from bashing immigrants, particularly Hispanics ("Anti-Immigrant" 1995, p. A-07).

A possible explanation for these divergent responses is the different economic situation of the two states in the early 1990s. Studies demonstrate that in times of economic crisis, especially of rising unemployment rates, opposition to immigration increases (Espenshade and Hempstead 1996, p. 539). Undoubtedly, California's economy has been ailing and has been the last in the country to recover from recession. Nevertheless, historically California's nativism has been more virulent than Texas, even at times of economic downturn for both states. Therefore, economics alone cannot account for the strikingly disparate reactions of the two states.

Four other factors might be more likely to explain the different treatment of immigrants in California and Texas. They are (1) the demographic composition of the two states, (2) the views of the role of immigrants, (3) the perceptions of economic interests in major areas of emigration, and (4) the composition, cohesiveness, and relative voting strength of immigrant communities.

Demographics

California is home to one-third of all immigrants in the United States. In addition, undocumented immigrants constitute 4.6 percent of the population in California, while they make up only 2 percent of the population in Texas (Suro 1994, p. A-25). In California's major cities the immigrant population is substantially larger and geographically more concentrated than elsewhere, so as to make it highly visible. Equally important, California's recent immigrants seem to be predominantly less skilled workers with poor educational backgrounds which explains the relatively large number of recent immigrants who are in poverty. Moreover, in contrast to Texas whose immigrants hail predominantly from Mexico, California's migrants stem not only from Mexico and other Latin countries but also from Asia and the islands in the Pacific.

The consequences that flow from the demographic picture in the two states are twofold. First, California's higher total percentage of (low-skilled) immigrants has caused a larger number of immigrants to be dependent on welfare benefits. This created substantial resentment toward immigrants among the population. Second, the data also indicate that the political power of the immigrant groups in the two states differs. A larger number of residents are disenfranchised in California; and ethnic and racial groups compete against each other in the political arena, fragmenting their potential influence. However, even though demographics, combined with the economic situation, may explain much of the differential between Texas and California, the case of New York City indicates that demographics alone cannot account for the differences in the treatment of immigrants.[8]

Divergent Views of the Role of Immigrants

Despite the myth of the United States as a country that welcomes all, extremes of encouragement of immigration and of xenophobia have dominated the American politics of immigration and naturalization. In the early years of the country efforts were made to limit naturalization or to restrict the political power of naturalized citizens rather than to stop immigration. In states where noncitizen residents were allowed to vote, throughout the nineteenth century efforts were underway to deny aliens such a right (Curran 1975, pp. 18-20, 31). Later, Congress restricted immigration numerically to keep out certain racial and religious groups labeled as undesirable.

While many of the anti-immigrant movements started in the East, California has a long and tortured history of exclusionary attempts. California's crusade against Chinese immigrants, for example, included legislation that barred Asian immigrants from the public school system. Despite countervailing economic interests, eventually a severe economic crisis in California led to successful lobbying for federal restrictions which manifested themselves in the first national race-based exclusions (Curran 1975, pp. 75, 82-88). The federal welfare act of 1996 and other restrictive federal immigration legislation merely continue this tradition and highlight California's persistent influence on national immigration policy and its success in nationalizing local immigration issues.

California's interaction with Mexican immigrants has always been particularly tragic. In the 1930s California was on the forefront of the indiscriminate mass deportation of U.S. citizens and noncitizens of Mexican ancestry. Los Angeles County participated in these repatriation efforts "to decrease the fiscal burden of providing welfare" to immigrants (Johnson 1995b, p. 1525).

Again, in the early 1990s fiscal concerns and only slightly hidden racism dominated the immigration discourse. A parody of Mexican immigrants that circulated in the California State Assembly in 1993 demonstrates the combination of the two issues most forcefully. It read:

"We have a hobby—it's called breeding. Welfare pay for baby feeding" (Johnson 1995b, p. 1510).

While California "feel[s] victimized by immigration" (Motomura 1994, p. 214) and blames undocumented immigrants "for almost every one of [its] problems" (Sherwood 1994, pp. 4, 11), Texas does not appear to share these sentiments, even though, historically, both states have treated Mexican immigrants and U.S. citizens of Mexican descent dismally.

Around the turn of the century regular killings of Mexicans and Mexican Americans along the Texas-Mexico border contributed to the oppression of those population groups. During the Depression Texas, along with California, participated rather enthusiastically in repatriating Mexican "immigrants" (Skerry 1993, p. 23). The obstacles erected to the political participation of U.S. citizens of Mexican descent were a major reason for Congress's decision in the mid-1970s to extend coverage of the Voting Rights Act to all Hispanics in Texas, while such protection seemed necessary in only a few of California's counties (Skerry 1993, p. 91).

Texas also pioneered the idea of denying public education benefits to undocumented immigrant children. The 1975 Texas education law challenged in the Supreme Court case *Plyler* v. *Doe* was allegedly designed to improve or at least maintain the quality of public education in Texas which was claimed to be threatened by the extra fiscal burden imposed by undocumented Mexican children.[9] Even though the legislation was motivated by resentment of undocumented immigrants (LaValle 1981, p. 1230), it was not intended to rid Texas of such migrants. The Texas legislature appeared tolerant of undocumented workers—it was just not inclined to provide any services for them or their families. Proposition 187, on the other hand, requires school districts to report suspected undocumented immigrant children or their parents to state and federal authorities—presumably so that the INS can initiate deportation proceedings. While this might seem only a rhetorical difference, it reflects a divergent view of immigration. In contrast to California, Texas traditionally appears to have understood the economic benefits it has gained from undocumented migration. Its efforts, therefore, have been directed at controlling immigrants rather than forcing them to leave. "Proposition 187 imposes a systematic program for driving 'illegal' aliens out of California" (Neuman 1995, p. 1445).

Trade and Foreign Policy

Perception *and* reality tend to determine how a state or country assesses the importance and condition of its economic situation and its (foreign) trade. Studies have indicated that "[t]hose who think that trad-

ing with other countries is bad for the United States, who oppose
NAFTA, and who feel that Japanese and German products are inferior
to those manufactured in the United States generally desire lower levels
of immigration" (Espenshade and Hempstead 1996, p. 556). In short,
the more isolationist individuals feel, the more likely they are to advo-
cate less immigration.

Historically the trade routes from Mexico City to Laredo, Texas were
more extensive and important than those to Tijuana on the Califor-
nia-Mexico border. Even though today California and Texas are among
Mexico's largest trading partners, the perception in both states as to the
importance of this economic relationship continues to differ. While
Texas sees its economic future closely tied to that of Mexico, California
views Mexico as only one of many trading partners in the Pacific Rim
area. Therefore, offending the Mexican government has not been a
major concern to California policymakers (Brownstein 1994, p. A-1).

When Governor Wilson campaigned in California for reelection by
advocating the cutting of benefits to illegal immigrants, former Democratic Texas Governor Ann Richards highlighted her efforts to trade
more extensively with Mexico (Suro 1994, p. A-25). She and Governor
Bush, her successor, have publicly promoted trade and other relationships with Mexico as beneficial to Texas.

California's Proposition 187 proves to be a boon to the Texas economy
since many Mexican entrepreneurs have shifted their business to Texas
which appears more hospitable to them (Spiro 1994, p. 166). However,
Governor Bush seems to fear that the anti-immigrant national political
climate which California incited might also affect the Texas-Mexico relations. He stated that "'[t]he relationship between Texas and Mexico has
never been better...but Washington can be very shortsighted'"
("Anti-Immigrant" 1995, p. A-07).

Voting Rights and Political Organization

Since all aliens are deprived of voting rights, "politicians have little
incentive to learn about and respond to their claims" (Schuck 1989, p.
13). This holds true even for PRAs, even though they are never too far
removed from citizenship. However, in the last few decades an increasing number of PRAs, especially from Latin countries, have failed to naturalize. In addition, even naturalized citizens often do not vote. For
example, sociodemographic factors, such as age, class, and education as
well as earlier exclusion from electoral politics, contribute to the low
turnout of Hispanic voters (de la Garza and DeSipio 1993, pp. 1509,
1513).

Even in spite of these considerations, with California's total population being 43 percent persons of color (Ramirez 1995, p. 961), and 26 percent Latino (Cervantes, Khokha, and Murray 1995, p. 3), one would expect this group—many, but not all of whom, would be relatively recent immigrants—to be rather well represented politically. However, California is also home to almost half the undocumented population in the United States (Johnson 1995b, p. 1546), and these individuals have no political rights. Overall, at least "40 percent of Latino adults cannot participate in electoral politics because of nationality" (de la Garza and DeSipio 1993, p. 1507). In addition, Mexican-American citizens tend to be more geographically dispersed in California, and therefore "less cohesive politically" (Skerry 1993, p. 95).

Among all states, prior to 1965 Texas most egregiously violated the voting rights of Mexican Americans (de la Garza and DeSipio 1993, p. 1482). Nevertheless, the political organization of Mexican Americans in Texas has always been stronger than in California. In addition, the 1965 Voting Rights Act has "successfully addressed each of the structural barriers faced by Latino voters" (de la Garza and DeSipio 1993, p. 1493), especially in Texas. The Hispanic national and state office holders from Texas include Henry Cisneros, the former mayor of San Antonio and former Secretary of Housing and Urban Development, Henry B. Gonzalez, a long-time member of the House of Representatives, and Dan Morales, the outgoing state Attorney General.[10] The numerical representation of Mexican Americans on the local, state, and even national level in Texas accurately reflects the effective power of that group which has largely been based on "the development of working-class, neighborhood-based political institutions" (Skerry 1993, p. 128).

The creation of voting districts tailored along racial or ethnic lines has assisted minority voters to some extent in electing "their" representatives. On the other hand, majority-minority districts ultimately reduce the political necessity for nonminority officials to respond to minority community concerns in their districts (de la Garza and DeSipio 1993, p. 1525). Minority districts, therefore, might underscore rather than camouflage the political weakness of the minority group.

Even if citizen voters do not support further immigration, they are often inclined to oppose legislation that might negatively affect their ethnic group. Mexican Americans in Texas, for example, have considered some efforts to control undocumented migration "as likely to exacerbate discrimination" (de la Garza 1985, p. 103). Therefore, voter self-interest might incidentally lead to some protection for immigrants.

While "Latinos of different national origins can have very different political interests despite their residence in the same jurisdiction or geographic area" (de la Garza and DeSipio 1993, p. 1525), Latinos of the same national origin but residing in different jurisdictions can also espouse very different views of immigration. Mexican Americans in Texas are likely to favor an immigration preference for immigrants from Latin America; California's Mexican Americans believe too many immigrants are in the country already. Since more noncitizens than citizens seem to espouse the California view (Espenshade and Hempstead 1996, p. 548), increased naturalizations could actually harm immigrants.

Particularly in California, "as districts become increasingly multiracial, and...only one candidate can win,...race-based politicking engenders conflicts between minority groups" (Ramirez 1995, p. 975). Different racial groups tend not to be politically cohesive,[11] and even though many of the anti-immigrant attacks are directed against all (nonwhite) immigrants, new citizens do not necessarily coalesce because of such attacks.

This analysis indicates that the rights of noncitizens might be protected by voters who belong to a sizable and cohesive minority population that values immigration of members of the same minority group. To be even more effective, these minority voters should be dispersed throughout all voting areas rather than be concentrated exclusively in majority-minority districts. Because of antidiscrimination legislation, the voters' attitudes and political clout ultimately will benefit all immigrants.

Immigrants will also profit from the existence and support of strong ethnically or racially based political organizations. Without such structural support, the political power of ethnic or racial groups will remain sporadic and dispersed in a system that is driven by racial divisions and classifications.

NATIONAL LEGISLATION—ONE STEP FURTHER

While the experience of California indicates that "[t]he dynamics of the political process may leave a group more vulnerable at the state level than at the federal level" (Neuman 1995, p. 1435), political developments in the last few years have indicated that this is not necessarily accurate. As the California movement against undocumented immigrants snowballed into a national campaign modeled on an extension of Proposition 187, immigrants throughout the United States, including those in more pro-immigrant states like Texas, were affected negatively.

After federal courts had stopped the implementation of Proposition 187, at least partially and temporarily, the California governor as well as members of Congress from California were on the forefront of the national campaign to deprive immigrants of benefits. According to a lobbyist for the city of Los Angeles, "Wilson's office 'spent a lot of time' on [federal] welfare reform legislation" (Donoghue 1996, p. 1). Not surprisingly, the invalidation of state legislation on grounds of federal supremacy over immigration issues caused the battle to be fought in the national capital. Ultimately, Governor Wilson's legal affairs secretary claimed that "'[t]he federal law in essence enshrines the objectives of Prop. 187, with the exception of Proposition 187's denial of primary and secondary education benefits'" (Donoghue 1996, p. 1).

Eventually, the U.S. Congress went further in many respects than the state of California by undertaking a full-blown national assault on all immigrants, irrespective of their legal status. While limitations on welfare benefits for PRAs are not unprecedented,[12] the scope of the undertaking was. The welfare bill made all immigrants, including PRAs, ineligible for Medicaid (if states choose to exclude them), food stamps, and Supplemental Security Income (SSI), which is targeted to the elderly, blind, and disabled. Exempt from the ban are asylees and refugees, immigrant veterans, members of the armed forces and their immediate families, and those who have worked 10 years or more without receiving any means-tested aid. Recent amendments also continue to guarantee SSI benefits to those who were present in the United States prior to August 22, 1996, the day the welfare bill went into effect. The onslaught on the welfare rights of immigrants was facilitated by the public's overall negative attitude toward welfare recipients and was driven by the widely held assumption that most new immigrants are in the country illegally rather than legally (Espenshade and Hempstead 1996, p. 553), by the blurring of "the distinction between legal and illegal migration..." (Scaperlanda 1996, p. 710), and by the belief that immigrants come to the United States to benefit from the welfare system.

While the federal welfare legislation explicitly keeps public education open to undocumented immigrant children, it constitutes an assault on legal immigrants initiated by the Congress and joined in by the President. The President's acquiescence was almost certainly due to the impending 1996 presidential election; states home to most immigrants, especially California, hold a substantial number of electoral votes (Sherwood 1994, pp. 4, 11).

Even though PRAs are perceived to be less vulnerable to the excesses of citizens because of their future ability to vote and their ethnic ties to citizens (Schuck 1989, p. 4, n.15), they also fell victim to the large-scale attack on welfare benefits and the public's and the legislature's apparent inability or unwillingness to distinguish between illegal and legal immigrants. The welfare legislation creates unprecedented distinctions among PRAs and increases the contributions immigrants are expected to make to the community before they can rely on its assistance.

The 1996 act is also indicative of a larger reconceptualization of the concept of membership in the American polity. No longer are future political membership and past financial contributions in the form of tax payments enough to justify reliance on the welfare state. The conception underlying the new immigrant model resembles that of the labor migrant in Germany. While German labor immigrants may claim payments from the funds into which they have paid directly, such as pension or unemployment insurance, they do not have a right to general welfare benefits for longer than three months. This approach is based on the notion that labor immigrants have a right to support only based on their active contributions to the economy. Once they no longer participate actively in the labor market, they are quickly assumed to have lost their usefulness and, therefore, to forfeit the right to benefit from the general welfare fund. The new U.S. welfare legislation also seems to assume that unless one has proven to have been a net contributor to the polity, one cannot rely on the charity of the general populace in the form of welfare benefits.[13] Obviously, the model of the welfare state has not replaced that of the nation-state, especially in a time of large-scale welfare cutbacks and a celebration of the work ethic.

THE FALLOUT FROM AND FUTURE CONSEQUENCES OF THE NEW APPROACH TO IMMIGRANTS

One of the consequences of Proposition 187, probably inadvertent and unplanned, and of the national drive to deprive PRAs of welfare benefits has been the attempt of hundreds of thousands of them to naturalize to become or remain eligible for welfare benefits. The 1996 welfare act also encourages naturalizations because it only removes immigrant's sponsor's financial responsibility for a PRA, which is now legally enforceable, when the PRA naturalizes. Such incentives to naturalize are not unprecedented, even though they have never been better publicized or more effective.

The Frank Amendment to the 1986 Immigration Reform and Control Act (IRCA) which imposed sanctions on employers that hire undocumented workers protects "citizens" or "intending citizens" under its antidiscrimination provisions. It does not cover "an alien who fails to apply for naturalization within six months of the date the alien first becomes eligible...to apply for naturalization...."[14] Both the welfare act and the Frank Amendment ultimately pursue the same goal—the naturalization of immigrants as soon as they are eligible. To accomplish this goal the federal government holds out a carrot and a stick. Should the immigrants reject the offer of assimilation through naturalization, they have forfeited the right to be treated as potential future citizens and, therefore, either lose or fail to gain certain protections.

Interestingly, the naturalization of scores of PRAs has led to divergent national responses. While some have greeted the scores of new citizens with enthusiasm, others have suggested the tightening of naturalization requirements (Schuck 1996, p. 2004). The latter argument has been connected to the controversy over the Clinton administration's naturalization drive and resulting claims of abuse. In addition, at least one member of Congress who lost his reelection bid, Robert Dornan of California, has claimed that noncitizens committed fraud by voting against him. Both charges reinforce the public perception of immigrants as abusing the system or even as criminals. The proposal to lengthen residency periods for naturalization is probably also tied to the perception that the new immigrants are more difficult to assimilate because of their racial makeup (Johnson 1996). Should naturalization standards become more onerous, immigrants will, of course, be even less protected since it will take even longer or become impossible for many of them to participate in the political process.[15]

The interaction between Proposition 187 and the federal welfare legislation will also have long-term effects on the relationship between the federal government and the states. "State efforts to strengthen enforcement of federal immigration laws—including Proposition 187—elevate the sense of state rather than national citizenship..." (Motomura 1996, p. 1946). Such effort, on the part of larger and more influential states, also increases state power over federal areas, such as immigration and foreign policy (Motomura 1994, p. 215f.). This is particularly troubling since, as indicated above, states historically have shown "propensities to oppress aliens" (Neuman 1995, p. 1436) and to nationalize their anti-immigrant campaigns. In addition, such federal legislation will negatively affect states like Texas that, for economic, political, and pragmatic reasons, would not have passed anti-immigrant legislation on their own.

Much of the implementation of the welfare bill has been left to the states. As the lobbying of some governors and mayors for a reversal of the welfare legislation as applied to PRAs indicates, the responsibility for PRAs has merely been shifted from the federal government to the states. For example, the states can decide whether to permit otherwise-eligible PRAs to receive Medicaid. So far, many states, including California and Texas, have opted to retain at least some welfare benefits for PRAs ineligible for federal assistance. On the other hand, California has been on the forefront of those states phasing out any services that might even indirectly benefit undocumented migrants (Carlsen 1997, p. A19).

Municipalities and counties may enforce different rules than those issued by the state. For example, "San Francisco County and a half-dozen other counties in Northern California have already announced that they will continue to provide prenatal care to illegal immigrant women if the state cuts off its aid" (Golden 1996, pp. A-1, C-24). Such developments will potentially lead to greater balkanization of the country and even of individual states. In addition, it might lead to further concentration of immigrants—PRAs and/or undocumented migrants—in small pockets of the country which will cause additional resentment and limit the organizational power of immigrants even more.

Finally, Proposition 187 sparked a national debate about the *ius soli* system that ascribes citizenship to almost anybody born on U.S. soil. In its education provisions, Proposition 187 draws distinctions between native-born citizens depending on their parents' immigration/citizenship status. Governor Wilson's rhetoric also seems to have affected some members of Congress, including Representative Dan Burton of Indiana who spoke of the birth of thousands of "illegal-alien children" in the United States for whom welfare payments are being made.[16] Under current U.S. law it is impossible for "illegal-alien children" to be born in the United States. Even though parents may be undocumented, if born in the United States, their children are U.S. citizens. In light of the rhetoric it is no surprise that constitutional amendments limiting birth-right citizenship to the children of PRA or citizens (mothers) are already pending in Congress.[17]

The *ius soli* system currently used in the United States is also attackable from a comparative perspective. After all, the European countries subscribe to a modified *ius soli* or to a *ius sanguinis* system which ties a child's immigration/citizenship status more closely to the parents. However, the proposal of such a scheme in the United States fails to consider that most European countries have smaller undocumented populations. More importantly, opponents of the *ius soli* system have not fully weighed the substantial difficulties such systems are causing. For example, Germany now has a sizable noncitizen population, including first-, second- and even third-generation "immigrants," who have no or only very limited political rights. Also the opponents of birth-right citizenship have failed to contemplate that a few European countries have granted legal residents the right to vote, at least in local elections. Local voting rights could provide immigrants with some indirect political protection on the national stage, with the necessary stake in the community to naturalize eventually, and with the requisite political skills to compete successfully in the regional and even national arena. However, while the abolition of the *ius soli* system is being discussed seriously in the United States, no thought is given to compensate immigrants by providing them with other, effective protections.

CONCLUSIONS

The repercussions of recent U.S. welfare legislation have not yet fully crystallized. However, its passage symbolizes how either virtually or effectively disenfranchised groups can easily fall prey to the country's anxiety about the so-called "under-class" and welfare abuse as well as its racial intolerance. The public's perception of immigrants as lazy criminal abusers of the welfare system contributed to the revocation of their social rights.

The recent development indicates the need for politically empowering currently disenfranchised immigrants. After all, if PRAs are "citizens in training," why not provide them with a "practice vote," for example, in local elections?[18] While representation in the political arena would be important in any country, it is particularly crucial in the United States. In contrast to Germany whose history makes the government's treatment of foreigners an object of scrutiny at home and abroad, the United States often does not feel constrained by regional or world public opinion. In addition, it is not sufficiently bound into a regional human rights body that could protect immigrants from the deprivation of rights.

Even more troubling than the welfare debate are its potential long-term consequences. The arguments surrounding the 1996 act seem designed to fragment the immigrant community further by separating the "deserving" from the "undeserving." In addition, they have shifted the focus of the immigration debate away from admission and the problem of border control to the question of who a person's parents are.[19] This novel focus may create multiple groupings of individuals with different sets of limited social rights, not unlike the current situation in Germany. Moreover, undocumented status appears infectious. Anyone related to illegally present immigrants, or possibly even intimately associating with them, will also be deprived of government benefits, independent of their own immigration/citizenship status. Ultimately, blood, indicative of worth as reflected in citizenship, will replace the much hailed equality of opportunity for all.

ACKNOWLEDGMENT

Special thanks to Douglas Haddock, Hermann Kurthen, Kevin R. Johnson, José Roberto Juárez, Jr., Michael D. Smith, and all the participants in the conference on Immigration and the Welfare State: Germany and the U.S. in Comparison, held at the Freie Universität Berlin in December 1996, and my research assistants, Karen Lee Johnson and John Jordan.

NOTES

1. *Public Law* (No.193, 104th Congress, 2nd session, August 1996).

2. Possibly the most important benefit of citizenship that recent immigrants desire is the preferred and extensive right of citizens to family unification.

3. The Supreme Court upheld the denial of Medicare benefits to immigrants who either were not in PRA status or did not fulfill the five-year residency requirement. 426 U.S. 67, 1976.

4. *Immigration and Nationality Act* (sec. 241(a)(5), 1996), *U.S. Code* (vol. 8, sec. 1251(a)(5), 1996). This deportation ground has been used only rarely.

5. The major difference is constitutionally prescribed. See *U.S. Constitution* art. II, sec. 1, cl. 4 (President must be "natural born Citizen").

6. This provision of Proposition 187 has been enjoined permanently. *LULAC* v. *Wilson*, 1997 U.S. Dist. LEXIS 18776 (C.D. Cal.), Nov. 17, 1997.

7. See *Georgetown* (1996, pp. 26-27), statement by Dr. Thomas Muller, author, *Immigrants and the American City*.

8. Suro (1994, p. A-25):

In New York, where the concentration of illegal immigrants and the economic woes are about as great as in California, Rudolph W. Giuliani (R) was elected mayor last year after opening his arms to all immigrants, including those who live and work there illegally.

Some of the distinctions between Texas and California do not apply to New York City, and, therefore, could not account for the difference in the treatment of immigrants. However, New York City appears to be such a unique case that, while interesting, the result of a study of the "Big Apple" might prove less relevant, comparatively speaking.

9. 457 U.S. 202, 1982.

10. The Texas congressman who chairs the House Subcommittee on Immigration, Lamar Smith, comes from a predominantly white district.

11. *DeGrandy* v. *Wetherell* (815 F. Supp. 1550, 1569. N.D. Fla. 1992), *aff'd in part, rev'd in part sub nom. Johnson* v. *DeGrandy* (512 U.S. 997, 1994).

12. See *Mathews* v. *Diaz* (426 U.S. 67, 1976), upholding federal statute denying aliens right to enroll in Medicare unless they are PRAs and have resided in United States for at least five years.

13. In the German as well as the U.S. model successful asylees are exempted from such stringent requirements, presumably because they are viewed as having suffered enough.

14. *U.S. Code* (vol. 8, sec. 1324b(a)(3)(B)(I), 1996).

15. Some proposals for campaign finance reform would also bar PRAs from making campaign contributions. In addition, PRAs might shy away from becoming politically active because they may "fear jeopardizing their legal status and possible deportation as well as undermining their eligibility for naturalization" (Johnson 1993, p. 1153).

16. 139 *Congressional Record* H4412, *H4418 (daily ed. July 1, 1993) (statement by Rep. Burton).

17. Neuman (1996, p. 187): "It seems historically appropriate that the political pressure for this proposal comes from California, just like Chinese exclusion and Japanese internment. This time, the United States should resist more firmly."

18. A number of municipalities already provide noncitizens with limited voting rights, see Raskin (1993, pp. 1461-1464).

19. See *Georgetown* (1996, pp. 22-23), statement by Warren Leiden, Executive Director of the American Immigration Lawyers Association.

REFERENCES

Abriel, E. G. 1995. "Rethinking Preemption for Purposes of Aliens and Public Benefits." *UCLA Law Review* 42: 1597-1630.

Aleinikoff, T. A. 1995. "The Tightening Circle of Membership." *Hastings Constitutional Law Quarterly* 22: 915-924.

"Anti-Immigrant Talk Angers Texas Governor." *Washington Post.* August 11, 1995, sec. A, pp. 07.

Brooks, C. W. 1994. "Health Care Reform, Immigration Laws, and Federally Mandated Medical Services: Impact of Illegal Immigration." *Houston Journal of International Law* 17: 141-175.

Brownstein, R. 1994. "Wilson Proposes U.S. Version of Prop. 187." *Los Angeles Times*, November 19, sec. A, p. 1.

Cervantes, N., S. Khokha, and B. Murray. 1995. "Hate Unleashed: Los Angeles in the Aftermath of Proposition 187." *Chicano-Latino Law Review* 17: 1-23.

Chia, D. et al. 1996. "Developments in the Legislative Branch." *Georgetown Immigration Law Journal* 10: 285-294.

Curran, T. J. 1975. *Xenophobia and Immigration, 1820-1930*. Boston: Twayne Publishers.

de la Garza, R. O. 1985. "Mexican American, Mexican Immigrants, and Immigration Reform." Pp. 93-105 in *Clamor at the Gates*, edited by N. Glazer. San Francisco: ICS Press.

de la Garza, R. O., and L. DeSipio. 1993. "Save the Baby, Change the Bathwater, and Scrub the Tub: Latino Electoral Participation After Seventeen Years of Voting Rights Act Coverage." *Texas Law Review* 71: 1479-1526.

Donoghue, K. 1996. "Federal Support for Prop 187?" *The Recorder* August, 28, sec. 1.

Espenshade, T. J., and K. Hempstead. 1996. "Contemporary American Attitudes Toward U.S. Immigration." *International Migration Review* 30(2): 535-570.

"Georgetown Immigration Law Journal 10th Anniversary Symposium—March 6, 1996 Transcript." 1996. *Georgetown Immigration Law Journal* 10: 5-28.

Golden, T. 1996. "In Anti-Immigrant Storm, the Pregnant Wait." *New York Times*, October 16, sec. A, p. 1; sec. C, p. 24.

Johnson, K. R. 1993. "Los Olvidados: Images of the Immigrants, Political Power of Noncitizens, and Immigration Law and Enforcement." *Brigham Young University Law Review*: 1139-1256.

Johnson, K. R. 1995a. "An Essay on Immigration Politics, Popular Democracy, and California's Proposition 87: The Political Relevance and Legal Irrelevance of Race." *Washington Law Review* 70: 629-673.

Johnson, K. R. 1995b. "Public Benefits and Immigration: The Intersection of Immigration Status, Ethnicity, Gender, and Class." *UCLA Law Review* 42: 1509-1575.

Johnson, K. R. 1996. "Fear of an Alien Nation: Race, Immigration, and Immigrants." *Stanford Law & Policy Review* 7: 111-126.

LaValle, K. M. 1981. "Equal Protection and the Education of Undocumented Children." *Southwestern Law Journal* 34: 1229-1259.

Lesher, D. 1997. "Deadlock on Prop. 187 has Backers, Governor Fuming." *Los Angeles Times*, November 8, sec. A, p. 1.

Martinez, G., and P. J. McDonnell. 1994. "Prop. 187 Backers Counting on Message, Not Strategy." *Los Angeles Times*, October 30, sec. A, p. 1.

Motomura, H. 1994. "Immigration and Alienage, Federalism and Proposition 187." *Virginia Journal of International Law* 35: 201-216.

Motomura, H. 1996. "Whose Alien Nation? Two Models of Constitutional Immigration Law." *Michigan Law Review* 94: 1927-1952.

Neuman, G. L. 1995. "Aliens as Outlaws: Government Services, Proposition 187, and the Structure of Equal Protection Doctrine." *UCLA Law Review* 42: 1425-1452.

Neuman, G. L. 1996. *Strangers to the Constitution*. Princeton, NJ: Princeton University Press.

"Q & A Pete Wilson, Governor of California." *San Diego Union-Tribune*, November 6, 1994, sec. G, p. 5.

Ramirez, D. 1995. "Multicultural Empowerment: It's Not Just Black and White Anymore." *Stanford Law Review* 47: 957-992.

Raskin, J. B. 1993. "Legal Aliens, Local Citizens: The Historical, Constitutional and Theoretical Meaning of Alien Suffrage." *University of Pennsylvania Law Review* 141: 1391-1470.

Scaperlanda, M. 1996. "Partial Membership: Aliens and the Constitutional Community." *Iowa Law Review* 81: 707-773.

Schuck, P. H. 1989. "Membership in the Liberal Polity: The Devaluation of American Citizenship." *Georgetown Immigration Law Journal* 3: 1-18; also published as pp. 51-65 in *Immigration and the Politics of Citizenship in Europe and North America*, edited by W. R. Brubaker. Lanham, MD: University Press of America.

Schuck, P.H. 1996. "Book Review: *Alien Rumination*." *Yale Law Journal* 105: 1963-2012.

Sherwood, B. 1994. "California Leads the Way, Alas." *New York Times*, November 27, sec. 4, p. 11.

Skerry, P. 1993. *Mexican Americans*. New York: The Free Press.

Spiro, P. J. 1994. "The States and Immigration in an Era of Demi-Sovereignties." *Virginia Journal of International Law* 35: 121-178.

Soysal, Y. N. 1994. *Limits of Citizenship. Migrants and Postnational Membership in Europe*. Chicago: University of Chicago Press.

Suro, R. 1994. "Same Issue, 2 Political Realities." *Washington Post*, October 27, sec. A, p. 25.

ANTECEDENTS AND CONSEQUENCES OF TIGHTENING WELFARE ELIGIBILITY FOR U.S. IMMIGRANTS

Thomas J. Espenshade and Gregory A. Huber

Dramatic changes are in store for U.S. immigrants as a result of major pieces of federal welfare and immigration reform legislation enacted in the latter half of 1996. The thrust of these reforms is to deny legal immigrants access to means-tested public benefits to which they had previously been entitled and otherwise to reduce eligibility by tightening criteria. The purposes of this paper are (1) to provide a framework for understanding these changes, (2) to describe the significant features of the new reforms, explaining how they have altered the fiscal landscape, and (3) to speculate about some of their possible implications.

Our main conclusion can be stated simply. Building on work by Calavita (1996), we argue that recent U.S. welfare policy reforms affecting immigrants can be linked to a convergence of anti-immigrant sentiment with the fiscal imperatives of balanced-budget conservatism and the ascendancy of dependency politics. Within this new fiscal politics of immigration, legal aliens are viewed as part of the reason for the high cost of welfare and other social services. Having little or no voice in the electorate and trapped by the forces of budgetary opportunism and

29

political expediency, immigrants are an attractive target for many policy-makers. A consequence of the shrinking welfare state is to ensure the metamorphosis of legal immigrants from public charges to windfall gains for the federal treasury.

BACKGROUND TO WELFARE REFORM[1]

It is not by coincidence that restrictions on immigrants' eligibility for welfare and other public benefits should come at this time. They are motivated by structural changes in the American economy and by a reconfiguration in the racial and ethnic composition of the U.S. population, stimulated in large measure by a rising level of immigration which is now the largest in U.S. history when measured in absolute terms (Fix and Passel 1994).

Economic restructuring has led to a growing feeling of frustration and anxiety among American workers, as average real wages have remained stagnant for the better part of two decades, corporations are downsizing and laying off white-collar workers, and there is a perception of high taxes and the threat of additional jobs lost to overseas production. A rising fraction of the U.S. labor force is engaged in part-time employment, as more manufacturing, low-wage service, and, increasingly, higher-skill computer-programming jobs are exported abroad. Rising income inequality accentuates the sense of relative deprivation among lower and middle-income families, and the weight of accumulating federal government budget deficits means that more than 15 percent of total federal expenditure now goes to pay interest on the national debt (Plotkin and Scheuerman 1994; Reischauer 1996).

Added to economic insecurity is the uncertainty produced by demographic disequilibrium. As of March 1995, 8.8 percent of the U.S. population, or nearly 23 million individuals, were foreign born (Hansen 1996). This proportion has increased from 4.8 percent in 1970 and is the highest since 1940, although during the latter decades of the nineteenth century and early years of the twentieth century it was not uncommon for immigrants to account for between 13 and 15 percent of the total population. Nearly one-quarter of the U.S. foreign-born population arrived during the 1990s and another 35 percent came during the 1980s, suggesting an accelerating tempo to migration. Because many of the newer immigrants are from Asia or Latin America rather than from Europe, immigration is affecting the demographic mix of the U.S. population and is gradually transforming the economic, social, and political mainstream. In combination, these changes are seen by many as having an unsettling effect on the status quo (Teitelbaum and Weiner 1995).

Declining economic prospects and demographic changes have produced in the United States a renaissance of isolationism, marked by both international and domestic aspects. On the international front it is reflected in reluctance to send American troops to Bosnia, a retreat from U.S. foreign-aid commitments, an expanding movement to make English the "official language" of the United States, and by a heightened anti-immigrant public sentiment coupled with proposed or recently enacted legislation to restrict the flow of legal and undocumented (or illegal) immigrants into the country. Domestically, social distances among people appear to be widening, contributing to a diminished sense of shared public responsibility for one's neighbors. Recent examples include new laws requiring police to inform local residents when a convicted sex offender moves into their community, dwindling public support for affirmative action programs, and mounting fiscal conservatism, exhibited most poignantly in the Republican-controlled Congress's Contract with America—an attempt to shrink the size of the federal government and give many traditional federal responsibilities to the states. Rising disenchantment with the welfare system itself has helped to fuel welfare reform. Indeed, part of President Clinton's appeal to voters in 1992 was his campaign pledge to "end welfare as we know it." In addition, immigrants have been accounting for a rising share of U.S. welfare rolls.

Anti-Immigrant Sentiment

We may interpret U.S. residents' increasingly nativist attitudes as one manifestation of neo-isolationism. Historically, these attitudes have shifted between tolerance, ambivalence, and outright dislike. In fact, ever since the Colonial period there have been attempts by former immigrants to keep out newcomers (Espenshade and Calhoun 1993). Recent trends in immigration attitudes can be gauged from the pattern of responses to a question asked repeatedly in U.S. public opinion polls beginning after World War II. The proportion of survey participants who believe that levels of immigration to the United States should be reduced remained relatively constant near one-third until 1965, when it rose sharply, indicating that tolerance for immigration has waned in the last three decades. By the early 1980s and again in the 1990s the proportion surpassed 60 percent (Simon and Alexander 1993; Espenshade and Hempstead 1996).

In June 1993 a nationwide public opinion survey conducted by CBS News and the *New York Times* sampled 1,363 American adults who were asked a series of questions about the kind of job President Clinton was doing, the condition of the U.S. economy, and attitudes toward foreigners and U.S. immigrants. One of the important findings in the data is a strong positive relation between having an isolationist mentality and believing that U.S. immigration levels should be reduced (Espenshade and Hempstead 1996). Those who think that trading with Japan and other countries is bad for the United States, who oppose the North American Free Trade Agreement (NAFTA) with Mexico and Canada, and who feel that Japanese and German products are inferior to those produced in the United States generally prefer less immigration. Respondents who have unfriendly feelings toward other countries, who pay little attention to international news, and who believe that the United States has no responsibility to intervene diplomatically, financially, or militarily in the affairs of other countries are also more likely to support lower levels of immigration. The analysis by Espenshade and Hempstead (1996) is the first to establish an empirical link between immigration attitudes on the one hand and having an isolationist outlook versus a more global perspective on the other, and it suggests that restrictionist attitudes toward U.S. immigration are one of several important examples of emerging neo-isolationist tendencies in the United States.

Balanced-Budget Conservatism

Ronald Reagan's election as President in 1980 signaled a change in how the public defined economic problems in the U.S. (Plotkin and Scheuerman 1994). No longer was the issue mainly one of slow growth in the private sector; rather the problem was that government had gotten too big. The electorate endorsed the ideas of a balanced budget and less government spending, but it resisted having fewer government services. Reagan's popular tax cuts were not followed by spending reductions, and the federal deficit ballooned as a result. Between 1981 and 1983 the annual deficit doubled as a proportion of total government spending (from 12 to 25%), and the sight of unprecedented $200 billion budget imbalances soon gave rise to what Plotkin and Scheuerman (1994, p.6) call balanced-budget conservatism, an "omnipresent political focus on deficits, spending cuts, and tax avoidance."

The Republicans' Contract with America, introduced into Congress with much fanfare after the 1994 elections, is the latest rebirth of balanced-budget conservatism. An important element of this contract was the omnibus budget reconciliation bill, passed by Congress in November 1995. After prolonged negotiations between Congress and the White House that included a partial shutdown of the federal government, Republicans succeeded in gaining President Clinton's support for a long-run spending plan that balances the U.S. budget in the year 2002.

Dependency Politics

A third factor behind recent welfare reform legislation is the rise in the last three decades of what Mead (1986, 1992) calls dependency politics. During the progressive era that ran through the 1960s the question that dominated domestic economic policy discussions was how to help ordinary American workers advance their standard of living. Debates between liberals and conservatives turned on whether the government or the private economy was more effective in closing the gap between blue- and white-collar workers. During the 1960s attention was redirected to the problems of the inner city, to poverty, and to the large and growing prevalence of non-work among the permanent underclass in U.S. society. In the era of dependency politics the great dividing line has shifted from one separating different classes of workers to that between workers and nonworkers.

This has also affected the American public's willingness to support public welfare programs. As long as poor Americans were working and perceived as trying to help themselves, the public supported or at least tolerated income redistribution policies. Now, however, given the greater prevalence of nonworking poverty, the American public seems less willing to endorse income transfer programs destined primarily to benefit the "undeserving" poor.

Rising Immigrant Social Service Use

Finally, welfare reforms that target immigrants have been spurred by the fact that the number of immigrants receiving public assistance has been rising since the 1970s, despite a long-standing exclusion of immigrants who are likely to become a public charge. Between 1983 and 1993, for example, the number of immigrants receiving Supplemental Security Income (SSI) more than quadrupled—from 151,000 to 683,000—as immigrants increased their share of the SSI caseload from 4 to 11 percent. Participation rates in the SSI program were higher in 1990 for immigrants than for natives—6.5 versus 3.7 percent (Borjas and Hilton 1996). In 1990 overall immigrant participation rates were also higher for receipt of Aid to Families with Dependent Children (AFDC), state general assistance, Medicaid, food stamps, and for total use of any government need-based social service (no author 1996). In the 1970s, by contrast, immigrants were less likely than natives to receive cash welfare (Borjas 1994).

Sorensen and Blasberg (1996) have demonstrated that much of the higher benefit use by immigrants is due to the fact that proportionately more older immigrants than their native counterparts are ineligible for

Social Security. Lacking a lengthy work history in the United States that would qualify them for retirement benefits, noncitizens turn to Medicaid, SSI, and food stamps for old-age support. Among persons 15-64 years old, immigrants' and natives' use of AFDC and SSI are similar, whereas immigrants are slightly more likely than natives to rely on food stamps and Medicaid (Sorensen and Blasberg 1996).

Furthermore, the greater reliance on public benefits by refugees accounts for the aggregate difference between aliens and citizens (Fix and Passel 1994). With approximately 45 percent of all current refugees receiving some form of public assistance during their first five years in the United States, refugees are the most likely noncitizen group to receive public assistance (Chikuhwa 1996). Refugee needs are also significantly greater than those of other immigrants because refugees are more likely to lack English language proficiency and other labor market skills (Fix and Passel 1994).

THE NEW FISCAL POLITICS OF IMMIGRATION

Major changes in noncitizen eligibility for welfare and in U.S. immigration policy are contained in two pieces of legislation enacted into law during August and September of 1996. The first, the Personal Responsibility and Work Opportunity Reconciliation Act of 1996 (Welfare Reform Act), reforms the entitlement policy for poor families and imposes new limits on alien access to welfare and other social services. The second, the Illegal Immigration Reform and Immigrant Responsibility Act of 1996 (Immigration Reform Act), provides for increased efforts to combat illegal immigration and imposes new standards of financial self-sufficiency for sponsored, legal immigrants. Both reforms are compromise measures resulting from policy changes proposed by Republican members of Congress and related to their Contract with America.

In this section we describe these newly enacted changes. To begin, it is important to note what the two laws do *not* do in relation to immigration policy. They do not directly reduce legal immigration or the number of refugee or asylee entrants. Nor do they alter the broad criteria for obtaining a permanent resident visa, including the preeminence of family reunification goals embedded in current immigration law. Finally, the reforms do not affect access to social services by illegal immigrants who are already ineligible for most public programs.[2]

The Welfare Reform Act

The Welfare Reform Act was signed into law by President Clinton on August 22, 1996. The law is a massive overhaul of U.S. welfare policy that reduces federal spending, eliminates the entitlement "right" of support for poor families, and requires able-bodied persons who receive government assistance to work. In particular, the Welfare Reform Act eliminates the Aid to Families with Dependent Children (AFDC) entitlement program, first established in 1935, and replaces it with a state-implemented Temporary Assistance for Needy Families (TANF) program designed to provide short-term cash assistance to poor families (National Conference of State Legislatures 1996a). The law also reforms such federally funded programs as food stamps, Supplemental Security Income, child care, and child support, and reduces the size of the Social Services Block Grant (SSBG). Data on total U.S. expenditures on major welfare programs in fiscal year (FY) 1995 are included in Table 1 to give readers a sense of the size and scope of programs affected by welfare reform.

One reform that is applicable only to legal immigrants affects affidavits of support. A support affidavit is a contract promise made by a financial sponsor who is a U.S. citizen or permanent resident alien to provide financial assistance to new immigrants to keep them out of poverty. Affidavits are required for all immigrants who are unable to demonstrate that they will not become public charges. These contracts were previously considered unenforceable because several courts had ruled that support affidavits were not legally binding (U.S. General Accounting Office 1995). Under the Welfare Reform Act, however, affidavits for future immigrants are legally enforceable against the sponsor, by either the immigrant or any government that provides a means-tested social service, until the immigrant becomes a U.S. citizen or performs 10 years of qualifying work. Moreover, the person who petitions for an immigrant to come to the United States must also be the financial sponsor, whereas in the past any citizen or permanent resident could present an affidavit of support.

Table 1. Total U.S. Welfare Expenditures in Fiscal Year 1991, by Program and Citizenship Status

Program	1995 Spending[a] (in billions of U.S. dollars)	Percentage of Noncitizen Beneficiaries
SSI	21.0	9
Food stamps	27.4	8
AFDC	25.6	7
Medicaid	156.3	8

Note: [a]Spending includes all federal, state, and local government expenditures.

Source: No author (1996); Green Book, House Committee on Ways and Means (1996, Tables 1-4, 8-22, 16-13, 16-14); Office of Management and Budget (1997).

The Welfare Reform Act also introduces significant changes in immigrant eligibility for social services by creating a three-tiered system. The broadest eligibility is reserved for refugees and asylees (hereafter refugees); there is newly limited access imposed on legal immigrants; and illegal immigrants are almost completely excluded from social services usage. Aliens who become naturalized U.S. citizens are eligible to receive benefits on the same terms as all other citizens, although benefits for citizens have also been limited by the Welfare Reform Act. Changes in alien eligibility are not uniform across programs, however, and their application to immigrants already residing in the United States also varies. Furthermore, several programs are now provided to legal immigrants and refugees at state discretion. It is useful to describe the most important of these changes on a program-by-program basis.

SSI and Food Stamps

SSI is a federally administered program that provides cash assistance to elderly, blind, and disabled persons who are economically disadvantaged (Congressional Budget Office 1995). The Food Stamps Program is administered by the U.S. Department of Agriculture and provides coupons that are redeemable for food purchases to households that qualify on the basis of family size and income (Congressional Budget Office 1995). The Welfare Reform Act reduces FY 1997-2002 spending for food stamps by $27 billion below previous levels. SSI funding is not directly affected, although changes in eligibility for immigrants and citizens are expected to lower spending when compared with previous trends.

Under the old welfare system refugees and legal immigrants were eligible for both SSI and food stamps from the time they entered the country, although sponsored legal immigrants were subject to deeming provisions when determining their income for eligibility purposes. Deeming means that a sponsor's income is considered or "deemed" to be available to an immigrant when determining the immigrant's eligibility for a means-tested public benefit program. Previously, applicants for SSI were subject to deeming only for their first five years in the United States, while food stamps applicants were subject to deeming for their first three years.

Under the new law refugees are eligible for SSI and food stamps only during their first five years in the United States, and legal immigrants are now denied access, although there are some exceptions. The new rules for refugees and legal immigrants apply retroactively during eligibility recertification throughout 1997. Illegal immigrants are ineligible for these programs under both the old and new laws.[3]

Other Federal Means-Tested Programs

These programs include all cash, medical, housing, food assistance, and social services of the federal government that are not mentioned above. Illegal immigrants were previously ineligible for other federal means-tested benefits (with some exceptions), while legal immigrants and refugees were eligible. Refugees and current legal immigrants retain their eligibility, and illegal immigrants remain ineligible. However, newly entering legal immigrants are ineligible, with significant programmatic exceptions, for their first five years in this country and are subject to deeming after that period, until they become citizens.

AFDC/TANF

AFDC is a joint federal/state program administered by the states with shared funding obligations. It provides cash benefits, in amounts determined by states according to federal limits, to families that meet financial need standards based on family size and income. Low-income female-headed households with children are the primary recipients. AFDC is being replaced over the next year by the TANF block grant, which allows states to make available temporary cash assistance, and programs that promote job preparation, work, and marriage.[4] Under the new system, individuals may receive TANF benefits for a total of five years during their entire lifetimes. Federal funding for TANF is frozen at 1996 levels of approximately $16.5 billion, and states are required to put half of all TANF recipients to work by 2002 (American Public Welfare Association 1996).

Illegal immigrants were ineligible for AFDC and are ineligible for TANF. Legal immigrants were eligible for AFDC, although sponsored immigrants were subject to deeming during their first three years in the United States. Now, legal immigrants who were in the United States at the time the Welfare Reform Act was passed are eligible for TANF coverage at a state's discretion. Legal immigrants who arrive after the law was passed are not eligible for TANF for their first five years in the United States, but they may be covered at a state's discretion after that period, and they are subject to the same exceptions as for the SSI and food stamp programs. Refugees were eligible for AFDC and remain eligible for TANF for their first five years in the country and, afterwards, at state discretion.

Medicaid

Medicaid is another joint federal/state program administered by the states with shared funding obligations. Medicaid provides basic and critical health care to poor persons who meet need and categorical criteria determined by states within federal guidelines. Emergency medical assistance is available for all persons who meet income standards but are not categorically eligible for full Medicaid. The Welfare Reform Act does not directly reduce Medicaid appropriations, although reductions in immigrant eligibility are expected to generate savings.

Before the latest reforms, illegal immigrants were eligible only for emergency medical assistance, whereas legal immigrants and refugees were eligible for full Medicaid. The Welfare Reform Act continues this policy toward illegal immigrants and establishes that legal immigrants who were already U.S. residents when the welfare bill was passed may be covered by full Medicaid at state discretion. New legal immigrants are eligible only for emergency assistance during their first five years in the United States and, after that, may be covered at a state discretion, subject to the same exceptions as for the SSI and food stamps programs. Refugees are now eligible for full Medicaid for their first five years in the United States, and coverage may be extended after that period at a state's discretion.

Other State and Local Programs and the SSBG

Numerous state and local public assistance programs provide in-kind and cash assistance to persons whose eligibility is usually determined by income or categorical need. Additionally, the SSBG, implemented by the states, provides services including prenatal care and outreach medical assistance. The size of the SSBG for 1997 is reduced by approximately $400 million dollars to $2.4 billion by the Welfare Reform Act (American Public Welfare Association 1996).

Previously, court rulings that applied the Equal Protection Clause of the 14th amendment to the U.S. Constitution prevented states from distinguishing among legal immigrants, refugees, and citizens, although illegal immigrants could be denied eligibility for most state programs or for federal programs targeted toward citizens.[5] With certain programmatic exceptions and subject to the same eligibility exceptions as the SSI and food stamp programs, the Welfare Reform Act explicitly grants the states authority to distinguish among citizens, refugees, and legal immigrants in the provision of both federally and state-funded social services.[6]

The Immigration Reform Act

The Immigration Reform Act was signed into law by President Clinton on September 30, 1996. The law's main purpose is to prevent the entry and employment of illegal immigrants. It doubles the number of border control agents, increases funding for the Immigration and Naturalization Service (INS), establishes pilot programs for employment-eligibility verification, sets federal standards for state personal-identification documents, reiterates the delegation of discretionary authority to the states to distinguish between legal immigrants, citizens, and refugees, and restricts the right of aliens to challenge INS action. Individuals who sponsor family members under the family reunification segment of current immigration law are now required to have an income of at least 125 percent of the federal poverty level, whereas previously there were no income requirements for sponsors.[7]

IMPLICATIONS OF THE REFORMS

Retrenchment in noncitizen eligibility for social services will have significant effects on both current and future legal immigrants and refugees. Alterations in sponsorship requirements and the institution of binding affidavits of support will affect future legal immigrants. Because legal immigrants and refugees have different needs and levels of benefit use, however, these changes will create differential impacts.

Effects on Current Immigrants

Table 2 summarizes estimated reductions in noncitizen social services access and programmatic spending resulting from the Welfare Reform Act. Approximately 500,000 immigrant SSI and AFDC recipients will lose eligibility over the next year, representing a case load reduction of approximately 35 percent. While most of those becoming ineligible are legal immigrants, some of the approximately 230,000 refugee recipients are no longer eligible, if they have been in the United States more than five years. Similarly, all of the approximately one million immigrants currently receiving food stamps and an additional 600,000 with full Medicaid coverage are expected to lose their benefits.

Reductions in benefits are likely to create economic hardship for some immigrants. Refugees and poorer legal immigrants, including the elderly parents of naturalized citizens, who lack extensive work histories in the United States will be the hardest hit by the new reforms. The degree of hardship is difficult to estimate, however, for several reasons. First, some analysts have argued that, although reductions in services are significant, current immigrants will be able to meet new needs by adjusting their behavior and increasing work efforts (Congressional Budget Office 1995). Second, the extent of reduction in access to other federal, state, and local programs is uncertain, because so much is left

Table 2 Estimates of the Case Load and Cost Impact
for Noncitizens of 1996 Welfare Reform

Program	Number of Noncitizens Losing Eligibility	Fiscal Year 1997 Savings From Noncitizens[a] (in millions of U.S. dollars)	Fiscal Years 1997-2002 Savings From Noncitizens[a] (in billions of U.S. dollars)
SSI[b]	500,000	375	13.3
Food stamps	1,000,000	365	3.7
AFDC/TANF	500,000[c]	N/A[d]	N/A[d]
Medicaid	600,000	105	5.3

Notes: [a]Savings from federal expenditures only.
[b]These SSI estimates have since been superseded by legislation to restore disability benefits to legal immigrants who were in the United States in August 1996 and receiving assistance. See text for details.
[c]Estimates are for heads of households only and do not include children.
[d]Estimates not available because funding is frozen at current levels and reallocated internally within the TANF program.

Sources: Congressional Budget Office (1996); No author (1996); U.S. General Accounting Office (1995).

to the discretion of individual states (Congressional Budget Office 1995). Third, it is difficult to estimate the impact of reductions in eligibility on the poverty status of current immigrants, because data relating income to household participation and eligibility for support programs do not distinguish the immigrant status of individual household members. Households often contain individuals with different immigrant statuses and lengths of residence in the United States. These differences affect eligibility for social services under the new reforms, but are not accounted for by current research. Fourth, in the presence of cutbacks, legal immigrants who face the loss of benefits have an incentive to become naturalized citizens in order to retain their eligibility and soften the impact of benefit reductions.

Effects on Future Legal Immigrants

Reductions in social service eligibility for future refugees, whose status in the United States is largely unplanned, are likely to have a significant impact, unless substantial increases in employment are achieved. For future legal immigrants, beyond the direct barriers to eligibility for services, the higher income standards imposed on sponsors and the fact that sponsors will be financially liable under the new affidavits of support are likely to affect poorer new immigrants the most, making it more difficult for them to locate qualified sponsors. At the same time, the enforcement of new affidavits of support means that immigrants who might otherwise be without support, due to deeming requirements or to the failure of sponsors to provide promised support, will have legal recourse against their sponsors.

Overall, potential legal immigrants who need financial sponsors will be less likely to find one, and these supply considerations may decrease legal immigration and shift the composition toward more skilled migrants (Espenshade, Baraka, and Huber 1997). Moreover, immigrants who do arrive will be less able to rely on government support during times of personal hardship. However, whether restrictions on social services eligibility will also reduce incentives (that is, the demand) for legal immigration is unclear. Although some authors have argued that the generosity of the U.S. welfare system toward immigrants has increased the attractiveness of immigrating to the United States (for example, Brimelow 1995), others insist that the data supporting such conclusions are weak, that foreign understanding of U.S. welfare policy is minimal, and that the relative desirability of the United States rests on such other factors as freedom and relative opportunity (Schuck 1996; Massey and Espinosa 1997; Cornelius 1998).

Cost Savings

Immigrants received a total of $4.5 billion in AFDC and SSI benefits in 1993 (U.S. General Accounting Office 1995). When food stamps are included, the total rises to $5.3 billion in 1996 under the previous eligibility system (Congressional Budget Office 1995). The total cost savings to the federal government from reduced eligibility for immigrants are estimated at $20-25 billion for the six-year period between 1997 and 2002. This is approximately 45 percent of the projected $54 billion savings from the entire welfare reform bill. Eighty-five percent of these reduced outlays arise from SSI, Medicaid, food stamps, and AFDC programs (Congressional Budget Office 1995). The cost of restoring SSI benefits to 500,000 elderly and disabled legal immigrants that was part of the 1997 balanced-budget accords is estimated at $11.4 billion over five years and represents nearly half of all the savings that were to have been realized by restricting benefits to immigrants under the 1996 welfare reform act (Pear 1997). Estimated savings associated with these programs for 1997 and later years are presented in Table 2. State expenditures and other forms of social service spending are also expected to decline, although reliable estimates are unavailable.

Projecting these savings beyond the indicated period is difficult. First, the number and composition of the incoming legal immigrant and refugee population determines much of the demand for public services, and this level is inherently difficult to gauge due to the possibility of new immigration legislation or a changing international climate that alters refugee admissions. Second, changes in deeming and sponsorship requirements may not only make it more difficult to gain entry to the United States for immigrants who would otherwise need to rely on public benefits, but may also encourage those who reside in the United States to work or turn to others for financial assistance.[8] This effect is likely to be largest for those who voluntarily choose to immigrate and less significant for refugees. Third, a greater propensity to naturalize may increase the eligibility of persons who are otherwise ineligible if they remain noncitizens.

In fact, rising trends in naturalization are likely to undercut the savings projected by the U.S. Congressional Budget Office (CBO). For example, the CBO calculation for SSI savings assumes that, of the 80 percent of immigrants receiving SSI who have been in the United States for more than five years, one-third of them will become citizens by 2000 (Congressional Budget Office 1995). However, rates of naturalization have surged dramatically in the last year. A record one million immigrants applied for U.S. citizenship in FY 1995, double the number in FY 1994, and three times as large as the number of 1992 requests (Cohen 1995). These figures suggest that immigrants who are eligible for citizenship are responding quickly to growing pressures for denial of social services, more forcefully perhaps than the CBO anticipated. Although the CBO is correct to note that older immigrants—who are most likely to use SSI—are less likely to naturalize, the prospect of a complete cutoff in aid is likely to be a substantial motivating force.

CONCLUSIONS

The changing political climate toward immigrants in the United States can be interpreted, as we suggested earlier, as an outgrowth of a rise in neo-isolationism and dependency politics that has encouraged a new fiscal politics of immigration (Calavita 1996). Growing anti-immigrant sentiment has merged with forces of fiscal conservatism to make immigrants an easy target of budget cuts. The latest round of welfare reforms directed at immigrants seems motivated not so much by a guiding philosophy of what it means to be a permanent member of American society as by a desire to shrink the size of the federal government and produce a balanced budget.

ACKNOWLEDGMENT

This is a revised version of a paper presented at the conference on Immigration and the Welfare State: Germany and the U.S. in Comparison, Freie Universität

Berlin, Germany, December 12-14, 1996. Partial support for this research was provided by a grant from the Andrew W. Mellon Foundation. We are grateful to Michael Hoefer, Lindsay Lowell, Lawrence Mead, Adam Shrager, Joyce Vialet, and Wendy Zimmermann for supplying valuable source materials, to Deborah Schildkraut and Adam Shrager for a careful reading of the paper, and to Melanie Adams for technical assistance.

NOTES

1.   Portions of this section draw on material in Espenshade (1996).

2.   An important exception concerns the right of illegal immigrant children to have a public school education, guaranteed by the U.S. Supreme Court in the 1982 case *Plyler* v. *Doe*.

3.   The 1997 balanced-budget agreement restored eligibility for SSI benefits to legal immigrants who were in the United States and receiving aid on August 22, 1996 when President Clinton signed the welfare reform bill. It would also allow legal immigrants who were here then to receive benefits if they became disabled in the future. The budget agreement does not restore SSI benefits for new legal immigrants or eligibility for food stamps (Pear 1997).

4.   A block grant gives financial assistance to a state and broad discretionary power to choose particular implementation methods. Federal program guidelines on state action under TANF are significantly fewer than with the AFDC program, although work participation requirements and restrictions on immigrants' usage are increased (National Conference of State Legislatures 1996c).

5.   The Equal Protection Clause states: "No State shall...deny to any person within its jurisdiction the equal protection of the laws." In *Graham* v. *Richardson*, 403 U.S.C. 365 (1971), the U.S. Supreme Court ruled that states may not distinguish between legal immigrants, refugees, and citizens in the provision of social services on the grounds that (1) states are not empowered to make legitimate distinctions between these classes of persons and (2) federal laws preempt state discretion. Discrimination based on refugee and legal immigrant status was deemed a "suspect classification" that cannot be justified without a compelling state interest, which the Supreme Court did not find in a state's desire to reduce spending (National Conference of State Legislatures 1996d).

6.   Programs excluded from state discretion are emergency medical care, emergency disaster relief, public health for immunizations and communicable diseases, and certain in-kind programs as determined by the Attorney General (National Conference of State Legislatures 1996b, p. 2).

7.   The act is also significant for what it does not contain: further restrictions on the eligibility of legal immigrants for social services, limitations on the number of legal immigrants, asylees, or refugees, the Gallegly amendment that would have denied public education to illegal immigrant children, or the automatic deportation of public charges. The restrictions on challenges to INS action are significant because they prohibit class-action lawsuits challenging INS malfeasance and further restrict the rights of aliens to challenge deportation or denial of legal resident status in court (Greenhouse 1996).

8.   Because many of the federal savings associated with deeming provisions are determined by state discretionary decisions about eligibility for programs with federal funding after an immigrant's first five years in the United States, the savings effects will be highly dependent on state action and on the subsequent naturalization behavior of immigrants.

REFERENCES

American Public Welfare Association. 1996. "The Personal Responsibility and Work Opportunity Reconciliation Act of 1996." August 22, Washington, DC.

Borjas, G. J. 1994. "The Economics of Immigration." *Journal of Economic Literature* 32(4): 1667-1717.

Borjas, G. J., and L. Hilton. 1996. "Immigration and the Welfare State: Immigrant Participation in Means-Tested Entitlement Programs." *Quarterly Journal of Economics* 111(2): 575-604.

Brimelow, P. 1995. *Alien Nation: Common Sense About America's Immigration Disaster*. New York: Random House.

Calavita, K. 1996. "The New Politics of Immigration: 'Balanced-budget conservatism' and the Symbolism of Proposition 187." *Social Problems* 43 (3): 284-305.

Chikuhwa, T. 1996. "Refugees and Welfare." *Research Perspectives on Migration 1(1)*. Washington, DC: Carnegie Endowment for International Peace and The Urban Institute.

Cohen, R. 1995. "Citizenship Applications Hit 1 Million." *The Star-Ledger*, December 9, p. 1.

Congressional Budget Office. 1995. *Immigration and Welfare Reform*. CBO Papers (February). Washington, DC.

Cornelius, W. A. 1998. "Appearances and Realities: Controlling Illegal Immigration in the United States." Pp. 384-427 in *Temporary Workers or Future Citizens? Japanese and U.S. Migration Policies*, edited by M. Weiner and T. Hanami. New York: New York University Press.

Espenshade, T. J. 1996. "Fiscal Impacts of Immigrants and the Shrinking Welfare State." Working Paper No. 96-1, Office of Population Research, Princeton University, Princeton, NJ.

Espenshade, T. J., and C. A. Calhoun. 1993. "An Analysis of Public Opinion Toward Undocumented Immigration." *Population Research and Policy Review* 12: 189-224.

Espenshade, T. J., and K. Hempstead. 1996. "Contemporary American Attitudes Toward U.S. Immigration." *International Migration Review* 30(2): 535-570.

Espenshade, T. J., J. L. Baraka, and G. A. Huber. 1997. "Implications of the 1996 Welfare and Immigration Reform Acts for U.S. Immigration." *Population and Development Review* 23 (4): 769-801.

Fix, M., and J. S. Passel. 1994. *Immigration and Immigrants: Setting the Record Straight*. Washington, DC: The Urban Institute.

Greenhouse, L. 1996. "How Congress Curtailed the Courts' Jurisdiction." *The New York Times*, October 27, p. D5.

Hansen, K. A. 1996. "Profile of the Foreign-Born Population in 1995: What the CPS Nativity Data Tell Us." Paper presented at the annual meetings of the Population Association of America, New Orleans, May 9-11.

Massey, D. S., and K. E. Espinosa. 1997. "What's Driving Mexico—U.S. Migration? A Theoretical, Empirical, and Policy Analysis." *American Journal of Sociology* 102(4): 939-999.

Mead, L. M. 1986. *Beyond Entitlement: The Social Obligations of Citizenship*. New York: The Free Press.

Mead, L. M. 1992. *The New Politics of Poverty: The Nonworking Poor in America*. New York: Basic Books.

National Conference of State Legislatures. 1996a. "Analysis of the Personal Responsibility and Work Opportunity Reconciliation Act of 1996." August 30, Washington, DC.

National Conference of State Legislatures. 1996b. "Immigrant Provisions in Welfare Reform: P.L. 104-193." September 17, Washington, DC.

National Conference of State Legislatures. 1996c. "Welfare Reform Update: TANF Briefing—Impact on Immigrants." September 19, Washington, DC.

National Conference of State Legislatures. 1996d. "Welfare Reform Update: Selected Constitutional Issues in Welfare Reform." Washington, DC.

No author. 1996. "Immigrants and Welfare." *Research Perspectives on Migration* 1(1): 1-7, 10-11. Washington, DC: Carnegie Endowment for International Peace and The Urban Institute.

Pear, R. 1997. "Legal Immigrants to Benefit Under New Budget Accord." *The New York Times*, July 30, p. A17.

Plotkin, S., and W. E. Scheuerman. 1994. *Private Interest, Public Spending: Balanced-Budget Conservatism and the Fiscal Crisis.* Boston: South End Press.

Reischauer, R. D. 1996. "The Future of the Public Sector." Paper presented at the conference on What's Ahead? Long Run Trends in the U.S. Economy, Center for Economic Policy Studies Symposium, Princeton University, Princeton, NJ, November 16.

Schuck, P. H. 1996. "Book Review: *Alien Rumination.*" *Yale Law Journal* 105: 1963-2012.

Simon, R. J., and S. H. Alexander. 1993. *The Ambivalent Welcome: Print Media, Public Opinion and Immigration.* Westport, CT: Praeger.

Sorensen, E., and N. Blasberg. 1996. "The Use of SSI and Other Welfare Programs by Immigrants." Income and Benefits Policy Center. Washington, DC: The Urban Institute.

Teitelbaum, M. S., and M. Weiner. 1995. "Introduction: Threatened Peoples, Threatened Borders: Migration and U.S. Foreign Policy." Pp. 13-38 in *Threatened Peoples, Threatened Borders: World Migration and U.S. Policy,* edited by M.S. Teitelbaum and M. Weiner. New York: W.W. Norton and Company.

U.S. General Accounting Office. 1995. *Welfare Reform: Implications of Proposals on Legal Immigrants' Benefits.* GAO/HEHS-95-58. Washington, DC.

THE STRANGERS AMONG US:
SOCIETAL PERCEPTIONS, PRESSURES, AND POLICY

Vincent N. Parrillo

In a democratic society leaders do not initiate state policy, nor do lawmakers pass legislation in a social vacuum. Rather, their actions typically follow what they discern is the will of the public resulting from economic, political, and social conditions that require amelioration, correction, or formalization. Perhaps this interdependency between leaders and led was best expressed by the legendary Hindu religious and political leader, Mahatma Gandhi, when he said, tongue-in-cheek, "There go my people. I must catch up with them, for I am their leader." The implication, of course, is that public perceptions and pressures—more so than research recommendations—do influence the political leadership, which is more often in a reactive rather than proactive posture. While many politicians have an ideology, few seem to have a real vision and, so often, fall prey to Michels's "iron law of oligarchy" (Michels 1949). That is, they typically respond to situations to keep their constituencies happy in order to ensure their own reelection. A good example of this is found in state policies relating to foreigners or *Ausländer*.

Two countries with large numbers of foreigners are the United States, an immigrant-receiving country throughout its existence, and Germany, whose history as an immigrant-receiving country is less well known (even by many Germans). Although the United States has customarily absorbed foreigners into its society, Germany's approach to foreigners, until recently, has been one of cultural isolation and severely limited integrative policies (Ardagh 1991). Nevertheless, in contradiction to their country's past practices, in 1992 two out of three Germans agreed that Germany needed immigrants, while 68 percent of American respondents thought current immigration was bad for the United States (Wiegand 1993, p. 9; Mandel and Farrell 1992, p. 115).

Almost always the issue of cultural homogeneity becomes one rallying point for opposition to foreigners. One hears either the lament for the "cultural purity" of yesteryear in contrast to present-day "multicultural mongrelization" or else the claim that today's cultural unity is undermined by non-assimilating recent arrivals. Such claims about past cultural homogeneity are often the result of the Dillingham Flaw.

THE DILLINGHAM FLAW

Senator William P. Dillingham of Vermont chaired the House-Senate Commission on Immigration (1907-1911) which conducted extensive hearings at a time of the largest immigration influx ever in U.S. history. When its investigation was completed, the commission issued a 41-volume report, partly based on social science research and statistics. Sadly, the report was flawed in its interpretation and application of the data. While commission members reflected the perceptions and biases of their times, the Dillingham Commission also committed several errors of judgment that led it to conclude that immigration from southern, central, and eastern Europe was detrimental to American society. The commission first erred in its use of simplistic categories and unfair comparisons of the "old" and "new" immigrants, ignoring differences of technological evolution in their countries of origin. It also erred in overlooking the longer time interval that immigrants from northern and western Europe had had in which to adjust, as well as the changed structural conditions in the United States that were wrought by industrialization and urbanization in the intervening decades between the two waves of immigration.

Because some of today's negative judgments of out-group members flow from the same faulty logic as that of this immigrant commission, this weakness is called the Dillingham Flaw. Put simply, the Dillingham Flaw is any inaccurate comparison based upon simplistic categorizations and anachronistic observations. The latter occur whenever we apply modern classifications or sensibilities to an earlier time when either they did not exist or, if they did, had a different form or meaning. To avoid the Dillingham Flaw, we must overcome the temptation to use modern perceptions to explain a past that its contemporaries viewed quite differently (Parrillo 1996, pp. 13-16).

Once people fall victim to the Dillingham Flaw, other misconceptions usually follow. Such victims falsely believe they understand their nation's past and confidently assess their own world in what they presume is a wider context. Certain that they have a knowledgeable and objective frame of reference, they tend to be highly critical of the present, culturally heterogeneous scene because they perceive it as different from the culturally homogeneous past. Like that old congressional commission, they are susceptible to mistaken impressions about a "threat" posed by recent immigrants whose presence and behavior they view as different from past immigrants. Pressures on legislators to enact restrictive policies often quickly follow.

THE CULTURAL HOMOGENEITY MYTH IN THE UNITED STATES

That the United States is a nation of immigrants is an undeniable fact, but Americans often do not connect their history to the current multicultural picture. Contemporary public views on multiculturalism or diversity often rest on the erroneous assumption that what occurred in the past were fleeting moments of cultural heterogeneity that yielded to fairly rapid assimilation. The cultural diversity that exists in America today is misperceived as different, more widespread, and resistant to assimilation, something to be celebrated, respected, and maintained, say its proponents, thus making it, in the eyes of alarmed others, not only a new construction but somehow also a threat to the cohesiveness of American society.

A brief look at the nation's past reveals its always-present diversity. At the time of the American Revolution, regional differences in the New England, middle, and southern colonies led to distinct cultures evolving in each of those areas (Fuchs 1990a; Hofstadter 1971). Second, religious diversity—in a time when religion exerted a significant influence on everyday life—created other social-distance barriers. Third, as the 1790 census of the then-13 states (Table 1) revealed, English Americans numbered less than half of the total population (48.3%).

By 1890, before the massive immigration from southern, central, and eastern Europe began in earnest, the melting pot still did not exist for at least 40 percent of the 63 million people living in the United States. For example, more than 9 million people of German descent were highly conscious of their German nationality, particularly after the unification of

Table 1.   Total U.S. Population Distribution, 1790

Ethnic background	Percent
English	48.3
African	18.9
German	6.9
Scottish	6.6
Scots-Irish	4.8
Irish	2.9
Dutch	2.7
Native American	1.8
French/Swedish	1.8
Unassigned	5.2

Source: U.S. Bureau of the Census, 1976.

their homelands in 1871. Mostly concentrated in rural villages and urban centers of the German belt and German triangle of the Midwest and linguistically isolated from the rest of the United States, they constructed their own ethnic world and demonstrated an overwhelming inclination for endogamy (Olson 1979, p. 194). And there were others. In addition to the 7 million-plus African Americans and 6 million Irish Catholics—unassimilated and socially ostracized—ethnic America also counted 1.5 million Scandinavians, 500,000 French Canadians in New England, 250,000 Native Americans, 200,000 Cajuns in Louisiana, 200,000 Dutch, and 150,000 French (Parrillo 1996, pp. 110f.). In response, the U.S. government passed a series of immigration bills and created federal immigrant processing stations at all port cites to keep out "undesirables." Ellis Island became the biggest and best known of these alien screening locales.

Still a land of unassimilated millions, the United States experienced the influx of another 23 million immigrants—mostly from southern, central, and eastern Europe—between 1880 and 1920. By 1910 the nation's older cities in the Northeast contained more foreign-born than native-born Americans, often as many as two-thirds to three-fourths of the cities' populations. Their physically and culturally distinct presence not only set them apart, but dramatically changed the character of these cities. In response to public concerns, the influential writings of people like Madison Grant and the demagoguery of such politicians as U.S. Senator William Bruce of Maryland, who called the Catholic and Jewish immigrants indigestible lumps in the national stomach, Congress passed restrictive immigration laws.

In 1990 the total of African, Asian, Hispanic, and Native Americans living in the United States totaled 25 percent. In 1790, however, the ethnoreligious, linguistically, or racially distinct groups living outside the mainstream but in the 13 states (Irish, Dutch, French, German, Swedish, Native American) totaled 35 percent. Also, African Americans comprised about 19 percent of the total compared to about 13 percent in 1990 (U.S. Census Bureau 1994, 1976).

The American public, however, is mostly unaware of these data showing the United States as less heterogeneous than 200 years ago because of the influence of the Dillingham Flaw. What they see is the aftermath of the 1980s, when 7.3 million immigrants arrived, the second-highest decade of immigration since 1910. If current trends continue, a record-level 9 to 10 million immigrants will enter in the 1990s. Only one in five immigrants now comes from Europe and many Americans worry about the short-term and long-range impacts of the current foreigner presence. In the mid-1990s public concern built, especially in the six major immigrant-receiving states which receive over 80 percent of all immigrants (California, Texas, Florida, New York, Illinois, and New Jersey), and where the school systems and social welfare agencies were overwhelmed by sheer numbers. Public pressure increased to restrict illegal and legal immigration, make English the official language, and eliminate welfare benefits to foreigners. So far six states have sued the federal government to recover these additional costs; the first positive response came from President Clinton who, in the midst of his reelection campaign, earmarked $280 million in relief to California.

THE CULTURAL HOMOGENEITY MYTH IN GERMANY

Speaking on American diversity during two recent USIA-sponsored lecture tours throughout Germany, the author often encountered German citizens in the audience who steadfastly maintained that their country was totally unlike the United States. Their contention was that, until recently, Germany had virtually no population heterogeneity. They believed theirs had essentially been a land of cultural unity that only now was threatened by new, different strangers. This impressionistic sense of public opinion was reaffirmed in a random sampling of 200 Germans in Berlin in November 1994 (see Table 2). About two out of three Germans questioned, regardless of age, believed their country had been culturally homogeneous throughout most of the twentieth century.

And yet Germany has been far from homogeneous. As in the United States, the Dillingham Flaw affects these erroneous perceptions. What looks like past cultural homogeneity in the light of today's cultural diversity was in fact seen differently by previous generations. Moreover, some-

Table 2.   German Perceptions About Cultural Homogeneity, 1994

Question: For most of the twentieth century until recently, Germany has been essentially a culturally homogeneous country.

	Age 18 to 30	Age 31 to 50	Age 51 to 70
Strongly agree	24%	22%	28%
Agree	39%	43%	40%
Disagree	19%	18%	21%
Strongly disagree	11%	10%	7%
No opinion	7%	7%	4%
Residence of respondents			
In Berlin	83%		
Outside Berlin	17%		

Source: Parrillo, survey conducted of 200 respondents in Berlin, November 1994.

thing else in Germany's history helps explain present-day denial of past diversity: The nationalistic fervor following Germany's unification in 1871, coupled with a determination to match its neighbors' more advanced imperialism, prompted pressures for homogenization and led to a government policy that suppressed its history of migration, cultural, and ethnic diversity (Kurthen 1995, p. 935). Several decades later it did not serve Nazi propaganda purposes to acknowledge the reality of ethnic diversity in Germany.

Prior to unification, inhabitants of the different kingdoms and small states saw one another as culturally distinct entities and for good reason. For centuries Germany had been a land of cultural, ethnic, and religious diversity due to extensive immigration and outmigration. Vestiges of those once more pronounced cultural differences can exist throughout Germany.

In the western part of the country, for example, six major German ethnic groups have persisted in their historic regions from Roman and early medieval times to the present, and their numerous subdivisions are of no small historic, linguistic, and cultural importance. They are the Alemannics, Bavarians, Upper Franks, Lower Franks, Saxons, and Frisians. In the east, seven German ethnic groups had their origin in later colonizations from the west, beginning in the ninth century. They are known generally as the Mecklenburgers, the Upper Saxons, the Brandenburgers, the Silesians, the Pomeranians, the Prussians, and the Baltic Germans.

Dialectal divisions in Germany were once of conspicuous significance for the ethnic and cultural distinctions they implied. Today, despite such leveling and standardizing influences as mass education and communication, and in spite of internal migration and the trend among the younger, better-trained, better-educated, and more mobile ranks of society to speak a standard, accentless German, three major dialectal divisions of Germany still persist. These coincide almost identically with the country's major topographic regions: Upper German, Central German, and Lower German. In fact, the varieties of German people are such that the *Encyclopaedia Britannica* makes the following value-laden observation:

> Although such generalizations fail to account for the exceptions, it can be stated that the people of the regions north of the Main River tend more toward the popular notion of the blond, blue-eyed, sober-sided, hard-working, and often dour German of legend. A conspicuous exception to this stereotype would be that of the Rhinelander, noted for his carefree disposition and almost Gallic affinities with Latin Europe. The Franconians in the south also share in the north German profile of being rather sturdily given to work and no nonsense, and they are rather conservative in the preservation of their traditional ways. A great contrast is found between the easygoing natives of Baden and their fellow Alemannians, the Swabians, who among other Germans are thought to be the hardest working, the thriftiest, the most inclined to introspection, and one of the most self-sufficient of German peoples. No greater regional contrasts could exist than that between the Swabians and the Bavarians, the latter noted for their garrulous and sometimes coarse temperament, rough humor, and vigorous pursuit of fleshly pleasures. Nonetheless, if Swabia has furnished Germany with its poets and great intellects, Bavaria is the home of its artists (Goetz 1990, p. 103).

While one might easily quarrel with such stereotypical statements in an authoritative—supposedly objective—source, when pressed the average German will admit to regional differences among Germans, yet still insist they are minimal compared to those displayed by non-Germans living in their country. To an extent they are right, of course. When a new group is more different, the older, less different group no longer seems as removed on the social distance scale as it once did. This was clearly the case in the United States, when the influx of southern, central, and eastern Europeans turned nativist hostility away from the large numbers of Irish and Germans who at least looked like Americans (Parrillo 1997, p. 165).

Beside the differences among Germans in Germany, one can also find various historical minority groups. Chief among them were the Jews, present since medieval times, and who numbered about 800,000 prior to the World War II genocide. Small pockets of the descendants of other nationalities can be found throughout the country. These include descendents of (1) the Dutch invited in the late eighteenth century by Frederick William II to build part of Potsdam and settle there; (2) the similarly invited Bohemian Hussites and French Huguenots in Berlin; and (3) the Italian artisans in Dresden.

During the industrial revolution in the nineteenth century the new enterprises in the Rhine-Ruhr area (the industrial heartland of Germany) recruited hundreds of thousands of laborers from Italy, Poland, Russia, and the Slavic region to dig out the coal, labor in the factories and mills, or else work on the farms in eastern Germany. Evidence of this period of worker heterogeneity remains in the non-German last names found throughout the Rhine-Ruhr region. Later, between 1955 and 1968, foreign workers were recruited from Italy, Spain, Greece, Turkey, Morocco, Portugal, Tunisia, and Yugoslavia to relieve labor shortages in Germany. The government of the German Democratic Republic also recruited workers, though in smaller numbers, from Vietnam, Mozambique, and Cuba. Called guest-workers because they were expected to return eventually to their homelands, the reality is quite different. About 40 percent of Germany's foreign residents have been there for more than 15 years, and 25 percent have lived in Germany for more than 20 years (Steiner 1996).

In 1982 Germany's foreign-born population numbered about 4.7 million, or 7.6 percent of the total population (OECD 1995). By 1995 foreigners had increased to almost 7.2 million, or 8.8 percent of the total population of 81.6 million (German Information Center 1996). This foreign-born population included 2.1 million Turks; 1.4 million ex-Yugoslavs; 586,000 Italians; 360,000 Greeks; 277,000 Poles; 184,000 Austrians; 109,000 Romanians; 107,000 Iranians; and 96,000 Vietnamese (*Statistisches Bundesamt* 1996). As in the United States, the large presence of so many strangers sparked a nativist reaction, both politically and sometimes violently.

PERCEPTIONS AND RESPONSES

Despite their personal and national immigrant heritage, several generations of Americans have consistently voiced their objections in public opinion polls against further immigration. In analyses of such polls since the 1930s—mainly Gallup, NORC, and Harris surveys—Rita Simon found that, although the strength of the sentiment varied, similar negative opinions against increased immigration were the general principle (Simon 1993, 1985, 1974). As another illustration of the Dillingham Flaw, these polls indicate that the only popular and valued immigrants were those who came long ago, whenever long ago happened to be, even though these same groups were reviled at the time of their arrival.

In 1921, for example, today's popular ethnic groups were then so reviled in the press and by the public that Congress enacted the National Origins Quota Act, followed three years later by the

Johnson-Reed Act, reducing annual immigration totals by 80 percent from the 1910-1914 average. Earlier, public pressures had influenced the passage of three literacy bills between 1896 and 1917 that were designed to keep out the large numbers of illiterate European peasants entering the United States. In defiance of Congress and public will, three different presidents vetoed these bills and paid a price for doing so. Presidents Cleveland and Taft consequently did not serve further terms and President Wilson failed to stop Congress from overriding his veto and never again had much political influence. Far-right nativist reaction in the 1920s brought the Ku Klux Klan to its height of popularity. With its newly embraced antiforeign and patriotic platform, it grew to over four million members, more living in the North (the locale of most foreigners) than in the South.

In a content analysis of the leading German magazines—*Der Spiegel, Stern, Quick*—from the 1960s into the 1980s, Galanis (1996) found a direct correlation between several economic indicators (balance of payments, gross national product, unemployment rate) and how these publications depicted the presence of foreign workers. In periods of economic prosperity, the depicted immigrant images were positive, but in periods of economic stagnation or crisis, the depicted photographic images and articles were much more negative. Another finding by Galanis was that articles dealing with the most visible minority, the Turks, were overrepresented in relation to their actual population while others, such as the Yugoslavs, were severely underrepresented, as "Turk" became equated with "foreigner." In times of economic crisis, articles on the Turks were more than negative; they were highly critical attacks.

Antiforeigner sentiment in Germany actually declined between 1980 and 1990, a time of relative prosperity. Public opinion for denying voting rights fell from 39 to 27 percent; those willing to expel foreigners during times of high unemployment dropped from 38 to 20 percent; and those opposing marriage between Germans and foreigners plunged from 33 to 18 percent (Wiegand 1993, p. 18).

However, after unification of Germany in 1990 refugees began pouring into the country and, by 1992, over 438,000 people from the Balkans, central Europe, and elsewhere claimed political asylum. This seemingly uncontrollable influx led to firebombings and antiforeigner violence by far-right groups and to a public clamor to cut back the flow of asylum-seekers (Whitney 1996). In response, the German Parliament changed the asylum law, keeping the constitutional guarantee of protection against political persecution but seeking to exclude persons coming to Germany for economic reasons. No longer could asylum-seekers enter the country freely and seek employment and/or social welfare benefits while waiting many months for their cases to be adjudicated and, even then, make years of appeals if their claim were denied. Now authorities could repel unqualified applicants at the point of entry and have them sent to safe third states (EU member states and Finland, Norway, Austria, Poland, Sweden, Switzerland, and the Czech Republic). They could also be returned to safe states of origin (Bulgaria, Gambia, Ghana, Poland, Romania, Senegal, Hungary, and the Slovak Republic). To deal with public objections to the large-scale presence of Gypsies, the federal government forged an agreement in which Romania agreed to accept deportees (even without valid identity papers) in exchange for German aid. As a result, asylum-seekers from Romania declined from 73,717 in 1993 to 3,522 in 1995 (Steiner 1996).

THE IMPACT OF THE FOREIGN PRESENCE

In 1996 the foreign labor force in Germany constituted 8.7 percent of the total, compared to 9.3 percent in the United States. Foreigners in Germany represented 8.8 percent of the total population in 1995, while in the U.S. foreigners made up 8.7 percent of the total (*Statistisches Bundesamt* 1996, U.S. Census Bureau 1996). The 7.1 million, non-EU, nonethnic Germans in Germany as of December 31, 1995, represented an increase of 26 percent since 1991.

Despite a declining birth rate, population growth in 1991-1995 was 2 percent, due to the influx of foreigners (German Information Center 1996). U.S. births have been declining also since 1990, falling below four million in 1994 for the first time since 1989. As a result, international migration generates a larger portion of U.S. population growth. In 1994 net international immigration accounted for 736,000 of the 2,471,000 (30%) total increase (U.S. Census Bureau 1996).

For these reasons a sizable segment of the U.S. citizenry believes immigration totals are too high. For example, a 1995 *New York Times* poll found that 55 percent of Catholics and 54 percent of non-Catholics wanted immigration decreased (Cronin 1995). Ironically, immigration is decreasing and without government intervention. In 1993 immigration declined 7 percent from 1992, dropping from 974,000 to 904,000; in 1994, it fell to 804,000, a further decline of 11 percent. Moreover, the immigration rate (the sum of immigration totals divided by the sum of U.S. population totals) for the 1980s and 1990s is lower than 11 other decades dating back to the 1840s (INS 1994).

The significance of the immigration rate is that the smaller its number, the less dramatic are the absolute numbers in terms of societal impact. To illustrate, the impact of 8.8 million immigrants in 1901-1910 when the U.S. population in 1910 was 92 million (a 10.4% immigration rate) is decidedly different than perhaps 10 million in 1991-2000 with a population of about 275 million, making the immigration rate about 2.8 percent.

Numbers notwithstanding, many Americans—through direct experience and mass media coverage—sense greater heterogeneity than in the past and clamor for action to curb what they perceive as an inundation of foreigners draining social welfare resources.

Germans also sense greater heterogeneity than ever before, in part because of the concentration of the foreigner population. Three-fourths of them live in the federal states of Bavaria, Berlin, Northrhine-Westfalia, and Hessia, where they make up between 12 to 15 percent of the population. In some densely populated areas such as Frankfurt or Offenbach, they make up more than 25 percent of the population (Steiner 1996).

Among those on the political right, immigration and asylum are highly charged emotional issues. However, anti-immigrant sentiment and the emergence/revival of far-right parties appealing to the neoconservative segment of the German population illustrate only one aspect of German public opinion. The Greens on the left and many Germans in the middle respond more favorably to the need for foreigners as a part of German society.

Yet even as Germans on both sides of the political spectrum ponder their nation's role as a receiving nation, the foreign worker population remained stable, and the severe drop in the number of asylum-seekers—down 26.4 percent in 1993 to 322,842 from 438,191 in 1992—continued in 1994, falling to 127,210. The numbers stabilized in 1995 at 127,937 and, as of November 1, 1996, the yearly totals were about five percent lower than 1995 (Steiner 1996).

FOREIGNERS AND JOB COMPETITION

Despite popular belief that foreigners take jobs away from natives, numerous research studies of both legal and undocumented immigrants show little evidence that they adversely affect the earnings of any group or cause unemployment, even in areas of high immigrant concentration (Rumbaut 1994; Fix and Passel 1994; Simon 1989; Muller and Espenshade 1985). Moreover, immigrants do not increase the rate of unemployment among native-born Americans, even among minority, female, and low-skill workers (Simon 1995). No empirical evidence documents any numerical importance in the displacement effect of natives from jobs (Borjas 1990, p. 92).

Several factors explain these two realities. Potential immigrants have considerable awareness of labor market conditions in the host country and tend not to come if their skills are in small demand. At the same time, immigrants increase the demand for labor across a range of occupations; they consume goods and services as well as produce them. In the long run they create as many jobs with their purchasing power and with the new businesses they start as the jobs they themselves occupy.

Beside the fact that immigrants fuel the economy both as consumers and workers, they also play another important role. While Germany and the United States have declining birth rates, they also have rapidly expanding retired populations, vast entitlement schemes, and expectations of constantly rising living standards. Consequently both countries require a growing supply of tax-paying foreign residents to balance their actuarial accounts and guarantee social security and welfare programs for the elderly in something like their current form. Foreign workers thus fill an important need, both for the industries unable to hire enough qualified domestic workers and for the government dependent on their payroll contributions.

FOREIGNERS AND SOCIAL WELFARE

Another major area of contention is social welfare costs. A 1986 *New York Times* poll found 47 percent of all Americans believed that most immigrants wind up on welfare and abuse the system. On this subject, research findings of studies completed after 1990 differ widely, ranging from immigrants generating a yearly surplus of $1,400 per capita to public coffers to causing an annual deficit of $1,600 per capita. The disagreements result from:

- varying definitions of immigrants (inclusion or exclusion of refugees and/or undocumented aliens);
- characteristics of different population segments of immigrants (age, national origin, social class, time of arrival, etc.);
- differences in measuring tax-dollar costs;
- differences in what is included as public services and revenue sources; and
- a variety of other complex conceptual issues (Vernez and McCarthy 1995).

Generally speaking, immigrant welfare costs increased significantly in the 1980s, more so than among the native born (Van Hook and Bean 1996; Borjas 1995). These higher welfare usage rates, however, are particularly clustered among refugees and elderly immigrants (Fix and Passel 1994). Refugees, because of their needy circumstances and immediate eligibility, normally have high rates of welfare assistance. Elderly immigrants, usually joining their adult children under family reunification, often secured Supplemental Security Income (SSI) and Medicaid welfare assistance after meeting their three-year residency requirements, driving these expenditures skywards. Key provisions of the 1996 welfare reform act addressed this problem.

However, if one excludes refugees and elderly immigrants, the rate of welfare use for new immigrants who entered between 1980 and 1990 is considerably below the rate for natives aged 15 and above. Even illegal aliens contribute more in taxes than they receive in benefits; new data suggests that the undocumented pay about 46 percent as much in taxes as natives do and use about 45 percent as much in services (Simon 1995).

One consistent fact about immigration for all countries and in all decades is that new immigrants—both legal and illegal—are more concentrated than natives in the younger age range of the labor force when individuals pay more in taxes than they draw in social welfare assistance programs. The native born typically are more concentrated in the childhood and elderly periods of economic dependence when social welfare payments far exceed revenue flows.

Immigrants typically arrive when they are young and healthy and therefore use fewer welfare services on average, than do native families who receive in greater proportion expensive Social Security, Medicare, and other aid to the aged. Furthermore, during its first several decades in the United States, the average immigrant family pays more in taxes than does the average native family. Altogether, the immigrant family contributes yearly about $2,500 more in taxes to the public coffers than it obtains in services (Simon 1995).

Immigrants who came to the United States between 1970 and 1992 had an aggregate income of $300 billion (9% of all U.S. personal income) and paid a total of over $70 billion in taxes of all kinds. When subtracting from those taxes the estimated costs for all forms of social services used by immigrants and their children, including education expenses disproportionately borne by state and local governments, these immigrants entering the United States between 1970 and 1992 generated a surplus of at least $25 billion to $30 billion (Passel 1994).

Another misconception is that undocumented aliens are flooding across borders to get social welfare benefits. In truth, very small proportions of illegals receive free public services, either because they see themselves as in the country temporarily, or they are afraid of being apprehended if they apply at government offices. The findings of North and Houstoun, corroborated by other studies, are representative (Simon 1989, p. 289). They reported these proportions of illegals using services: free medical care, 5 percent; unemployment insurance, 4 percent; food stamps, 1 percent; welfare payments, 1 percent; child schooling, 4 percent. Virtually no illegals receive Social Security, the costliest program of all, but 77 percent paid social security taxes, and 73 percent had federal income taxes withheld (North and Houstoun 1976, p. 142). In Germany 2.1 million foreigners paid into social security through their jobs in 1994 (Steiner 1996).

A poll of eminent U.S. economists found remarkable consensus that twentieth-century immigration had (and has now) a positive effect on the economic condition of the United States. Included in the surveys were 38 persons who had been president of the American Economic Association, as well as those who had been members of the President's Council of Economic Advisers. These economists also extended their backward assessment into a forward-looking policy judgment. When asked, "What level of immigration would have the most favorable impact on the U.S. standard of living?" 56 percent said "more," 33 percent said "same number," and none said "fewer." Only 11 percent said "don't know" (Simon 1989, pp. 357-364).

Similarly, in Germany—despite some outcries that foreigners are an economic burden—the data shows the opposite. In 1992 the Institute of German Business found that foreign workers generated 10 percent of the country's gross national product. Another leading German economic institute calculated that recent migrants to Germany contributed about 14 billion Deutsche marks ($8.4 billion) more in taxes and social security contributions in 1991 than they received in various welfare payments.

ETHNOGENESIS AND ASSIMILATION

Even if economic fears are overcome, the acceptance of visibly distinct ethnic groups still requires a breaking down of cultural barriers. Movement from subcultural isolation to full assimilation is aided by the process of ethnogenesis (Alba 1985, pp. 9-12; Greeley 1977). As it absorbs some elements and modifies others of the host culture, an ethnic group also retains, modifies, or drops elements from its cultural heritage in adapting to the new country. Consequently, the group develops cultural traits and values still unlike the natives but also unlike the nonmigrating people in their homeland.

Because ethnogenesis is a gradual process, many natives become impatient with their slow acculturation and even fearful that societal cohesion—particularly in language and culture—is in jeopardy. Public pressure to enact protective measures often results. By 1995 in the United States, for example, 22 of the 50 states had passed English-only legislation (Parrillo 1997, p. 537). A 1995 poll revealed that 73 percent of Americans thought English should be the official language of the country, a view supported by more than a third of the members of Congress, where such legislation was proposed but not yet enacted (Hedden 1995).

Despite claims of English-only proponents that such laws are necessary, numerous studies show them to be unnecessary. In practice and attitude, the newcomers reflect a desire to learn the new language. Most U.S.-born Latinos and Asians use English as their primary language at home (de la Garza 1992). About nine in 10 Hispanics believe it is their duty to learn English as quickly as possible, and almost all think it is essential for their children to become competent in English (AJC 1987).

Moreover, children of immigrants typically identify with the country in which they grow up, not the land of their parents. As any educator in the United States or Germany can explain, children pick up a new language rather easily. After a short time they converse as easily as if they were native born. This language acquisition and socialization in the host country leads to an ease in identifying with one's adopted country. Although many factors determine how fully foreigners assimilate, including their motivation, a key one is official policy.

DEFINING CITIZENSHIP

Naturalization is the ultimate step for an immigrant and the host country. It denotes formal movement toward structural assimilation and inclusion into the national identity. It is here where foreigners indicate their desire to integrate into the host society, and where state policy demonstrates the society's willingness to accept as one of its own a stranger from another place. When the strangers' physical features or ethnoreligious marks challenge the similarity-attraction bond, their ease or difficulty in acquiring citizenship is the quintessence of that country's actions matching or contradicting its rhetoric.

The concept of determining citizenship rests on one of three principles: *ius soli*, the law of the birthplace; *ius sanguinis*, the law of parentage; or *ius domicilii*, the law of naturalization under certain conditions, including length of residency. *Ius soli* has its historic roots in the United States, Canada, and Australia—countries colonized by immigrants of different European nationalities who wanted their children to become Americans, Canadians, or Australians. Britain and France, which after World War II took in large numbers of European and non-European residents of former colonies, added the *ius soli* principle to their nationality laws. However, determining citizenship by descent or bloodline (*ius sanguinis*), originally set down in the 1791 French *Code Napoléon*, is the more globally applied principle. It has governed the nationality laws of Islamic countries, Japan, and most European countries, including Germany. Citizenship through naturalization (*ius domicilii*) is of recent origin in some modern nation-states formerly predisposed only to *ius sanguinis* citizenship.

Differences in nation-state origins and in the evolution of naturalization laws partially explain some distinctions between Germany and the United States in their official policies toward foreigners today. Recent legislation in each country, however, reflects lawmakers' efforts to charter a new course that is a notable departure from the past but reflective of current public sentiment.

In recent months the U.S. Congress flirted with the idea of passing new immigration restrictions, but election-year pressures caused the legislators not to act. However, prompted by other pressures to overhaul the welfare system to eliminate abuses, move people from dependency to work, and reduce the deficit, Congress passed the welfare reform bill, placing restrictions on immigrants, who were perceived as driving up welfare costs despite substantial evidence that they have always pulled their own weight.

The new law bars most legal immigrants who have not become naturalized citizens, including permanent residents and refugees granted asylum, from receiving food stamps and Supplemental Security Income (SSI), which benefits the elderly and the disabled. Legal immigrants are also denied welfare and Medicaid benefits in their first five years in the country, the waiting period before one can become a citizen. According to the Congressional Budget Office in 1996, it was anticipated that more than 500,000 immigrants would lose SSI benefits and about one million would lose food stamps. Legal immigrants represent only about 5 to 9 percent of those on public aid, yet they would absorb about 40 percent of the cuts in welfare. More than half of the legal immigrants destined to lose their benefits had lived in the United States for more than five years and were thus likely eligible for naturalization (Soros 1996).

Not surprisingly, an upsurge in citizenship applications arose. Over one million residents applied for citizenship in the 1997 fiscal year, an unprecedented number. Many were, no doubt, motivated more by self-protective economic concerns for their old age or that of their parents than by patriotic enthusiasm and the desire to formalize their national identities. Unwittingly, the federal government thus redefined what U.S. citizenship means to foreigners and will not reap as much savings in social welfare as it anticipates.

While the unintended consequence of U.S. government policy to restrict foreigners benefiting from social welfare is increasing citizenship applications, liberalized German laws of 1991 and 1993 deliberately sought to increase naturalization. After several years of deliberation, the government acted to close the gap between de facto immigration and the restrictive definition of naturalization for *Ausländer* (Kurthen 1995, p. 933). Under current law second-generation Germans can apply for naturalization without the previously required German-language fluency and assimilation into the German culture. Moreover, the reduction of the naturalization fee from US$3,000 to US$60 further serves to encourage foreigners to apply for citizenship.

Non-Germans aged 16 to 23 can now become naturalized if they have (1) resided in Germany for eight years, (2) attended a school in Germany for six years, (3) given up their previous citizenship (except for those accepted with multiple citizenship), and (4) not been convicted of a major felony. Those older can file if they have resided in Germany for 15 years and are able to support themselves and their family (condition waived if an individual was not responsible for going on public assistance).

More Turkish Germans are thus opting for citizenship. In the first year of liberalized citizenship qualifications, their numbers increased 73 percent, from 2,016 in 1990 to 3,502 in 1991. In 1994, 19,000 Turkish Germans acquired citizenship, an increase of 442 percent (Whitney 1996). Still, the numbers are small, given the two million Turks who live in Germany. Part of this is due to the minimum length of residence before residency.

Another reason may be the fairly close geographic proximity of their homeland. In the United States there is a greater likelihood of immigrants from greater distances becoming citizens than those whose homelands are nearer. To illustrate, for immigrants admitted in 1982, seven of the top 10 countries with the highest naturalization rates through 1993 were from Asia. Those with the lowest rates were mostly from Canada, Mexico, and the Caribbean (INS 1996).

In addition to Turkish Germans, citizenship applications from the other major ethnic groups in Germany are proportionately even lower. Many simply do not want to become German citizens, as revealed in a 1995 survey in which 51 percent of foreign parents in Germany objected to the naturalization of their children, while just 24 percent said they would support it (German Information Center 1996).

CONCLUSIONS

Falling victim to the Dillingham Flaw, natives in Germany and the United States often see their countrymen as part of the cultural homogeneity of the land now under threat by dissimilar newcomers. In reality, the similarity-attraction bond among today's native-born population did not exist among their ancestors, for those generations viewed themselves as different from one another.

Economists and many government officials recognize that one important benefit of immigrants is their human capital. One of their greatest contributions is the impetus they give to a country's growth and vitality, enhancing its productivity as workers and consumers. Self-selected for boldness and determination among the populations they come from, driven by necessity to work hard, and stimulated by the tension of living in two cultures, foreigners are likely to be an energetic, positive force in their adopted country. Data from numerous economic analyses support this position.

Enactment of state policy typically reflects the public will, and in the United States an anti-immigrant sentiment influenced passage of voter referendums in California, English-only laws in 22 states, and a national welfare reform act eliminating benefits for noncitizens. Although in the 1996 election the right-leaning Republican party suffered setbacks in states with large numbers of immigrants (California, Florida, Illinois) and lost seats in the House of Representatives, it gained seats in the U.S. Senate, making that body more conservative for 1997-1998. With a smaller House margin and a Democrat as President, the fate of pending bills on a national English-only law and immigration restrictions is uncertain.

Despite liberalized naturalization laws, Germans and their lawmakers still subscribe to the myth that theirs is not an immigrant-receiving country. Newcomers of German descent are perceived as returning nationals, not immigrants, despite language and cultural differences. Asylum-seekers are temporary aliens, and guest workers are not labor migrants, even if they have put down roots in Germany. Despite recent changes in citizenship regulations based on the principle of *ius domicilii*, naturalization rates are only about half those of the United States. Proximity to the homeland and a still-prevalent ethos of an ethnocultural national homogeneity, despite its nonexistence, are the two most likely explanations for this lower level. Even so, the processes of ethnogenesis, acculturation, and integration are social dynamics that, from a multigenerational perspective, should lead to a higher naturalization rate.

Virtually all immigrant subcultures in the United States have been convergent over several generations, despite their early vitality, apparent resistance to assimilation, and the public perception of nonassimilability. As detailed earlier in this paper, cultural and structural assimilation were not rapid processes. Although it does not even approximate the atmosphere of a melting pot, Germany still needs time for more of its second- and third-generation residents—as products of German education and socialization—to manifest their desire for absorption into the German national identity.

Meanwhile, public sentiment and state policy in Germany and the United States will be critical determinants of the level of assimilation attained by those seeking it. The United States, hailing itself as a nation of immigrants, and Germany, denying the reality of its immigrant presence, have embarked on paths not only contradictory of each other but of their past philosophies as well. Germany has liberalized its approach to its foreigner population, while the United States has curtailed its commitment to the social welfare of its foreigners. As the millennium approaches, the perceptions, pressures, and policies in both countries for the remaining years of the twentieth century will shape, for the early part of the next century at least, the cohesiveness and social welfare of their pluralistic populations.

REFERENCES

Alba, R. D. 1985. *Italian Americans: Into the Twilight of Ethnicity*. Englewood Cliffs, NJ: Prentice-Hall.

American Jewish Committee. 1987. "English as the Official Language." New York.

Ardagh, J. 1991. *Germany and the Germans: After Unification*. New York: Penguin Books.

Borjas, G. J. 1990. *Friends or Strangers: The Impact of Immigrants on the U.S. Economy*. New York: Basic Books.

Cronin, A. 1995. "Catholics and the Line Between Church and State." *New York Times*, October 8, p. E5.

de la Garza, R. O. 1992. *Latino Voices: Mexican, Puerto Rican, and Cuban Perspectives on American Politics*. Boulder, CO: Westview Press.

Fix, M., and J. Passel. 1994. "Setting the Record Straight: What are the Costs to the Public?" *Public Welfare* 52 (Spring): 6.

Fuchs, L. H. 1990. *The American Kaleidoscope: Race, Ethnicity, and the Civic Culture*. Hanover, NH: Wesleyan University and the University Press of New England.

Galanis, G. 1996. "A Picture of Immigrants as Revealed by the Mass Media of West Germany." Paper presented at the Pan-Hellenic Convention of Psychological Research, Rethimno, Crete (May).

Goetz, P. W., ed. 1990. "Germany: The People." *The New Encyclopdia Britannica*, vol. 20. Chicago: Encyclopedia Britannica.

Greeley, A. M. 1977. *The American Catholic: A Social Portrait*. New York: Basic Books.

Hedden, S. 1995. "One Nation, One Language?" *U.S. News & World Report*, September 25, pp. 38-42.

Hofstadter, R. 1971. *America at 1750*. New York: Knopf.

Kurthen, H. 1995. "Germany at the Crossroads: National Identity and the Challenges of Immigration." *International Migration Review* 29 (4): 914-938.

Mandel, M. J., and C. Farrell. 1992. "The Immigrants." *Business Week*, July 13, pp. 114-122.

Michels, R. 1949. *Political Parties*. Glencoe, IL: Free Press; orig. 1911.

Muller, T., and T. J. Espenshade. 1985. *The Fourth Wave: California's Newest Immigrants*. Washington, DC: Urban Institute Press.

North, D. S., and M. F. Houstoun. 1976. *The Characteristics and Role of Illegal Aliens in the U.S. Labor Market: An Exploratory Study*. Washington, DC: Linton and Company.

OECD. 1993. *Système d'Observation Permanente des Migrations Internationales (SOPEMI)*. Paris: OECD.

Olson, J. S. 1979. *The Ethnic Dimension in American History*. New York: St. Martin's Press.

Parrillo, V. N. 1996. *Diversity in America*. Thousand Oaks, CA: Pine Forge Press.

Parrillo, V. N. 1997. *Strangers to These Shores* (5th ed.). Boston: Allyn and Bacon.

Passel, J. S. 1994. "Immigrants and Taxes: A Reappraisal of Huddle's 'The Cost of Immigrants.'" PRIP-U1-29, Washington, DC: Urban Institute.

Rumbaut, R. G. 1994. "Origins and Destinies: Immigration to the United States since World War II." *Sociological Forum* 9 (December): 615.

Simon, J. L. 1989. *The Economic Consequences of Immigration*. Cambridge, MA: Basil Blackwell.

Simon, J. L. 1995. *Immigration: The Demographic and Economic Facts*. New York: Cato Institute and National Immigration Forum.

Simon, R. J. 1974. *Public Opinion in America, 1936-1970*. Chicago: Rand McNally.

Simon, R. J. 1985. *Public Opinion and the Immigrant*. Lexington, MA: Lexington Books.

Simon, R. J. 1993. "Old Minorities, New Immigrants: Aspirations, Hopes, and Fears." *The Annals of the American Academy of Political and Social Science* 30 (November): 61-73.

Soros, G. 1995. "Immigrants' Burden." *The New York Times*, October 2, p. A19.

Statistisches Bundesamt. 1995. Cited on German Information Service website (http//www.germany-info.org/close-up/facts.htm).

Steiner, S. 1996. "Foreigners in Germany and the New German Asylum Law." German Information Center, unpublished manuscript.

U.S. INS (Immigration and Naturalization Service). Various years. *Statistical Yearbook*. Washington, DC: U.S. Government Printing Office.

U.S. INS (Immigration and Naturalization Service). Various years. *Annual Report*. Washington, DC: U.S. Government Printing Office.

Van Hook, J. V.W., and F. D. Bean. 1996. "Welfare Reform and SSI Receipt Among Immigrants in the United States." Paper presented at the conference on Immigration and the Welfare State, Freie Universität Berlin, December 13.

Vernez, G., and K. F. McCarthy. 1995. *The Costs of Immigration to Taxpayers: Analytical and Policy Issues*. Washington, DC: Rand.

Whitney, C. R. 1996. "Europeans Redefine What Makes a Citizen." *The New York Times*, January 7, p. E6.

Wiegand, E. 1993. "Zunahme der Ausländer-feindlichkeit? Einstellungen zu Fremden in Deutschland und Europa." *ZUMA-Nachrichten* 16 (31):7-28.

IMMIGRANTS, MARKETS, AND RIGHTS

James F. Hollifield and Gary Zuk

International migration reached "crisis" proportions in America and Western Europe in the last two decades, both in terms of the numbers of migrants involved and their impact on the politics and societies of the receiving countries. Compounding the problem, the influx came in an era of rising unemployment, sluggish growth, and political change and uncertainty. The foreign population more than doubled in the United States, for example, from less than 10 million to more than 20 million during this span, and the percent unemployed crested at 9.5 percent in the 1970s before settling at its current rate of 5.5 percent (Cornelius, Martin, and Hollifield 1994; Fix and Passel 1994). Among the European states, France and Germany bore the brunt of the postwar population movements.[1] The latter's migrant population swelled nearly 20 percent from 1980-1990 alone, and France has a greater number of foreigners than all the OECD nations except the United States and Germany (OECD 1993). At the same time the two European republics, which enjoyed very low unemployment levels in the early 1970s, faced rates that topped 8 percent in Germany, and 10 percent in France a decade later, and today hover between 8 and 12 percent (Cornelius, Martin, and Hollifield 1994). Not surprisingly, all three countries began searching for ways to defuse the potentially explosive issues of immigration and unemployment.

AMERICAN EXCEPTIONALISM

It is important to put the American experience into a comparative and historical context, because we find many of the same political and economic dynamics at work in Europe and the United States driving immigration policy in liberal directions, in spite of growing popular and political opposition to admissionist policies. Yet migration scholars resist comparing America's immigration experiences with Europe's, drawing attention to singular or defining characteristics distinguishing the former from the latter (Fuchs 1990a; Horowitz and Noiriel 1992). First, there is the U.S. system of separation of powers which, through the process of judicial review, gives judges a kind of veto over many public policies. This fundamental feature helps to explain the course of the civil rights movement, and the rise of a new liberal-republican consensus in the 1950s and 1960s.[2]

Then there is America's legacy of slavery. The American republic was founded on a contradiction: equality before the law for everyone except blacks. This peculiarity led de Tocqueville to predict that "if ever America undergoes great revolutions, they will be brought about by the presence of the black race...that is to say, they will owe their origin, not to the equality, but to the inequality of condition" (de Tocqueville 1945, p. 270). This is precisely what happened in the Civil War and, again, in the civil rights movement of the 1950s and 1960s. These turning points completely changed attitudes toward citizenship (Kettner 1978; Archdeacon 1990; Fuchs 1990a).[3]

A third special feature arises from what can be called a "founding myth" of the republic, namely that the United States is a "nation of immigrants," founded as a refuge from the religious and ethnic conflicts of Europe and, therefore, more tolerant of newcomers than the "older," more established nation-states of Western Europe. Many scholars indeed draw a sharp distinction between nations of immigrants and countries of immigration (see, for example, Freeman and Jupp 1992). The practical import of this myth is that legal immigration has much greater legitimacy in the United States than in Europe.[4] As a consequence, immigration policy in the United States took an expansive turn after World War II, becoming more liberal after the passage of the Immigration and Nationality Act of 1965, which repealed the restrictive national origins quotas and made family unification and skills the centerpiece of U.S. policy. Twenty-five years later, the Immigration Act of 1990 raised the ceiling on legal immigration by 40 percent.

The partial exception to the new liberalism was the Immigration Reform and Control Act (IRCA) of 1986, which instituted employer sanctions for those who knowingly hire undocumented immigrants; but

IRCA became an expansive policy, nonetheless, because millions of illegals were granted amnesty and adjustments of status under its auspices, and the employer sanctions have prove to be very difficult to enforce. Since the end of the cold war, we have seen a weakening of the rights-markets coalitions which sustained the more liberal immigration and refugee policies of the 1970s and 1980s. This has been accompanied by a rise of nativist and populist politics in certain states, especially California, which held a referendum on restricting illegal immigration by cutting social services to illegal immigrants and their children—the Save Our State (SOS) Initiative—Proposition 187.

THE POLITICAL ECONOMY OF IMMIGRATION

The varied national responses to the migration crisis would seem to indicate that there is little to link one national experience with another. Moreover, comparisons to the American experience are often rejected: as noted above, America is seen as a nation of immigrants, with a much larger territory, and a civic or political culture that is more tolerant of ethnic and cultural differences.[5] Indeed, especially since the end of the cold war, the American "model" of a multicultural and immigrant society was derided as a bad one that could only lead to greater social and political conflict (Wacquant 1992; Body-Gendrot 1993; Todd 1994; Hörder 1993; Hollifield 1994, 1996). The riots in Los Angeles in 1992 provided more grist for the mill of European critics. But, we contend that the problems of immigration control (and ultimately the assimilation of foreign populations) in Europe and America are much the same.

The global economic dynamic, which historically drove migration, affected the two regions in similar ways. Indeed, the great postwar population movements began, for the most part, in response to the demand for cheap labor and the pull of high-growth economies, which in the 1950s and 1960s literally sucked labor from poorer countries of the periphery. These international labor migration and demand-pull forces were subsequently legitimized by the receiving states through guest-worker and *bracero* policies (Miller and Martin 1982; Straubhaar 1986; Calavita 1992; Steinert 1995). The economically beneficial movement of labor from south to north was in keeping with the liberal spirit of the emerging global economy (Keohane and Nye 1977; Ruggie 1982; Gilpin 1987). Under the *Bretton Woods* system, international institutions like the IMF, GATT, and the World Bank—in addition to the OECD—were set up to encourage and promote international exchange, including trade, foreign investment, and—when necessary to maintain high, noninflationary rates of economic growth—labor migration.

What started as an efficient transfer of labor from south to north, however, quickly became a social and political liability in the 1970s, as growth rates in the OECD countries slowed in the aftermath of the recession of 1973-1974, leading to major policy shifts in Western Europe (but not in the United States) to stop immigration or, at least, the recruitment of foreign workers (Miller and Martin 1982; Martin 1991). At the same time demand-pull forces were reinforced by supply-push ones, as the populations of peripheral countries continued to grow rapidly, while their economies weakened. Informational and kinship networks had been established between immigrants and their home countries, helping to spur immigration, in spite of efforts by receiving states in Western Europe to stop all forms of it.[6]

Global economic (push-pull) forces provided the necessary conditions for the continuation of immigration in Western Europe after the implementation of restrictionist policies in the mid-1970s; and they helped to account for the surge in immigration (the so-called fourth wave)[7] in the United States beginning in the late 1970s. Yet to understand fully the crisis of immigration control in the 1980s and 1990s, we must look beyond markets to liberal-republican and social democratic developments in the three major receiving states, the United States, France, and Germany. The struggle to win civil and social rights for marginal groups, including ethnic minorities and foreigners and the institutionalization of these rights in the jurisprudence and public policy of liberal-republican states provide the sufficient conditions for continued immigration. It is this new, more expansive type of citizenship which has led to a convergence of the European and American experiences (Hollifield 1992).

The victory of the United States in World War II and the political settlement which followed, especially the establishment of a liberal republic in West Germany, led to the creation and institutionalization of a liberal international order, backed in large measure by U.S. economic and military power. This new international regime helped to disseminate information and to encourage trade and the exchange of ideas through new technologies of transportation and communication. The cold war accentuated the process by forging ever-stronger political and economic alliances between Western Europe and the United States and by creating new (rights-oriented), political coalitions, which pushed the United States to live up to its "liberal creed" (Dahl 1956; Myrdal 1962; Fuchs 1990b; Smith 1993; Tichenor 1994; Zolberg 1994).

The civil rights "revolution" in America led also to a more expansive immigration policy, one having repercussions far beyond its borders, that helped to transform relations among states and between states and individuals (Schuck 1984, 1993; Tichenor 1994). In short, rights became increasingly important in international relations (Keohane and Nye

1980; Ruggie 1982; Gilpin 1987). World politics entered an unprecedented phase of openness (in the West), which had dramatic effects on the ability of states to control their borders. The migration tides of the 1950s and 1960s created new and reluctant lands of immigration in Western Europe, and they brought to the fore questions of citizenship, the rights of minorities, and multiculturalism. The crisis also awakened xenophobic sentiments, spawning new social movements and political parties opposed to the extension of rights to noncitizens, ethnic minorities, and asylum seekers (Betz 1993; Thränhardt 1993; Faist 1994; Ireland 1994). The political backlash against immigrants and immigration notwithstanding, civil and social rights for foreign and ethnic minorities had become entrenched in the jurisprudence, institutions, and political processes of the United States, as well as the West European states. A new sensitivity to the rights of minorities and refugees grew out of the experiences of World War II and the cold war and made it difficult for states simply to expel or deport unwanted migrants, Operation Wetback notwithstanding (Herbert 1991; Bade 1992; Calavita 1992; Hörder 1993). In postwar Western Europe as well as the United States, immigration provoked constitutional debates, and it severely tested the capacity of political, judicial, and administrative authorities to "manage" the crisis (Hollifield 1992; Cornelius, Martin, and Hollifield 1994).

IMMIGRATION TRENDS, LABOR MARKETS, AND THE BUSINESS CYCLE

The literature on immigration tends to fall into three broad categories: historical, economic, and sociological. Among the classic works in the field are Higham (1955) and Fuchs (1990a) on the United States, Noiriel (1988) and Weil (1991) on France, and Bade (1992) on Germany. All offer solid overviews of immigration, whereas the economic literature tends to focus more on labor markets and the human capital effects of immigration (see, for example, Simon 1989; Borjas 1990). The most extensive literature on immigration is that of sociologists and demographers (e.g., Portes and Bach 1985; Portes and Rumbaut 1990; Waldinger 1994) or demographers and policy analysts (e.g., Papademetriou 1989; Teitelbaum 1992; Fix and Passel 1994). The political science or political economy literature is much sparser, and there are fewer studies on the issue of control, especially comparative analyses of the political economy of immigration (see, however, Hollifield 1992; Miller 1992; Freeman 1993; Castles and Miller 1994; Cornelius, Martin, and Hollifield 1994; Weiner 1995).

To bridge theoretical and empirical gaps in the political-economic literature on immigration control, we seek to address empirically issues which hitherto have been the subjects of conjecture. Specifically, what is the relationship between immigration and the business cycle in advanced industrial democracies?[8] And how is it related to the expansion of civil and social rights in these societies? Is increased immigration somehow a consequence of the civil rights revolution and the rise of the liberal welfare state? Is there an electoral effect (left versus right) on immigration flows? Here we have chosen to focus on questions relating to (1) immigration, the labor market, and the business cycle, (2) the effects of civil rights politics on immigration and refugee policy, and (3) electoral effects. The analyses are limited to the American case, but we have tried to keep the United States in a comparative perspective.

Most immigration analysts simply assume (or assert) that immigration flows are, to a large extent, a function of economic conditions in the sending and receiving countries. This is the logic of push-pull. A recent study (Martin and Midgley 1994, p. 21) neatly captures this relationship. The number of immigrants to the United States fluctuated with economic conditions here and abroad and with U.S. immigration policies. No doubt supply-push conditions in the sending countries clearly influence immigration flows. However, it is important to keep in mind that throughout the modern era, but especially in the twentieth century, supply-push migration has been more or less constant. Indeed, there is a virtually unlimited supply of migrants ready to cross international borders when the opportunity presents itself; but, as we shall argue, the determining factors are demand-pull and the rise of rights-based politics. Each of these will be examined in turn. First, we will explore demand-pull factors in the United States during the last century. It was not until the third wave (1880-1914) that serious attempts were made by the federal government to regulate immigration. The 1882 Chinese Exclusion Act suspended immigration for Chinese workers for a period of 10 years, barred them from naturalization, and provided for the deportation of undocumented Chinese workers. The Immigration Act of 1891 was the first comprehensive, federal immigration policy. It created a Bureau of Immigration (under the Treasury Department) and established procedures for the deportation of illegal aliens.

Figure 1 depicts trends in legal immigration to the United States, percent change in nominal GNP, and fluctuations in the unemployment rate. We see the apparent effects of this new regime for regulating immigration on the flow data, which decreased from about 600,000 per annum in 1892 to 250,000 by the end of the decade. Even so, the decline coincided with the 1893-1897 recession, suggesting that flows continued to respond to economic conditions even during a period of tighter control.

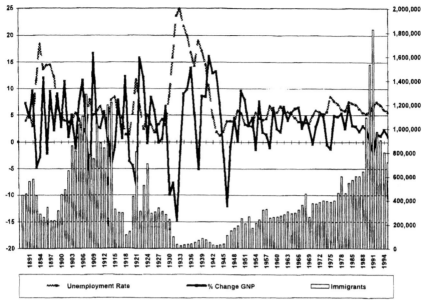

Source: INS Statistical Yearbook and *Statistical Abstracts of the United States.*

Figure 1. U.S. Immigration, Unemployment, and GNP Change, 1889-1996

Immigration rebounded strongly at the turn of the century, as did the economy, reflected in positive growth trends and shorter and more shallow economic cycles (except 1908). Meanwhile, in the labor market unemployment rates were well below the average, historically (depicted by the broken line). In short, demand-pull factors were especially conducive, and immigration flows reached record levels. Indeed the foreign-born population of the United States climbed to 15 percent, an all-time high. No major immigration legislation was passed during this period, except for literacy tests imposed by Congress in 1917, restrictions that were rendered moot by the effects of the First World War which, parenthetically, abruptly ended the third wave of immigration.

In the interwar years, immigration revived but fluctuated markedly presumably in reaction to the volatile economic conditions of the "Roaring '20s." The 1924 Immigration and Naturalization Act brought the nation's first permanent numerical limits on immigration. These restrictive measures codified the national-origins quota system, writing racial bias (in favor of northern and western Europeans) into law. The new measures also introduced skill-based, human capital criteria into immigration policy for the first time. Nevertheless, countervailing economic forces, for example, low unemployment, dampened the effects of the 1924 act. The migration mix began to shift away from Europe and toward the Western Hemisphere, with Canadians and Mexicans comprising the largest number of newcomers.

The onset of the Great Depression in 1929-1930 demonstrates quite clearly the powerful effect of business cycles on immigration flows in the pre-1945 period. Demand-pull forces ceased virtually overnight, as the economy shrank and unemployment soared (see Figure 1). At the same time the New Deal reforms ushered in a new era in American politics, expanding the concept of citizenship to include social and economic, as well as civil rights. This period marked the beginning of the end of racial and ethnic exclusion across a range of American public policies. The experience of the Great Depression, together with the effects of the Second World War, fundamentally altered American domestic and foreign policy.

Immigration laws did not come immediately to reflect the more expansive view of citizenship and the greater openness and self-confidence of trade and foreign policy. The McCarran-Walter Immigration and Nationality Act of 1952, for example, continued the system of national origins quotas that was put in place in the 1920s. It established a preference system based on family unification and skills but set new limits on immigration from the Eastern and Western Hemispheres. The recovery of the economy during the Second World War led to a rapid decline in unemployment rates and a surge in GNP but no real increase in legal immigration. Once again the disruptive effects of war in Europe had cut the United States off from its traditional sources of immigrant labor, forcing employers to turn to Mexico and Central America—a trend that would continue for the rest of the twentieth century.

As a way of further illustrating the relationship between immigration and the business cycle during the period from 1890 to 1945 bivariate correlations were calculated. These reveal no significant association between percent change in GNP and immigration flows; however, there is a correlation ($r = -0.42$; significant at the .001 level) with changes in the unemployment rate. This suggests that immigration was sensitive to demand-pull forces, even though the overall performance of the American economy (in terms of national income) had less effect in this regard.

Concerning the post-1945 period, immigration trended upward for virtually the entire era, producing the so-called fourth wave in the 1970s and 1980s, a trend that shows no sign of cresting. It is hard to find any dramatic effect of policy interventions during this roughly 50-year period, with the notable exception of the Immigration Reform and Control Act of 1986 (IRCA), which led to the legalization of 2.8 million people over a five-year period from 1987 to 1992. If we extract the IRCA admissions, the curve is still sloping upward from the late 1980s into the 1990s. We also must take into account the effects of the 1990 act, reforming legal immigration, which contributed to the upward trend by increasing legal immigration ceilings (40%), and expanding categories for admission, based on skills, diversity criteria, and temporary protected status for those fleeing natural or human-made disasters.

The postwar rise in immigration often is attributed to the effects of the Immigration and Nationality Act of 1965, which repealed the national origins quotas; but it is important to keep in mind that these quotas had lost much of their punch as a consequence of changes in immigration policy in the 1950s, for example, the admission of over 300,000 war brides and their dependents (many of whom were Asian), following the Second World War. The "revolution" in civil rights, from *Brown* v. *Board of Education of Topeka* in 1954 to the Civil Rights Act of 1964, also helped to weaken the ethnic and racial dimensions of immigration policy. Yet, looking at the flow data, the effect of the 1965 act is not immediately obvious. Indeed, we see only a slight increase in immigration in the late 1960s, then a leveling off in the early 1970s. What is most intriguing, however, is that the rise in unemployment, associated with the oil shocks and the two recessions of the 1970s, seems to have had only a minimal effect on immigration flows. We see a sharp climb in immigration in 1977, followed by a marked decline in 1979—swings of one to two hundred thousand. Then the curve is more or less flat, until we reach IRCA in the late 1980s, when the upward trend continues. The Immigration and Nationality Act of 1976, which extended the 20,000-per-country limits to the Western Hemisphere, seems to have had little effect on flows; likewise, the Refugee Act of 1980 had no discernible effect, the *Mariel* boatlift from Cuba notwithstanding.

By far the most important immigration reforms of the postwar period, at least in terms of their impact on flows, were IRCA (1986) and the Immigration Act of 1990. The effects here are clearly visible. The effects of the business cycle and labor market trends on immigration flows are less evident. If we look at the simple bivariate correlations for the postwar period (1945-1993), we again find no significant relationship between percent change in GNP and flows; however, there seems to be one between labor market performance (as measured by the unemployment rate) and flows, but the correlation (−0.36, significant at the .01 level) is the opposite of what we would expect. Clearly, as a way of sorting out and distinguishing economic and policy or political effects, we need to develop a preliminary model that incorporates the two.

IMMIGRATION AND POLICY INTERVENTIONS

Toward this end we constructed a time-series model that enables us to separate economic and political effects. The results of the analyses are presented in Tables 1 to 3. The first thing to note is that, conforming to the conventional wisdom, economic conditions in the receiving country, in this case the United States, have an impact on legal immigration flows. Specifically, demand-pull forces, as measured by unemployment rates and percent change in GNP, seem to have a modest impact on flows in the United States for the period 1891-1993. The omega (θ) coefficients, which assess the influence of a unit change (here 1%) in unemployment/ GNP on immigration flows (percent change), is −1.5 and 0.8 percent, respectively, and significant at the .05 level. In the model, we control for (but do not report) a variety of policy interventions, as well as the effect of World War I. Note that labor market conditions have almost twice the impact of changes in GNP, which again conforms to the literature.

Recalling our argument developed in the first sections of this paper, we predicted a weakening of economic effects over time, as immigration policies changed to reflect the rise of rights-based politics, a new legal culture, and more expansive definitions of citizenship and membership, especially during the 1950s and 1960s. Accordingly, we segmented the data into two (pre- and postwar) periods. Table 2 reports the effects of political and economic change on flows from 1891-1945. Once again, we find a highly significant labor market effect. Percent change in unemployment has a strong, inverse relationship with legal immigration flows, (−1.1, significant at the .05 level). Percent change in GNP has a somewhat more modest effect (= 1.0, statistically significant at the .10 level). We also controlled for the effects of World War I, which curtailed flows −69.6 percent each year that the war progressed; and the 1924 National Origins Act, which wrote into law the principle of racial/ethnic exclusivity and served to reduce immigration dramatically (−137.1%). Mean immigration for the entire period averaged 4.3

Table 1.   Labor Market and Economic Effects on Immigration, 1981-1993

	Impact	t
Labor market	−1.5	−2.1[1]
(% unemployed)	(.07)	
GNP	0.8	2.0[2]
(% change)	(0.4)	

Notes: [1]Significant at the .05 level, one-directional test (standard errors in parentheses).
[2]Significant at the .10 level, one-directional test (standard errors in parentheses).

Source: *INS Statistical Yearbook* and *Statistical Abstracts of the United States.*

Table 2. Labor Market, Economic, and Policy Effects on Immigration, 1893-1945

	Impact	*t*
Labor market	−1.1	−1.5[2]
(% unemployed)	(.07)	
GNP	1.0	2.4[1]
(% change)	(0.42)	
WWI	−69.6	−2.0[1]
	(35.2)	
National Origins Act	−137.1	−5.6[1]
	(24.6)	
Mean immigration (% change)	4.3	

Notes: [1]Significant at the .05 level, one-directional test (standard errors in parentheses).
[2]Significant at the .10 level, one-directional test (standard errors in parentheses).

Source: *INS Statistical Yearbook* and *Statistical Abstracts of the United States.*

percent per annum. Thus, even when controlling for policy interventions and The Great War, business cycles and labor market conditions had a sizable and significant impact on immigration flows in the prewar period.

Table 3 reports the results for the period 1946-1993. Several interesting and counterintuitive findings stand out. As expected, demand-pull effects weaken over time, despite a more highly integrated global labor market than ever before, because of improvements in transportation and communication. Migration networks, however, are even more efficient, with chain migration much in evidence. Indeed the omega coefficient shows no sig-

Table 3. Labor Market, Economic, and Policy Effects on Immigration, 1946-1994

	Impact	*t*
Labor market	−1.9	
(% unemployed)	(1.8)	−1.0
GNP	0.4	
(% change)	(0.9)	0.5
1965 Act	−1.6	
	(13.2)	−0.1
1986/1990 Acts	7.7	
	(18.7)	2.0*
Mean immigration (% change)	6.2	

Notes: [1]Significant at the .05 level, one-directional test (standard errors in parentheses).
[2]Significant at the .10 level, one-directional test (standard errors in parentheses).

Source: *INS Statistical Yearbook* and *Statistical Abstracts of the United States.*

nificant labor market effect, while GNP is negligible for the postwar period. A number of policy interventions, by contrast, are significant. The McCarran-Walter Act of 1952, for example, is linked to a 31.4 percent decline in immigration net of demand-pull forces and other policy effects.

Surprisingly the Immigration and Nationality Act of 1965, which often is cited as the most important immigration reform since the 1924 Act (Reimers 1985), has *no* discernible empirical effect (−1.6, not significant) on legal immigration. The caveat, of course, is that the 1965 act led to a gradual change in the composition of these flows by stimulating family unification (which was, after all, the purpose of the act) and encouraging larger flows from non-European sources (which was an unintended consequence of the act). The two major immigration reforms of the late twentieth century, the Immigration Reform and Control Act of 1986 (IRCA) and the 1990 Immigration Act, however, combined to have an enormous influence on immigration that simply dwarfed all others. Indeed the combined effect of these two acts spurred immigration by 164 percent.[9] In sum, the analyses show the impact of expansive (rights-based) policies in limiting the heretofore close relationship between business/labor market cycles and legal immigration flows.

THE RIGHTS-MARKETS COALITION

Policy interventions (by themselves) are perhaps not the best measures of the rise of rights-based politics. In terms of future research, the most challenging task will be to devise indicators of changes in the legal culture, including civil and social rights in all three liberal republics, France and Germany, as well as the United States. We anticipate using the value of benefits to immigrants as one (interval level) measure of new, rights-based politics. These data generally have been limited to scholars studying the United States (see, for example, Borjas 1990; Fix and Passel 1994). Data are available, for example, on Supplemental Security Income, Medicaid, food stamps, and AFDC payments to resident aliens and political refugees.

As a proxy measure of rights-based politics and its impact on immigration flows, we incorporated an electoral (left-versus-right) effect into our time-series model, using Democrat and Republican administrations. Not surprisingly, we found no significant association between the two. Looking at the history of immigration politics and policy it is hard to find a clear partisan split, since both parties lurch from one consensus to another—for restriction or admission—depending upon the historical context (Tichenor 1994). Indeed, as noted by Zolberg, immigration politics in the United States often creates strange bedfellows of the (economically liberal) Republican right and the (politically liberal) Democratic left (Zolberg 1994).

As a way of exploring this rights-markets coalition, we looked at the history of voting on rights, immigration, and trade issues in the Congress, from the 1964 Civil Rights Act to the 1993 NAFTA vote. What we expected to find was a great deal of consistency in voting on these issues over roughly a 30-year period, but with a breakdown of the coalition starting in 1990 with the end of the cold war. To this end, we looked dyadically at voting on six bills in the Senate and the House: (1) the 1964 Civil Rights Act and the 1965 Immigration and Nationality Act; (2) the 1986 Immigration Reform and Control Act and the 1988 Canadian-American Free Trade Agreement (CAFTA); and (3) the Immigration Act of 1990 and the North American Free Trade Agreement (NAFTA).

By dyad and starting with the Senate, we found that the Civil Rights Act and the 1965 INA passed by exactly the same vote (76 aye and 18 nay), with the principal opposition coming from Southern Democrats, who voted (four to 18) against civil rights and (nine-13) against the INA. Eighty-two percent ($N = 75$) voted the same way on the two bills, indicative of a growing rights coalition and a close affinity between issues of civil rights and immigration, with the boll weevils (Southerners) in the minority. Over 20 years later the rights coalition, which includes left-liberal Democrats and right-liberal or libertarian (free market) Republicans, is still intact. When we looked at voting on the next dyad, IRCA and CAFTA, the vote was 75-21 for the former and 83-nine for the latter. Here we see more dissent on the immigration issue and less on trade, perhaps because trade with Canada is not viewed as terribly threatening for any major interest or constituency. Still the coalition is not as strong as it was in the 1960s, with only 68 percent of the senators voting the same way on the two bills ($N = 54$). If we break out seven high-immigration states (California, Texas, Florida, New York, Illinois, New Jersey, and Massachusetts), we find an overwhelming support for both measures, with only one dissenting vote (on IRCA) among senators from these states.

Voting on the last dyad (the 1990 Act and NAFTA) in the Senate shows the continued strength of the rights-markets coalition, even well into the post-cold war period. The vote was 81-17 in favor of the 1990 Act and 61-38 for NAFTA. In this case 71 percent of the senators ($N = 45$) voted the same way. In the seven high-immigration states (see above), the vote was more nuanced, seven to five in favor of NAFTA and 10-two for the 1990 act. Thus, at least in the Senate, the rights-markets coalition remained relatively strong throughout this period, with two-thirds to three-fourths of the members voting the same way on issues of rights, markets, and immigration. As we shall see, however, this pattern did not hold in the House.

Table 4. Roll-Call Voting on Rights, Markets, and Immigration Issues,
U.S. Senate

	1964 Civil Rights and 1965 Immigration and Nationality Acts	
	Rights	INA
	76-18	76-18
D	46-18	52-15
R	30-0	24-3
SD+	4-18	9-19
Same-way voting: 82% (*N*=75)		
	Canadian-American Free Trade Agreement and the Immigration Reform and Control Acts	
	Markets	ICRA
	83-9	75-21
D	43-7	41-4
R	40-2	34-17
M*	10-0	11-1
Same-way voting: 68% (*N*=54)		
	North American Free Trade Agreement and Visa Quota Restrictions Acts	
	Markets	VQR
	61-38	81-17
D	27-18	40-14
R	23-10	41-3
M*	7-5	10-2
Same-way voting: 71% (*N*=45)		

Notes: + Southern Democrat.
          * Major immigration state.

Source: *The Congressional Record.*

With the first dyad (1964 Civil Rights Act and 1965 INA), in the House the votes were 289-126 for civil rights and 320-69 for immigration, again with chief opposition on both bills coming from the boll weevils. Southern Democrats voted 12-88 against civil rights and 36-52 against immigration. On this dyad, in the House voting consistency was 65 percent ($N = 222$), not nearly as high as in the Senate.

On the second dyad (IRCA and CAFTA), the tallies in the House were 230-166 on the immigration issue (note that IRCA was designed to deal primarily with the problem of *illegal* immigration) and 366-40 on the issue of freer trade with Canada. Unlike the Senate, we do not find strong bipartisan support for these measures. Republicans in the House opposed the IRCA by a vote of 62-105, and votes in our seven high-immigration states were much closer: 91-61 on NAFTA, compared to 136-nine on CAFTA. This is probably an interest/constituency-driven vote, in the sense that freer trade

Table 5. Roll-Call Voting on Rights, Markets, and Immigration Issues, U.S. House

	1964 Civil Rights and 1965 Immigration and Nationality Acts	
	Rights	INA
	289-126	320-69
D	153-91	202-59
R	136-35	118-10
SD+	12-88	36-52
Same-way voting: 65% (*N*=222)		

	Canadian-American Free Trade Agreement and the Immigration Reform and Control Acts	
	Markets	ICRA
	366-40	230-166
D	215-30	168-61
R	151-10	62-105
M*	136-9	91-61
Same-way voting: 52% (*N*=153)		

	North American Free Trade Agreement and Visa Quota Restrictions Acts	
	Markets	VQR
	234-200	231-192
D	102-156	186-65
R	132-43	45-127
M*	93-76	101-57
Same-way voting: 34% (*N*=92)		

Notes: + Southern Democrat.
 * Major immigration state.

Source: *The Congressional Record.*

with Mexico is viewed as much more threatening than freer trade with Canada. Fifty-two percent of the representatives (*N* = 153) voted the same way on IRCA and CAFTA. We can see more volatility in the coalition and the beginning of the breakdown of bipartisan, rights-markets (or strange-bedfellow) coalitions.

On the last dyad (the 1990 Act and NAFTA), the vote on reforming legal immigration was opposed by Republicans (45-127), as was the case with the IRCA; but it passed anyway by a vote of 231-192; whereas the vote on NAFTA was a bit closer (234-200), with Democrats leading the opposition to this trade agreement. They voted 102-156 against it. If we break out the major immigration states, we can see that, on balance, they favored the immigration bill (101-57), as well as the trade agreement (93-76). Overall, only 34 percent of the House members (*N* = 92) voted the same way on the 1990 Immigration Act and NAFTA.

We can see distinct differences between the two legislative bodies on trade and migration matters. The rights-markets coalition seems to have held together in the Senate, even with the end of the cold war, whereas it has fallen apart in the House. How can we explain this divergence? At least three explanations are possible. First is that the Senate is simply less partisan (more bipartisan) than the House. The second explanation, which is closely linked to the first, is that the Senate is capable of taking a longer term (less electorally driven) view of trade and migration, both of which have important foreign policy ramifications. Finally, it's possible that the House is driven more directly by the interests of much smaller districts/constituencies and is, therefore, more sensitive to any distributional (or allocational) consequences of trade and migration policies. Moreover, in the House Democrats seem to form rights-markets coalitions in support of trade and migration issues, but the Republicans, who continue to support freer trade, have lost their attachment to rights, especially in the immigration area. This is borne out in recent votes on welfare reform, as the Republican-controlled House has pushed for eliminating welfare benefits for legal as well as illegal immigrants.

CONCLUSIONS

The argument advanced in this paper is that, historically, immigration in liberal/industrial democracies has been a function of markets, as defined by demand-pull and supply-push forces, and rights. With the rapid rise in immigration in Western Europe and the United States in the postwar period, states have tried to intervene to regulate or, in some cases, to stop immigration; but these efforts have been confounded by market forces and by shifts in the political and legal cultures of these states. For this reason we have seen a convergence of immigration policy outcomes across a range of cases, despite important historical, cultural, and institutional differences.

To test the argument about the increasing importance of rights as a mitigating factor in the relationship between economic conditions and immigration flows, we constructed a time-series model using U.S. data. What we found is that there is a modest historical relationship between legal immigration flows, labor market conditions, and the business cycle (for the period 1891-1993), even when we control for policy change. However, when we performed the same analysis on data from the prewar (1891-1945) and postwar (1945-1993) periods, we found that the economic effects weaken in the postwar period. The biggest policy effects are those of the 1924 National Origins Act, depressing immigration by 137 percent, and the 1986/1990 acts, which had a cumulative, positive impact of 164 percent. We also found that the 1965 Immigration and

Naturalization Act had no discernible effect on immigration flows, when we controlled for changes in the labor market and business cycles.

These results tend to confirm the argument that the rise of rights-based politics and policies has broken the historical relationship between economic conditions in the United States and legal immigration flows, at least temporarily. But the breakdown of rights-markets coalitions (especially in the House of Representatives) and changes in law and policy could reverse this trend, which has contributed heavily to the fourth wave of immigration in American history. The cold war may have created an artificial political environment which made it easier to overcome partisan differences on issues of rights, trade, and migration. This would explain the long-standing consensus (from the late 1950s to the early 1990s) for maintaining more open (i.e., less protectionist and less restrictionist) trade and migration policies. As the cold war has waned (along with American hegemony), it has become more difficult to sustain the rights-markets/strange-bedfellows coalition. It is harder to sell free trade and admissionist immigration policies on the basis of rights (a more just and open world order) or markets (greater efficiency in labor markets). Politicians are now more sensitive to the distributional (as opposed to the allocational) consequences of these policies.

In conclusion we argue that economic explanations of immigration capture only part of the story. To get a complete picture of the migration crisis and problems of control, it is essential to look at the impact of changes in the legal and political cultures of receiving states.

NOTES

1. Germany has the largest concentration of immigrants of any state in Europe (roughly 6.8 million or 8.5% of its total population). France, with a foreign population of 3.6 million, is second in this respect. For an overview of the global migration crisis, see Cornelius, Martin, and Hollifield (1994) and Weiner (1995).

2. We can see, however, a similar institutional dynamic (expanding rights) at work in France and Germany (Hailbronner 1984; Schuck 1984; Lochak 1985; Aleinikoff and Martin 1995), and some measure of separation of powers, and judicial review. Moreover, as citizenship and membership have expanded in the two societies (thanks, in part, to active judiciaries), so, too, has the level of associational and political activity among immigrant and minority groups (Ireland 1994).

3. It is debatable whether other liberal republics have been marked by such a recent and traumatic past; but some parallels can be found in France (fascism and Vichy, as well as colonialism and the independence struggle in Algeria) and Germany (Nazism and the Holocaust). Indeed, in all three countries, hideous crimes committed in the name of the nation and the "people" helped to transform the politics of the present and the future, leading to constitutional and institutional reforms. French immigration and refugee policy was established in the *Ordonnances* of 1945, in the wake of the fascist Vichy regime, whereas the liberal German asylum policy was written into the Basic Law (Article 16) with the founding of the

Federal Republic (*Bundesrepublik*) in 1949, and it remained unchanged until 1993 (Noiriel 1988; Weil 1991; Bade 1992).

4.   On this point, cf. Simon (1989), Archdeacon (1990), Teitelbaum (1992). However, as Martin Schain and others have noted, the development and legitimization of this myth of the melting pot and *e pluribus unum* were very difficult, and there were periods when America's immigration policy was rife with nativism and racism (cf. Higham 1955; Body-Gendrot and Schain 1992; Smith 1993; Schain 1994). Moreover, in the history of polling on the issue of immigration, never more than 10% of the public have supported an expansive immigration policy (Archdeacon 1990; Teitelbaum 1992). Indeed, in the current debate over U.S. immigration policy, we can see sharply contrasting views over its costs and benefits. The libertarian economist, Julian Simon, for example, contends that immigration has been a tremendous boon to the economy, and, therefore, the government should not tamper with the basic market mechanisms that determine immigration flows (Simon 1989). The labor economist, George Borjas, by contrast, argues that the "ethnic capital" of today's immigrants is much lower than in previous waves. Government should, then, control the borders, stop illegal immigration (especially from the poorer countries of Latin America), and select more carefully legal immigrants according to strict human or ethnic capital criteria (Borjas 1990).

5.   The stark contrast between the "American model" and various European ones finds its origins in the works of de Tocqueville, especially *Democracy in America*. This essentially nineteenth-century view argues that there is a wide gap between American and European experiences with immigration. The Tocquevillian perspective has been reinforced in some of the contemporary literature on comparative immigration history (see, for example, Safran 1989; Horowitz and Noiriel 1992).

6.   For more on supply-push forces, see Bean (1989), Garcia y Griego (1989), Martin (1991), and Weiner (1995).

7.   Martin (Martin and Midgley 1994) chronicles four major waves of immigration to the United States: the English-led movement of the 1790-1820 era; the German-Irish settlements of 1821-1860; the Southern European exodus of 1861-1914; and the Latin-American and Asian influx that continues up to today.

8.   The argument that immigration is largely a function of economic and social forces, and that it is closely linked to the business cycle, has been made by, *inter alios*, Piore (1979) and Straubhaar (1988). Both (structural) Marxist theories of immigration, which stress the importance of maintaining an industrial reserve army and dual labor markets in advanced capitalist economies, as well as neoclassical economic theories of immigration, which stress push-pull forces, assume that immigration is closely connected to the business cycle.

9.   The cumulative impact of IRCA and the 1990 act was derived by taking the ratio of the impact (omega) coefficient to 1 minus the or delta (rate decay) parameter.

REFERENCES

Aleinikoff, T.A., and D.A. Martin. 1995. *Immigration Process and Policy*, 3rd ed. St. Paul, MN: West Publishing.

Archdeacon, T. 1990. *Becoming American*. Hanover, NH: Wesleyan University and the University Press of New England.

Bade, K., ed. 1992. *Deutsche im Ausland—Fremde in Deutschland. Migration in Geschichte und Gegenwart*. Munich: Beck.

Bean, F. B. 1989. *Mexican and Central American Population and U.S. Immigration Policy*. Austin, TX: University of Texas Press.

Betz, H-G. 1993. "The New Politics of Resentment: Radical Right-Wing Populist Parties in Western Europe." *Comparative Politics* 25 (4): 413-427.

Body-Gendrot, S. 1993. *Ville et violence: l'irruption de nouveaux acteurs*. Paris: Presses Universitaires de France.

Borjas, G. J. 1990. *Friends or Strangers: The Impact of Immigrants on the U.S. Economy*. New York: Basic Books.

Calavita, K. 1992. *Inside the State: The Bracero Program, Immigration, and the I.N.S.* New York: Routledge.

Castles, S., and M. J. Miller. 1994. *The Age of Migration - International Population Movements in the Modern World*. New York: MacMillan.

Cornelius, W. A., P. L. Martin, and J. A. Hollifield, eds. 1995. *Controlling Immigration. A Global Perspective*. Stanford: Stanford University Press.

Dahl, R. 1956. *A Preface to Democratic Theory*. Chicago: University of Chicago Press.

de Tocqueville, A. 1945. *Democracy in America*, vols. 1-2. New York: Alfred A. Knopf.

Faist, T. 1994. "Immigration, Integration and the Ethnicization of Politics." *European Journal of Political Research* 25: 439-459.

Fix, M., and J. S. Passel. 1994. *Immigration and Immigrants: Setting the Record Straight*. Washington, DC: The Urban Institute.

Freeman, G. P. 1993. "Why the Immigration Intake is too Large in Democracies." Unpublished paper presented at the annual meeting of the American Political Science Association. Washington, DC.

Freeman, G. P., and J. Jupp, eds. 1992. *Nations of Immigrants: Australia, the United States, and International Migration*. Melbourne: Oxford University Press.

Fuchs, L. H. 1990a. *The American Kaleidoscope: Race, Ethnicity, and the Civic Culture*. Hanover, NH: Wesleyan University and the University Press of New England.

Fuchs, L. H. 1990b. "The Corpse That Would Not Die: the Immigration Reform and Control Act of 1986." In *L'Immigration aux États-Unis*, edited by J. F. Hollifield and Y. Charbit (special issue of the *Revue Européenne des Migrations Internationales*) 6: 111-127.

Garcia y Griego, M. 1989. "The Mexican Labor Supply, 1990-2010." *Mexican Migration to the United States: Origins, Consequences, and Policy Options*, edited by W.A. Cornelius and J.A. Bustamente. San Diego, CA: Center for U. S. Mexican Studies, University of California, San Diego.

Gilpin, R. 1987. *The Political Economy of International Relations*. Princeton NJ: Princeton University Press.

Hailbronner, K. 1984. *Ausländerrecht*. Heidelberg. C.F. Müller.

Herbert, U. 1991. *A History of Foreign Labor in Germany, 1880-1980: Seasonal Workers—Forced Laborers—Guest Workers*. Ann Arbor, MI: University of Michigan Press.

Higham, J. 1955. *Strangers in the Land: Patterns of American Nativism, 1860-1925*. New Burnswick, NJ: Rutgers University Press.

Hollifield, J. F. 1992. *Immigrants, Markets and States: The Political Economy of Postwar Europe*. Cambridge: Harvard University Press.

Hollifield, J. F. 1994. "Entre droit et marché." In *Le défi migratoire: questions de relations internationales*, edited by B. Bade and C. W. de Wenden. Paris: Presses de la F.N.S.P.

Hollifield, J. F. 1996. "The Migration Crisis in Western Europe: The Search for a National Model." In *Migration-Ethnizität-Konflikt: Systemfragen und Fallstudien*, edited by K. Bade. Osnabrück: Universitätsverlag Rasch.

Hörder, D. 1993. "People on the Move: Migration, Acculturation, and Ethnic Interaction in Europe and North America." Annual Lecture Series, German Historical Institute, Washington, DC. No. 6. Oxford: Berg Publishers.

Horowitz, D. L., and G. Noiriel. 1992. *Immigrants in Two Democracies: French and American Experience*. New York: New York University Press.

Ireland, P. 1994. *The Policy Challenge of Ethnic Diversity: Immigrant Politics in France and Switzerland*. Cambridge, MA: Harvard University Press.

Keohane, R. O., and J. S. Nye. 1977. *Power and Interdependence: World Politics in Transition.* Boston, MA: Little Brown.

Keohane, R. O., and J. S. Nye. 1980. "The Theory of Hegemonic Stability and Changes in International Economic Relations, 1967-1977." In *Change in the International System,* edited by O. Holsti. Boulder, CO: Westview Press.

Kettner, D. 1978. *The Development of American Citizenship, 1608-1870.* Chapel Hill, NC: University of North Carolina Press.

Lochak, D. 1985. *Étrangers: de quels droits?* Paris: Presses Universitaires de France.

Martin, P. L. 1991. *The Unfinished Story: Turkish Labor Migration to the Federal Republic of Germany.* Geneva: International Labor Office.

Martin, P. L., and E. Midgley. 1994. "Immigration to the United States: Journey to an Uncertain Destination." *Population Bulletin* 49 (2): 2-45.

Reimers, D. 1985. *Still the Golden Door.* New York: Columbia University Press.

Miller, M. J. 1992. "Never Ending Story: The U.S. Debate over Illegal Immigration." In *Nations of Immigrants,* edited by G.P. Freeman and J. Jupp. Melbourne: Oxford University Press.

Miller, M. J., and P. L. Martin. 1982. *Administering Foreign-Worker Programs.* Lexington MA: D. C. Heath.

Myrdal, G. 1962. *An American Dilemma: The Negro Problem and American Democracy.* New York: Harper and Row.

Noiriel, G. 1988. *Le creuset français.* Paris: Seuil.

Papademtriou, D. 1989. *The Effects of Immigration on the U.S. Economy and Labor Market.* Immigration Policy and Research Report 1. Washington, DC: U.S. Department of Labor.

Piore, M. J. 1979. *Birds of Passage: Migrant Labor in Industrial Societies.* Cambridge: Cambridge University Press.

Portes, A., and R. Bach. 1985. *Latin Journey: Cuban and Mexican Immigration to the United States.* Berkeley: University of California Press.

Portes, A., and R. G. Rumbaut. 1990. *Immigrant America: A Portrait.* Berkeley: University of California Press.

OECD. 1993. *Système d'Observation Permanente des Migrations Internationales (SOPEMI).* Paris: OECD.

Ruggie, J. G. 1982. "International Regimes, Transactions, and Change: Embedded Liberalism in the Postwar Economics Order." *International Organization* 36 (Spring): 379-415.

Safran, W. 1989. "The French State and Ethnic Minority Cultures: Policy Dimensions and Problems." In *Ethnoterritorial Politics, Policy, and the Western World,* edited by J.R. Rudolph and R.J. Thompson. Boulder, CO: Lynne Reinner.

Schain, M. A. 1994."The Development of the American State and the Construction of Immigration Policy (1880-1924)." Unpublished paper delivered at the annual meeting of the American Political Science Association. Schuck, P. H. 1984. "The Transformation of Immigration Law." *Columbia Law Review* 84 (January): 1-90.

Schuck, P. H. 1993. "The New Immigration and the Old Civil Rights." *The American Prospect* Fall: 102-111.

Simon, J. L. 1989. *The Economic Consequences of Immigration.* Cambridge, MA: Basil Blackwell.

Smith, R. M. 1993. "Beyond Tocqueville, Myrdal, and Hartz: The Multiple Traditions in America." *American Political Science Review* 87 (3): 549-566.

Steinert, J-D. 1995. *Migration und Politik. Westdeutschland- Europa- Uebersee 1945-1961.* Osnabrück: Universitätsverlag Rasch.

Straubhaar, T. 1986. "The Causes of International Migration—A Demand Determined Approach." *International Migration Review* 20: 4.

Straubhaar, T. 1988. *On the Economics of International Labor Migration.* Bern and Stuttgart: Verlag Paul Haupt.

Teitelbaum, M. 1992. "*Advocacy, Ambivalence, Ambiguity: Immigration Policies and Prospects in the United States.* Proceedings of the American Philosophical Society 136 (2): 188-206.

Thränhardt, D. 1993. "Die Ursprünge von Rassismus und Fremdenfeindlichkeit in der Konkurrenzdemokratie." *Leviathan* 21 (3): 336–357.

Tichenor, D. J. 1994. "The Politics of Immigration Reform in the United States, 1981-1990." *Polity* 26 (3): 333-362.

Todd, E. 1994. *Le Destin des Immigrés.* Paris: Seuil.

U.S. Congress. *Congressional Record: Proceedings and Debates of the U.S. Congress.* Washington, DC: U.S. Government Printing Office, various years.

U.S. Department of Commerce. Bureau of the Census. 1997. *Statistical Abstract of the United States 1996.* Washington, DC: U.S. Government Printing Office.

U.S. Immigration and Naturalization Service. 1997. *Statistical Yearbook of the Immigration and Naturalization Service.* Washington, DC: U.S. Government Printing Office.

Wacquant, L. 1992. "The Zone." Les Actes de la Rocherche en Sciences Sociales (June). Paris: Presses de la F.N.S.P.

Waldinger, R. 1994. "The Making of an Immigrant Niche." *International Migration Review* 28 (1): 3-30.

Weil, P. 1991. *La France et ses étrangers.* Paris: Calmann-Lévy.

Weiner, M. 1995. *The Global Migration Crisis. Challenge to States and to Human Rights.* New York: Harper Collins.

Zolberg, A. 1994. "Reforming the back door: perspectives historiques sur la réforme de la politique américaine d'immigration." In *Logiques d'états et immigrations*, edited by J. Costa-Lascoux and P. Weil. Paris: Editions Kimé.

SECTION II

CITIZENSHIP AND IMMIGRANT INCORPORATION

CONTEXTS OF IMMIGRANT INCORPORATION:

LOCATING DIMENSIONS OF OPPORTUNITIES AND CONSTRAINTS IN THE UNITED STATES AND GERMANY

Barbara Schmitter-Heisler

In the general discourse on immigration and immigrant incorporation, the United States and Germany appear frequently as examples of opposite regimes. The United States is identified as the prototypical immigration country where policies and laws are generally geared to welcome immigrants by facilitating the naturalization of newcomers and providing automatic citizenship to their offspring born there (*ius soli*). Germany is identified as the prototypical non-immigration country,[1] where in the face of substantial immigration, naturalization is difficult and the offspring of immigrants generally take on the citizenship of their parents (*ius sanguinis*).[2] The need to facilitate access to political citizenship, reflecting the reality of immigration, has become an increasing issue in Germany and has engendered a variety of legislative proposals.[3] In the United States, where naturalization has been relatively easy, many legal immigrants, foremost among them those coming from the Western Hemisphere, in particular Mexicans, have not always been very eager to naturalize, until recently when the new welfare legislation which has

91

threatened to severely limit the access of legal immigrants to welfare programs is virtually pushing many into becoming citizens.[4]

In Germany the political and scholarly debate has tended to focus on the fact that the German government has stubbornly failed to recognize officially that the "guest-workers" first recruited in the 1950s had become de facto immigrants and that immigration issues will remain an important policy area in the future. In this situation, it is argued, immigrants have been subject to considerable legal insecurity and socioeconomic inequality, as well as discrimination and racism. While I agree that the acquisition of political citizenship for legal immigrants and their descendants must be facilitated, and that Germany must develop immigration and naturalization policies more in tune with the current reality, I do not think that official recognition that Germany has become a country of immigration would change significantly the current anti-immigrant, anti-foreigner climate or substantially alter the process of immigrant incorporation.[5]

In the case of Germany's de facto immigrants, the former guest-workers, their families, and descendants, this process is well underway.[6] In the mid-1990s the majority of this population has been in Germany for more than 20 years and includes a growing second and third generation. Although the immigrant population has been particularly hard hit by continued high unemployment rates, a growing empirical literature on labor market position and educational attainment indicates some improvements in these areas, especially for members of the second generation.[7] Although naturalization remains a difficult process, and the children of long-term foreign residents do not have birth-right German citizenship, immigrants are entitled to participate in a comparatively large welfare state that provides a variety of social citizenship rights, absent in the United States (Marshall 1965; Heisler and Schmitter-Heisler 1991; Schmitter-Heisler 1991). Yet, there have been no systematic attempts to locate these differences in a general model of immigrant incorporation.[8]

In order to address the incorporation of immigrants it is necessary to distinguish between immigration policies (policies that control the flow and composition of newcomers) and the process of incorporation which may or may not include specific integration/incorporation policies (e.g., special assistance given to newcomers in the form of language training, housing, education). While immigration policies set the parameters for the process of incorporation, this process builds on existing social institutions, in particular labor markets, education, religion, and social welfare. In short, the incorporation of newcomers is a social process that develops its own dynamic.[9]

In this paper I explore the comparative usefulness of a model of immigrant incorporation developed inductively in the context of the United States (Portes 1995). Despite some limitations, the comparative exploration of the model allows me to address several issues and questions concerning the process of immigrant incorporation in Germany and the United States. Comparison, as Castles has pointed out, "is not only a means of explanation and hypothesis testing, but also of locating and exploring phenomena as yet insufficiently understood" (1989, p. 9). In addition, cross-national comparison allows us to discover and explore questions that may not be relevant or obvious in a single country (Keating 1991).

LOCATING THE COMPARATIVE CONTEXT FOR IMMIGRANT INCORPORATION

If social scientists have learned anything from the varied experiences of post-World War II immigration, it is that the incorporation of immigrants and their descendants is not the kind of step-wise process first put forth by the assimilation model developed in the United States (Park 1950; Gordon 1964, 1981). Nor is it necessarily one defined by social exclusion resulting from racism and discrimination, as much of the European literature seems to suggest (Hargreaves and Leaman 1995; Wrench and Solomos 1993). Instead, the incorporation of newcomers is a process which is frequently punctuated, always uneven and segmented, and, above all, multidimensional. In short, it is considerably more varied and complex than either of these models suggests.

The complex and varied reality of immigrant incorporation becomes evident when examining the differences and similarities between various immigrant groups within a host society, and/or by comparing the differences and similarities among immigrant groups between host societies. In case of the former, possible differences may concern the legal status (e.g., legal immigrants, refugees, temporary workers), family composition, human and cultural capital, and geographic location of newcomers. In the case of the latter, we need to consider possible differences in the socioeconomic and political structures of host societies and their institutions. In other words, a comparative analysis of immigrant incorporation must consider both systematic variations between immigrants and variations between host societies.

American scholars have begun to explore systematically the complexity and variability of the incorporation process in the United States. Here, the work of Alejandro Portes and his collaborators has made substantial contributions toward understanding the complex and variable reality of

immigrant incorporation (Portes and Rumbaut 1990; Portes and Sensenbrenner 1993; Portes 1995). Based on empirical evidence from the
American experience, Portes has developed a framework for conceptualizing the varied processes of immigrant incorporation. This framework
is multidimensional, identifying "three levels of reception," the level of
government policy toward different immigrant groups (e.g., refugees,
asylum seekers, and legal immigrants), the level of civic society and public opinion, and the characteristics of ethnic communities. Each level is
relatively independent of the others (1995).

Portes's model reminds us that, despite the relatively easy access to
political citizenship granted to legal immigrants in the United States,
the economic success and social position of various immigrant groups
differs substantially. Such differences cannot be reduced to individual or
economic factors (e.g., human capital) but must be understood within
the varied social and economic contexts which differentially structure the
process of incorporation of immigrant groups.

Comparisons between the United States and Germany frequently focus
on differences at the level of government policy, especially the observation that, compared to Germany, the United States has been an immigration country, par excellence, that provides easy access to citizenship. An
implicit assumption underlying this literature (especially by German
authors) is that because American immigration and naturalization policies are more receptive, legal immigrants in the United States encounter
fewer obstacles and are relatively painlessly incorporated. This is particularly the case for the children of immigrants born in the United States
who automatically benefit from full citizenship rights. In other words, it is
assumed that first-level government policy differences determine different outcomes for immigrants and their descendants in these two societies.

Yet, in addition to its long and varied history of immigration and, to a
large extent, because of it, American society also displays many "exceptional" social, economic, and political characteristics that structure the
opportunities and constraints at the second and third level (Lipset 1996).
In terms of public effort, benefits, and employment, the United States
stands out as the least statist among Western nations (Rose 1985). American preferences for private efforts in the arena of welfare and in business
are well reflected in the low levels of state involvement in the economy,
the weakness of trade unions, the large low-wage sector, and the country's
history as a "welfare laggard" culminating in the welfare reform of 1996
which also includes measures that deny a variety of benefits to legal
immigrants.[10] Given the multidimensional character of immigrant incorporation, any comparison between the United States and Germany must
take into account the characteristics of American exceptionalism.

To my knowledge, Portes did not intend to develop a comparative model. Providing a framework for analyzing the process of immigrant incorporation in the United States, the model is not only based on American immigration and refugee policy (level one), it also takes the "exceptional" characteristics of American society as given (levels two and three). Given American exceptionalism, however, these characteristics become variables in a comparative context. While it appears that differences between the United States and Germany are most obvious at the first level, the level of political reception, we can identify substantial differences at each of the three levels. This suggests that the German context provides different opportunities and constraints for action and different modes of incorporation.

PLACING PORTES'S TYPOLOGY IN A COMPARATIVE CONTEXT

As indicated, Portes's model of immigrant incorporation identifies three levels of reception. At the first level—government policy—the model distinguishes between three types of policies, labeled as "receptive," "indifferent," and "hostile." Here, the receptive category applies to refugees who receive resettlement assistance in the United States; legal immigrants fall into the indifferent category; the hostile category applies to populations whose entry and permanence is actively opposed.

At the second level, the level of societal reception and public opinion, each of the above-three categories is further subdivided into two types: prejudiced and non-prejudiced reception, where prejudiced reception is accorded to nonwhite groups (i.e., the majority of legal immigrants), while white immigrants enjoy non-prejudiced reception. At the third level, the level of the ethnic community, Portes distinguishes between weak and strong ethnic communities, where weak communities are either small or predominantly composed of manual workers, while strong communities are characterized by geographic concentrations and a more diversified occupational structure, including significant numbers of entrepreneurs and professionals.

This framework then creates 12 possible contexts of immigrant incorporation. The location of an immigrant group within one of these contexts shapes the limits and possibilities, the assistance, and constraints of individual and group action. For example, the context of legal Mexicans immigrants is shaped by indifferent policies of reception, prejudiced responses from civil society and public opinion, and a weak ethnic community structure, whereas that of Koreans is structured by indifferent policies of reception, prejudiced responses from civil society and public opinion, and strong ethnic communities. As immigrant destinies depend heavily on the specific context of incorporation, this model helps to explain why Mexican immigrants (and most immigrants from Central America and the Caribbean) tend to occupy low socioeconomic positions (Schoeni, MacCarthy, and Vernez 1996).

Transposing Portes's typology to the German context raises several questions and issues. While the most obvious concern the first level, in particular the extent to which the three categories identified by Portes may be comparable or useful for the German case, these are less obvious, but equally important questions flow from the consideration of American exceptionalism at the second and third levels and Portes's observation that the three levels are relatively independent of one another.

First-Level Types

As is the case in the United States, settled foreigners in Germany occupy a variety of legal statuses. Having instant access to full citizenship and benefiting from a variety of special integrative measures, including housing and language instruction, ethnic Germans (*Aussiedler*) clearly enjoy the most receptive government policies.[11] Although asylum seekers and refugees also receive government assistance, the vast majority of asylum seekers and refugees confront an increasingly hostile environment. Yet, what about the category that most closely resembles legal immigrants in the United States, the former guest-workers, their families, and descendants? Can they be placed in Portes's indifferent category? If so, is there a significant difference in the way this category may be defined in the German case?

Compared to legal immigrants in the United States, who are entitled to citizenship if they fulfill the necessary requirements (five years of uninterrupted residence and in the case of spouses of U.S. citizens three years, no criminal record, knowledge of English and of U.S. government and history, and good moral character),[12] access to political citizenship for immigrants in Germany is hardly an entitlement and considerably more restricted. Even if they fulfill the necessary requirements (10 years of residency, the ability to read and write German, a voluntary affiliation to Germany, and some knowledge of the political order and commitment to the constitution) naturalization must be "in the public interest." While the United States does not require that naturalized citizens renounce their original citizenship and tolerates multiple citizenship, Germany has opposed to dual and multiple citizenship.[13]

While the new foreigners' law of 1991 has not made naturalization an automatic entitlement for all legal immigrants, young people who have resided in Germany for a minimum of eight years, attended German schools for a minimum of six years, and apply for naturalization between the ages of 16 and 23 (paragraph 85), and foreigners with long-term residency (at least 15 years, paragraph 86) now have a legal right to citizenship. Those seeking citizenship under the *Ermessenseinbürgerung* (discretionary naturalization) (in contrast to *Anspruchseinbürgerung (entitled naturalization)*) must still renounce their previous citizenship. Although the continued refusal of the German government to formally accept dual citizenship runs counter to trends in other European Union countries and has been subject to a continued debate and criticism from immigrants and their supporters, in reality exceptions are granted frequently. Dual citizenship is tolerated increasingly and has proliferated considerably in recent years (Die Beauftragte der Bundesregierung für die Belange der Ausländer 1995).

While the restrictive naturalization and citizenship policies in Germany have contributed to the low rates of naturalization (in the case of *Ermessenseinbürgerungen*),[14] the American experience indicates that naturalization is not an automatic outcome for legal immigrants, nor does it solve a myriad of social problems associated with immigration. Instead, while naturalization represents a relatively uncomplicated legal process, at the level of the individual immigrant it is considerably more complex. It involves the considerations of a variety of economic, political, social, cultural, and geographic conditions in the country of origin and in the immigrant ethnic community (Yang 1994a, 1994b). While research in the United States is beginning to shed some light on the many variables involved in this process, in the German case there is little information at this point.[15]

Among the variables that define the political and social conditions in the host country are the legal, social, and political distances between the status of long-term residents (denizen) and citizens. Three major advantages accrue to citizens over denizens in both countries: full voting rights (both passive and active), protection from deportation, and full access to social citizenship. Of these, protection from deportation applies equally in both countries—citizens cannot be deported. As for political and social rights, the distance between denizens and citizens is greater in the United States. Only citizens can vote at any level, local, state, or federal in the United States. In Germany immigrants who are citizens of member states of the European Union can vote in local elections (since 1994) and participate in elections for the European Parliament. Unlike in the Netherlands and Sweden, immigrants from nonmember states, however, do not have local voting rights. Yet, immigrants are not without a political voice. They can exercise secondary political rights by participating in political parties and trade unions. While union membership is also open to immigrants in the United States, the labor market position of many immigrants and the weak position of unions in the social and political system make membership less likely and even less effective as an alternative political voice.

As for social citizenship entitlements, long-term immigrants in Germany have equal rights to all entitlements of the welfare state (e.g., social assistance, child benefit, housing benefit). In contrast, the 1996 welfare law in the United States revoked food stamp and Supplemental Security Income (SSI) entitlements for legal immigrants. While the ensuing protests led to a limited reinstatement of SSI, and several states have moved to pick up the tab, the debate surrounding these policy changes demonstrate that legal immigrants cannot claim access to the same social citizenship rights as citizens.[16]

This suggests that while naturalization laws and procedures are more welcoming in the United States, the legal distance between citizen and denizen is smaller in Germany. In the United States the road to citizenship is relatively painless and short, and the advantages accruing to citizens over legal residents are greater. In Germany the road to citizenship remains comparatively difficult. Yet, the new law facilitating naturalization for young people and for those residents of more than 15 years has made this road less difficult for some. While there is a significant difference between five and 15 years, the reality in the United States has been that immigrants frequently postpone naturalization for many years after they become officially eligible.[17] Finally, the legal advantages associated with citizenship over long-term legal-residency permits (*Aufenthalts-berechtigung*) are less significant than those in the United States. This is particularly the case for immigrants who are citizens of European Union member states and who constitute one-quarter of the legal immigrant population.

In short, when transposing Portes's first-level categories of reception, we need to take into account the inherent legal differences (i.e., naturalization and citizenship policy) that define the content of the indifferent category and the relative advantages inherent in political citizenship over denizenship. These differences alone, however, may be considerably less consequential in shaping the overall contexts of incorporation of legal immigrants than is frequently suggested. For this, it is important to consider the second and third levels, and the manner in which all three are articulated to create the possible contexts of incorporation.

Second-Level Types

At the second level, the level of societal reception, Portes's model identifies two types of reception, prejudiced and non-prejudiced, where the former is accorded to nonwhite (who are the majority of legal immigrants) and the latter to white immigrants. While ethnicity, in general, and prejudice and racism, in particular, are clearly important in defining the societal reception of the majority of immigrants in Germany today, Portes's two categories are more reflective of American social reality. Although the United States is a highly segmented and fragmented society, in general, race (or racialized ethnicity), not class, has been the most fundamental and enduring cleavage and has played an important role in structuring American social institutions (Orfield 1988; Quadagno 1994; Edsall and Edsall 1991).

Any comparison between the United States and Germany must consider the significant structural/institutional differences between what Faist has aptly named "ethnically segmented pluralism" and "class oriented corporatism" (Faist 1993). Although class-oriented corporatism in Germany has been under some strain (including that emanating from immigration), the historically created social and political differences have produced different institutional conditions. These are particularly relevant when considering the contexts of incorporation at the second and third levels. Taking the societal characteristics of ethnically segmented pluralism, where ethnic hierarchies are more defining than class hierarchies, as given, it follows that the social context of members of ethnic groups located at the bottom of that hierarchy will be defined by prejudice and racism. In this context, access to strong ethnic communities clearly affords members of low-status ethnic groups social and economic advantages which are not available to those in weak communities.

A large literature attests to the fact that prejudice and racism have been important factors in defining the position of immigrants in Germany. Yet, instead of reflecting already-established ethnic-status hierarchies, such attitudes and ideologies occur in a different institutional context, the context of previously existing class segmented corporatism. In this context, ethnic hierarchies do not reflect long-existing divisions, but should be considered emergent within existing class-oriented corporatism. This means that the emerging patterns of ethnic and class segmentation may not mirror those of the United States. Instead, ethnic and class segmentation may follow different lines. In Germany the class dimension still remains salient in many social institutions (e.g., employment, schooling and training, and welfare) whereas the ethnic dimension is more dominant in others (particularly religion but, to some extent, also in housing). The extent to which ethnic considerations may come to overlap or replace class dimensions is ultimately an empirical question which cannot be addressed in this paper.[18]

Third-Level Types

Portes's third-level types, strong and weak coethnic communities, reflect the low level of state penetration in the area of business and labor activities in the United States. The virtual absence of laws governing store opening hours, the lax enforcement of employment laws and disincentives for collective bargaining, and generous bankruptcy laws aimed at stimulating business activities represent necessary, if not sufficient, conditions for the establishment of strong coethnic communities.

As German laws have discouraged rather than encouraged such activities (for both immigrants and citizens), the possibilities for strong ethnic communities have been more limited.[19] Indeed, the level of self-employment, in general, is much lower in Germany than in the United States. While the self-employment gap between immigrants and native populations was very large during the first two decades of immigration, recent data indicate that it is closing slowly (Sen and Goldberg 1996). Although employment and training opportunities offered by ethnic enterprise continue to represent a very small (if growing) fraction of employment opportunities in Germany, compared to the United States, where the majority of some immigrant groups (Koreans, Cubans and, to a lesser extent, Chinese) have access to strong ethnic communities, the German situation has been more limited. At the same time, nonwhite immigrants in the United Ststes who have few skills and little education face prejudice and weak ethnic communities, are subject to the many vicissitudes of low-wage, dead-end work in the secondary sector of the economy, where unemployment benefits do not exist, where labor laws are rarely enforced, and labor unions are noted for their conspicuous absence. In terms of their immediate economic and social situations, these may fare worse than their German counterparts.

The Relative Independence of Each Level

In the United States the low degree of "stateness" and preference for private solutions and initiatives have fostered a comparatively high degree of institutional independence and fragmentation which is manifested at each level.[20] In Germany (and in European societies more generally), characterized by higher levels of stateness and greater institutional integration, the three levels are more interdependent and the possibilities at each level are more limited.

The observation that degree of stateness and institutional structures vary between these societies is not new (Hollifield 1992; Faist 1995a, 1995b). Yet, because they have chosen to focus primarily on one of the levels, scholars of immigration in Europe have not considered the combined articulation of all three levels of reception in shaping the limits and possibilities, the opportunities and constraints of immigrant group action in Germany (and for that matter in Europe).

First, greater state penetration throughout the three levels and, with it, greater interdependence between the levels restrict the variety of possible contexts of immigrant incorporation in Germany. Thus, within the indifferent category, there is only one (not four) context: prejudiced societal reception and weak co-ethnic communities. This creates fewer possibilities and more constraints for individual and group action. At the same time, the conditions found in this single context are not identical to the corresponding American contexts. While each places limits on upward mobility and equality with the dominant population, the lines that limit them are drawn differently. In the United States this context is defined by an ethnically segmented labor market, characterized by low wages, the virtual absence of unions and collective bargaining and minimal, if any, work-related benefits (e.g., health insurance, vacations, unemployment benefits, sick pay). In Germany the labor market conditions of class-oriented corporatism do not only provide more work-related social benefits, they also provide opportunities for individual and collective action in unions and works councils.[21]

Outside the workplace, the more extensive (albeit somewhat shrinking) German welfare state still provides additional benefits such as child allowances, housing benefits, and social assistance for citizens and long-term immigrants alike. Thus, the distinction between prejudiced and non-prejudiced reception which reflects the American experience and American institutions must be modified in the German case to take account of built-in institutional opportunities available through class-structured mechanisms that may soften a prejudiced reception.

In the United States immigrants whose context is defined by prejudiced societal reception and who lack strong ethnic communities confront limited opportunities. They tend to be confined to the low-wage sector of the economy with little protection, and they are frequently confined to substandard housing in crime-ridden neighborhoods with substandard educational opportunities. In such situations, and in the context of prevailing ethnic (not class) politics, in general, political citizenship represents a dimension of equality and the potential for political voice.[22] In Germany, where class-based social institutions and social citizenship rights have imposed some limits on "negative opportunities," political citizenship for immigrants and, especially, for their descendants remains a moral and political imperative. Its effects on the process of immigrant incorporation, however, will be considerably less dramatic than generally anticipated.

CONCLUDING REMARKS

The large-scale immigration to the advanced industrial countries of Western Europe and the United States that began in the 1960s was not fully anticipated by politicians, policymakers, and scholars. All have grappled with the results and ongoing processes that have affected virtually all aspects of social life. Although the multiple processes associated with immigration and immigrant settlement and incorporation continue to unfold, we are in a position to study the vast array of changing conditions and circumstances produced by these processes. Many of them appear to be subject to easy generalizations: immigrants occupy low positions in the labor market, immigrants are less successful in education, immigrants encounter racism and discrimination, and immigrants are geographically and spatially concentrated in certain regions and in cities. Yet, within these sweeping generalizations, we can also detect significant differences, differences between immigrant groups within societies as well as differences between societies. Much can be learned by studying these differences, both within societies and between societies.

To date, most comparative work has focused on one of the three levels of immigrant incorporation outlined above, predominantly on the first level. While there are hosts of empirical studies on labor market position and education, housing conditions, and spatial concentration of immigrants in the United States and Germany, only Faist's comparative study of a specific and important aspect of the second level—the transition from school to work—provides a glimpse of the different dynamics of incorporation in the United States and Germany (1995). This study suggests that while the less regulated, more fragmented American system may be more "immigrant friendly" overall, it also produces high levels of immigrant poverty.[23] In contrast, the more regulated German system tends to generate higher levels of unemployment.

While the transition from school to work and insertion into the labor market represent only one dimension of the overall process of incorporation, albeit an important one, it should be viewed within the larger context. In this paper I have made an initial attempt at conceptualizing the major differences that structure these contexts in the United States and Germany. Given its history as a country of immigration and its social, economic, and political structures, the United States provides a greater variety of contexts and, with them, more opportunities and fewer constraints than Germany. It also fosters the impression that there is plenty of opportunity to go around, while playing down the fact that these opportunities also include the opportunity to be poor, not to have access to health care, and to live in deplorable neighborhoods, where housing conditions and social institutions, in particular, schools, are hardly conducive to social mobility. Because the German context is characterized by fewer opportunities and more constraints, the overall impression it presents is more negative. Ultimately, these questions cannot be answered without the benefit of more substantial and systematic comparative research that takes account of all three levels.

NOTES

1. Although politicians of the Christian Democratic Party, including Chancellor Kohl, like to make reference to the tired phrase *"Wir sind kein Einwanderungsland"* (We are not an immigration country), I believe that social scientists must look beyond such hollow ideological slogans for a full understanding of the current situation.

2. The exception are *Aussiedler* (ethnic Germans), who automatically have access to German citizenship, and before the demise the former German Democratic Republic, *Übersiedler* (those allowed to move to the Federal Republic).

3. *Der Spiegel* (June 24, 1996).

4. An additional incentive for the recent rush in naturalizations has been the fact that citizens are in a preferred category over legal immigrants in sponsoring relatives to immigrate.

5. While it would help to have a more balanced and clear immigration policy (for example a quota system), I do not believe that such a policy would change current perceptions of immigrants. In her review and analysis of public opinion data in Canada, Germany, the United States, and Britain, Hoskins concludes that "immigrants in the 1980s were defined primarily as problems" (Hoskins 1991, p. 140). With the exception of Canada where she found slightly more positive orientations toward immigrants, unreceptive opinions were independent of national contexts and situations.

6. This is frequently overlooked in the context of the 1990s when the threat of massive population movements associated with the disintegration of the Eastern bloc, as well as the enormous challenges associated with reunification and with controlling the influx of ethnic Germans, was superimposed on the lingering asylum issue of the 1980s.

7. For examples, see the contributions by Seifert and Wagner/Büchel/Haisken-DeNew/ Spiess in this volume.

8. In this paper I use the term immigrant for the former guest-workers and their descendants. Although they were not originally conceived as such, their long-term presence has made them de facto immigrants.

9. Societies with liberal immigration policies do not necessarily provide newcomers with incorporation assistance. For example, the United States provides little assistance for newcomers (with the exception of refugees). In contrast, Canada pursues a liberal immigration policy and provides considerable assistance toward the incorporation of newcomers.

10. Supplemental Security Income and food stamps.

11. The special position of *Aussiedler* is frequently mentioned as an indicator of the "perverse" features of German policy. While it has no equivalent in the United States, it is not exceptional in the world. Israel's policy of giving full citizenship to all Jews is one obvious example, but there are also examples of measures facilitating the citizenship of returning emigrants who have taken the citizenship of another country. Italy is a case in point (Schmitter 1984).

12. The latter two requirements may be waved for elderly persons.

13. It is frequently overlooked that by taking the oath of allegiance to the United States, immigrants are also expected to renounce allegiance to the nation of their original citizenship.

14. For example, survey data in Germany indicate that many immigrants would more strongly consider the option of naturalization, if they could be dual citizens, and data from the Netherlands, where dual citizenship has become possible recently, indicate increases in naturalizations.

15. The German case presents a very different dynamic in terms of the relationship between sending and receiving societies as well as other variables. There has been the assumption that the major stumbling blocks for naturalization have been the complexity of the process and the official unavailability of dual citizenship. While these clearly play a role, there is a need for considerably more research in this area. More detailed research on the variables involved should become easier as more immigrants choose to naturalize. Recent changes in the Dutch Nationality Act (1992) specifically allowing dual citizenship also shed some light on this issue. Contrary to expectations, the acquisition of Dutch nationality did not increase equally for all immigrant groups. Furthermore, a survey among four minority groups, Turks, Moroccans, Cape Verdians, and Tunisians, indicated that, for many, Dutch nationality meant the possession of "the Dutch passport," not of Dutch nationality (Van den Beden 1994).

16. Dominican President Leonel Fernandez Reyna has openly urged legal Dominican immigrants (who as a group receive more public assistance than any other non-refugee group in the United States), to become citizens in order to safeguard their welfare rights (*The New York Times* October 12, 1996). The Mexican Congress's recent vote (December 1996) for constitutional amendments permitting dual citizenship for Mexicans who adopt American citizenship follows similar lines of reasoning. It has prompted restrictionist interest groups in the United States, in particular, FAIR (Federation for American Immigration Reform) to call on the U.S. Congress to pass a law requiring naturalized citizens to relinquish their previous nationality (*Los Angeles Times* December 12, 1996).

17. This is changing in the wake of the new welfare legislation and more restrictive immigration policies.

18. The available empirical evidence on labor market positions of first- and second-generation immigrants and on the education and skills of the second generation, in particular, suggests that while the immigrant population in Germany remains more concentrated in low socioeconomic positions than the native German population, their relative positions have clearly improved. The questions is how to evaluate the data. As is the case in the United States, there are differences between ethnic groups that must be taken into account.

19. This is partially due to the manner of original recruitment (i.e., a system of contract labor) in which workers were initially tied to specific industries and workplaces. Most importantly, these laws significantly reduce the economic and social advantages stemming from coethnic unity in the context of the United States.

20. The example also reflects the history of the United States as an immigration country, where various successive waves of immigrants have been incorporated over time. To illustrate, he gives the example of illegal Irish immigrants who may confront less social prejudice than legal immigrants or refugees from Iran, Ethiopia, or Jamaica. This, of course, is not only a consequence of the fact that the Irish are white (although, historically, they were not treated as equals by natives), but also of the fact that Irish immigrants may find refuge in a well-developed and established Irish-American community. Thus, for undocumented Irish immigrants, the undocumented nature of their presence is less defining than it is for undocumented immigrants from Mexico.

21. Participation in trade unions and works councils have played a considerable role in the integration process. See essays in Kühne, Oztürk, and West (1994).

22. This became apparent in the last election, where newly naturalized citizens turned out to vote in large numbers in response to the anti-immigrant rhetoric of the Republican Party.

23. Recent U.S. Census data indicate that while median household income rose for every other American ethnic and racial group, it dropped 5.1 percent for the nation's 27 million Hispanics. The poverty rate among Hispanics has surpassed that of blacks for the first time, and Hispanics make up 24 percent of the nation's poor. This downturn does not only apply to the recently arrived, but it also applies to the American-born Hispanic population, sug-

gesting that Hispanics may become entrenched as America's working poor (*The New York Times* January 30, 1997).

REFERENCES

Bedem, R. van den. 1994. "Towards a System of Plural Nationality in the Netherlands. Changes in Regulations and Perceptions." Pp. 95-109 in *From Aliens to Citizens: Redefining the Status of Immigrants in Europe*, edited by R. Bauböck. Aldershot: Averbury.

Castles, F. 1989. "Introduction: Puzzles of Political Economy." Pp. 1-15 in *Comparative History of Public Policy*, edited by F. Castles. Cambridge: Polity Press.

Die Beauftragte der Bundesregierung für die Belange der Ausländer. 1995. Bericht über die Lage der Ausländer in der Bundesrepublik Deutschland. Bonn.

Edsall, T., and M. Edsall. 1991. *Chain Reaction: The Impact of Race, Rights, and Taxes on American Politics*. New York: W.W. Norton.

Faist, T. 1993. "Ein- und Ausgliederung von Immigranten: Türken in Deutschland und mexikanische Amerikaner in den USA." *Soziale Welt* 44: 275-299.

Faist, T. 1995a. *Social Citizenship for Whom? Young Turks in Germany and Mexican Americans in the United States*. Aldershot: Avebury.

Faist, T. 1995b. "Ethnicization and Racialization of Welfare-state Politics in Germany and the USA." *Ethnic and Racial Studies* 18: 219-250.

Gordon, M. 1964. *Assimilation in American Life: The Role of Race, Religion, and National Origins*. New York: Oxford University Press.

Gordon, M. 1981. "Modes of Pluralism: The American Dilemma." *Annals of the American Academy of Political and Social Science* 454: 178-188.

Hargreaves, A., and J. Leaman. 1995. *Racism, Ethnicity and Politics in Contemporary Europe*. Brookfield: Ashgate Publishing Co.

Heisler, M., and B. Schmitter-Heisler. 1991. "Citizenship—Old, New, and Changing: Inclusion, Exclusion, and Limbo for Ethnic Groups and Migrants in the Modern Democratic State." In *Dominant National Cultures and Ethnic Identities*, edited by J. Fijalkowski, H. Merkens, and F. Schmidt. Berlin Freie Universität.

Hollifield, J. F. 1992. *Immigrants, Markets and States: The Political Economy of Postwar Europe*. Cambridge: Harvard University Press.

Hoskin, M. 1991. *New Immigrants and Democratic Society: Minority Integration in Western Democracies*. New York: Praeger.

Keating, M. 1991. *Comparative Urban Politics*. Aldershot: Edward Elgar.

Kühne, P., N. Ozturk, and K-W. West, eds. 1994. *Gewerkschaften und Einwanderung: Eine Kritische Zwischenbilanz*. Köln: Bund Verlag.

Lipset, S. 1996. *American Exceptionalism: A Double-Edged Sword*. New York: W.W. Norton.

Marshall, T. H. 1950/1965. *Class, Citizenship, and Social Development*. Cambridge: Cambridge University Press/Garden City, NY: Anchor Books.

Orfield, G. 1988. "Race and the Liberal Agenda: The Loss of the Integrationist Dream, 1965-1974." Pp. 313-356 in *The Politics of Social Policy the United States*, edited by M. Weir, A. Shola Orloff, and T. Skocpol. Princeton: Princeton University Press.

Park, R. 1950. *Race and Culture: Essays in the Sociology of Contemporary Man*. Glencoe, IL: Free Press.

Portes, A. 1995. "Economic Sociology and the Sociology of Immigration: A Conceptual Overview." Pp. 1-41 in *The Economic Sociology of Immigration: Essays on Networks, Ethnicity and Entrepreneurship*, edited by A. Portes. New York: Russell Sage Foundation.

Portes, A., and R. G. Rumbaut. 1990. *Immigrant America: A Portrait*. Berkeley: University of California Press.

Portes, A., and J. Sensenbrenner. 1993. "Embeddedness and Immigration: Notes on the Social Determinants of Economic Action." *American Journal of Sociology* 98: 1320-50.

Quadagno, J. 1994. *The Color of Welfare: How Racism Undermined the War on Poverty*. New York: Oxford University Press.

Rose, R. 1985. "National Pride in Cross-National Perspective." *International Social Science Journal* 37(1): 85-96.

Schmitter-Heisler, B. 1984. "Sending States and Immigrant Minorities—The Case of Italy." *Comparative Studies in Society and History* 26: 325-334.

Schmitter-Heisler, B. 1991. "A Comparative Perspective on the Underclass: Questions of Urban Poverty, Race, and Citizenship." *Theory and Society* 20: 455-483.

Schoeni, R., K. McCarthy, and G. Vernez. 1996. *The Mixed Economic Progress of Immigrants*. Santa Monica: Rand Corporation, Center for Research on Immigration Policy.

Sen, F., and A. Goldberg, eds. 1996. *Türken als Unternehmer: Eine Gesamtdarstellung und Ergebnis neuerer Untersuchungen*. Opladen: Leske+Budrich.

Wrench, J., and J. Solomos, eds. 1993. *Racism and Migration in Western Europe*. Oxford: Berg.

Yang, P. 1994a. "Explaining Immigrant Naturalization." *International Migration Review* 28: 449-477.

Yang, P. 1994b. "Ethnicity and Naturalization." *Ethnic and Racial Studies* 17: 593-618.

VOLK NATION OR NATION OF IMMIGRANTS?
THE CURRENT DEBATE ABOUT IMMIGRATION IN GERMANY AND THE UNITED STATES IN COMPARATIVE PERSPECTIVE

Herbert Dittgen

The United States as a model of an "immigration country" has always played an important role in the German political debate on immigration. Germany's official declaration that it is a country not of immigration but rather a *Volk* nation implicitly distances it from the United States, a "nation of immigrants."[1] In fact, in Germany, the reference to the United States—as both an exemplary model and a warning—has been used for quite some time, beginning in 1913 when the German parliament (*Reichstag*) deliberated its citizenship law up to today's debate revolving around whether Germany should adopt an immigration policy or not.

During the debate in the German Reichstag in 1913, Freiherr Hartmann Oswald von Richthofen, deputy of the National Liberal Party, pointed out that the United States tried to limit "undesirable" immigration from south European Slavic states and questioned why, then, Germany would want to welcome these immigrants.[2] While the secretary of the ministry of the inte-

rior was referring to foreigners as *"Stammfremde"* (alien tribe), deputies of
the Social Democratic Party pointed out that Germany had already become
a multicultural society. Eduard Bernstein also used the American example
but this time to imply that immigration is advantageous for the recipient
society as well as for the immigrants themselves.[3] Eighty years since, not
much progress seems to have been made. The German Ministry of the Interior still maintains that Germany is not a country of immigration, whereas
most of the academic experts and the enlightened public are demanding
overdue recognition of Germany's real history and reality of immigration.
In the latter's push for an immigration policy, classic countries of immigration—such as the United States—are upheld as models (Bade 1994;
Oberndörfer 1991).

New, however, is the interest the U.S. government and public are express-
ing about Germany's response to illegal immigration. Germany's use of
identity cards is frequently regarded as the key for successfully containing
undocumented immigration. Officers of the San Diego Border Patrol
described their difficult task by comparing their manpower (5,000) on a
2,000 mile border with the size of the Federal Border Protection Force
(Bundesgrenzschutz) (5,300) at the comparatively short 600-mile eastern border of Germany.[4]

In the United States "illegal immigration" is the most important aspect
in the immigration debate and Germany frequently serves as a model for
an effective political strategy. Dominating the debate in Germany is the "crisis of asylum policy" and the need for an immigration policy—two separate
issues which are frequently confused. In this regard, the U.S. system of immigration quotas frequently serves as a model for Germany.

Thus, as can be seen, the debate concerning immigration in the
United States and Germany is close and, though not often recognized,
interrelated. However, in spite of this relationship, it would still appear
strange to compare the politics of immigration in Germany with that of
the United States. The United States is often seen as a traditional settler
society whose national identity is based on republicanism, a cosmopolitan tradition that facilitates the inclusion of newcomers. In contrast,
Germany is considered a hotbed of exclusionary nationalism. Why
should one compare the country which George Washington described as
"open to the oppressed and persecuted of all nations and religions" with
a country that has been notorious for its difficulties in dealing with "foreigners"?[5] The silent suspicion about German pathologies was seemingly
confirmed when, after its unification, it again became the site of a wave
of antiforeigner attacks. Small towns like Hoyerswerda or Rostock-Licht-
enhagen, where asylum-seekers were assailed by xenophobic hordes
while bystanders applauded, became catchwords worldwide for the new
Germany.

In short, if one looks at the stereotypes, political traditions, and histories of both countries, comparisons between their immigration experiences might seem unfounded. In fact, this alleged difference is an important part of the official rhetoric in Germany. The German Minister of the Interior and other bureaucrats frequently state that Germany is different from America—that its situation should not be compared with a country of immigration tradition. Their rationale is that even though there are many people entering Germany, it is not a typical immigration country and as a historically densely populated territory cannot afford to become a nation of immigrants. Often this goes with the notion that labor migrants are still to be considered "guest workers," and that the majority of asylum-seekers are "economic refugees" abusing the asylum right.

These doubts concerning the value of a comparison between the two countries were, of course, only meant to be rhetorical. That both countries consider themselves exceptional and in some ways incomparable is, in itself, an interesting parallel. Comparing Germany and the United States is valid since both—like other wealthy countries in the northern hemisphere—face similar challenges. Both countries must regulate immigration, and both must decide which and how many people to admit. Further, both countries must determine how they will enforce these regulations, control their borders, and distinguish the legal status of the people within their borders. Regulations concerning the rights of migrants and whether integration is perceived within a context of multi-culturalism or assimilation represent the core issues of national identity and sovereignty.

For many societies immigration policy is about nothing less than who they have been, who they are, and most crucially, who they will become. Therefore, immigration policy is much more than a rational calculation of economic factors. National debates about immigration are almost always fought on the ideological turf, however rarely this is admitted. In Germany, as well as in the United States, national traditions are frequently evoked in immigration debates. In fact, they center on national identity.

In their book, *Controlling Immigration*, Wayne Cornelius and his co-authors have shown that there is a growing convergence among industrialized, labor-importing countries regarding policy instruments for controlling immigration. This increasing similarity is also true regarding the efficacy of immigration control measures, that is, there is a gap between the goals of national immigration policies and the actual results (Cornelius, Martin, and Hollifield 1994). This paper will not focus on policies and their effectiveness, but rather on the politics of immigration in terms of public debate and decision making. The questions posed are: *what determines the debates in both countries? Why and how do policies change?*

I will begin with some basic considerations concerning "immigration" as a political issue in Germany and the United States. Following this I will address the question of how to approach a comparison of immigration politics. For a closer analysis of the political debate, I find that the concept of a "policy paradigm" is a helpful interpretive framework. Finally, I will explain the immigration paradigms in the United States and Germany and try to explain why these shift over time.

IMMIGRATION AS A POLITICAL ISSUE

Some observers claim that political decisions and debates related to immigration have a different character than other issues, such as fiscal or economic policy. Immigration tends to be either a nonissue or a hot one with divisive consequences and usually emotional overtones. It is not at all easy to determine why the debate ignites at particular moments. When debated, immigration is usually presented as a threat to the country, a danger that aggravates the nation's social problems. In this respect it is similar to the topic of crime. In fact, both are frequently debated as closely connected. For many, the problem seems obvious: there are too many acts of violence and too many people entering the country. Solutions are also seen as obvious: more law and order and stricter control of the borders. Immigration and crime are objects of sensational media reporting. Both generate fears, even though the majority of people neither experience crime in their daily lives nor have significant contact with immigrants.[6] The reasons, then, for these rather diffuse fears have to be related to other sources. Because crime and immigration generate strong feelings and opinions, they can also serve as hot buttons for politicians to exploit during election campaigns, particularly by characterizing their opponents as soft on crime or unwilling to limit unwanted immigration.

There is, however, an important difference between crime and immigration as political topics. Crime is almost always an issue; not so immigration. Moreover, there is always a major segment, though never a majority, that welcomes immigrants and defends their rights. In fact, immigration is a basic element of U.S. identity. But there remains a paradox. In a country where people speak proudly about their immigrant heritage, most recent immigration is at least controversial, if not bitterly debated.

Another peculiarity of immigration as a political topic is that it creates "odd couples" whose pairings cut across the usual ideological alignments of left and right (Zolberg 1990). Conservatives can be pro immigration because they are basically market oriented and view the supply of cheap labor as advantageous for the economy. At the same time, conservatives concerned with the cultural implications of immigration view the influx of people from different cultures as a danger for the community and national identity as a whole. The former look at immigration in terms of economics, the latter in terms of culture.

U.S. liberals and their German counterparts (social democrats and socially oriented members of the CDU) are either concerned about the effect of immigration for domestic workers or in terms of civil liberty rights, such as the defense of family reunion or open borders for humanitarian reasons. But there are also confessed liberals who are deeply concerned about multiculturalism and the "balkanization of the United States" or the "overforeignization" of Germany.

In the United Sates "immigration" is an important element in political rhetoric whenever the national tradition is celebrated. It is a source of national pride. This was most evident in the July 1986 centennial celebration of the Statue of Liberty, culminating in Liberty Weekend at New York Harbor. Even though the statue originally had little to do with immigration, it had, as Roger Daniels writes, "become the symbol, par excellence, of the nurturing aspects of American society" (1990, p. 407).

This, of course, is not true of Germany with its tradition of *Volk* nation. However, there are proponents of a generous asylum policy who sometimes argue that such a policy could serve as a kind of compensation for the horrors of the Nazi regime. As a matter of fact, the reason for incorporating the most liberal asylum law in the Western world into the German constitution stemmed from the experience that asylum was the only way to escape Nazi terror. This type of reasoning, however, will always be confined to a rather small segment of the German public.

The terminology used in debates on immigration is particularly revealing and worthy of a comparative study in its own right. In Germany only a few people use the term immigration. At issue are "foreigners," "foreigner politics," and "asylum-seekers." Germany has not an immigration law but an asylum law and an "alien law." The language indicates the exclusionary and legal way the issue is approached. In both countries one consistent metaphor for immigration is water. Immigration is a flow, a flood, a tide, a wave, an influx, a stream, or, after restrictions, a trickle. The country is inundated, swamped, submerged, engulfed, awash.[7] The vocabulary of Germany's extreme right reveals a special connotation, in that it uses these metaphors to describe foreigners in terms of pollution. These not only expose contempt for immigrants, but their fixation on the idea of a pure nation. In both countries the language of nativism appeals to national sentiments based on notions of national homogeneity (Higham 1955; Oberndörfer 1993; Kurthen and Minkenberg 1995). Since the issue of immigration is so closely linked to national identity, I will analyze more closely the ideology of immigration, how it determines the national debate, and its impact on policy decisions or nondecisions.

COMPARING THE POLITICS OF IMMIGRATION

Policy Paradigms

The politics of immigration are not frequently addressed in immigration literature. The main reason is that from an international migration perspective, the dominant analytical framework is an economic one, where politics are disregarded or are treated solely as dependent variables. The character of national labor markets, the informal or global economy, the differentials of earnings, and migrant networks are all viewed as the main determinants of migration and, therefore, represent the main focuses of research.

Saskia Sassen has argued that a "transnationalization of migration policy making" is taking place. Migration policy from this perspective has to be analyzed as embedded in a larger dynamic of transnationalization of economic spaces and human rights regimes.[8] Soysal and Jacobson have argued that traditional national citizenship has lost its meaning, because the rights of citizens are increasingly being laid down in international human rights regimes (Soysal 1994; Jacobson 1996). From this perspective national discourse about immigration would also have only marginal relevance. The growing importance of the international human rights regime is certainly an important development, but the interstate system remains profoundly illibera, and the institution of citizenship remains a powerful instrument for exclusionary and inclusionary politics (Brubaker 1995a, p. 230).

I argue, however, that the economic explanation has to be complemented by the political explanation. This is to say that the politics of states matter, and that their policies are an important factor in explaining migration. These assumptions certainly require more in-depth explanation which, due to the scope of this paper, cannot be done at this time (Weiner 1993).

From the perspective of states (internal view) various questions arise. How do states determine their immigration policies? Do they react mainly to external development, to new immigration pressures, or does immigration policy reflect the imperatives of domestic politics and the economy?

Gary P. Freeman has recently made a controversial point about the common characteristics of immigration politics in liberal democracies (1995b). He argues that they are "broadly expansionist and inclusive." The remaining differences are, as Freeman explains, a result of their peculiar immigration histories, and a common feature of debate about immigration in liberal democracies is the "constrained discourse." Arguments about the ethnic composition of migrant streams are precluded. In my opinion this approach obscures many of the crucial differences in the politics of immigration and I am going to argue that, on the contrary—using Germany and the United States as examples—the ethnic composition of those being admitted is an important topic of the public discourse. Freeman is correct about the importance of the respective immigration histories and the so-called national traditions. But they are part of the ideology and do not necessarily reflect historical and social realities.

Rogers Brubaker (1995b) has made this point very convincingly in a critique of Freeman's article. Immigration policy making cannot be explained by looking only at the structural features of liberal democratic policies. The historical, cultural, and political context have to be analyzed to get some meaningful explanations in comparative perspective. "In immigration policy debates, the boundaries of legitimate discussion are one of the crucial stakes of the debates." He correctly points out that "these boundaries change over time in response to broader developments in the environing culture and polity" (Brubaker 1995b, p. 905). I would also add that the notion of liberal democratic states neglects to take into account important differences between policy making in parliamentary and presidential systems, between a democracy defined by coalition building and a democracy defined by party politics.

In the following analysis I will argue that a simple political economy model of policy making is not sufficient to explain the change in immigration policy. The politics of immigration are not just reacting along business circles. Mere structural explanations are not satisfactory either. Policy debate, policy decisions by party politics, or interest group politics are taking place within a framework that is determined by ideas and ideologies. These ideas determine what kind of policies are possible, and which policies are taboo. Policy changes are usually preceded by a shift in the ideas and debate concerning the policy. In his work on British economic policy, Peter Hall (1993) aptly pointed out that political science typically neglects the influence of ideas in favor of structuralist and rational choice accounts of public policy and political change.

I have already explained the peculiar character of immigration as a political issue. It is highly loaded with value orientations. Therefore it would be highly appropriate to look more closely at the ideological dimension of the issue. The policy paradigm, or interpretive framework, that Hall proposes seems to be the most helpful tool for discussing the making, changing, and comparative analysis of immigration policy. As he states, "Policy makers customarily work within a framework of ideas and standards that specifies not only the goals of policy and the kind of instruments that can be used to attain them, but also the very nature of the problems they are meant to be addressing" (Hall 1993, p. 279). In many areas public policy is frequently more about defending and reaffirming symbols than it is about substance. Drug policy, for instance, has been placed in a punitive paradigm (Bertram, Blachman, Sharpe, and Andreas 1996, pp. 55-59). Another striking example of how important the framework of ideas is for policy making is the case of foreign policy. For 45 years the idea and dogma of containing Soviet power determined U.S. foreign policy. When the threat suddenly disappeared, foreign policy lost its internal compass—or paradigm—and confusion ensued (Dittgen 1996b).

The terminology policymakers use is an important dimension of the policy paradigm, because much of it is taken for granted and unamenable to scrutiny as a whole. If politicians, academics, and media continuously talk about the "migration crisis" or the "foreigner problem" the main parameters for the continuing debate are determined and hard to challenge. By using a certain language, the perception of a new, unprecedented *threat* is almost predetermined.

I argue that immigration policy making in Germany and the United States has clearly revolved around this sort of policy paradigm. It should be noted, however, that the explanation of "paradigm shifts" as a process of "social learning," by way of policy experimentation and policy failures—as Hall uses it for economic policy making in Britain—is not applicable for immigration policy. Thus, with immigration, "paradigm shifts" are connected to shifts in the broader political and cultural environment.

While the quality of most policy ideas can be tested in reality, the evaluation of immigration policy outcomes is extremely controversial. This is due to the highly ideological character of the issue. People look at the same political reality and give different accounts about the success and failure of immigration policy. This also holds true for scholarly analysis. Economic analysis is particularly controversial. In the United States the range of estimates of immigrants' impact on government spending is so wide that the research is virtually useless for policy making (Cornelius 1996b). Consequently, policy changes can be made without a clear-cut relation to policy results.

All immigration countries see their respective policies based on certain ideas that are closely connected to the national tradition. In the United

States, the "the classic country of immigration," legal immigrants are welcome and are expected to be integrated as citizens quickly. Cultural diversity is a source of national identity and unity (Fuchs 1990). Germany, the *Volk* nation or *Kulturnation*, is not a country of immigration. When people are permitted to enter, they are expected to be of German descent or expected to adopt German folkways (Hoffmann 1990). In France immigration policy is based on the "republican model," which implies a policy of assimilation that transforms immigrants into French citizens (Schnapper 1991). These national ideas about immigration are not static. They are a part of a political and cultural change, and their relation to historic and social reality could be vague if not fictitious.

GERMANY: THE POLITICS OF
DENIAL AND DETERRENCE

A German Information Center brochure provides us with a good description of its government's approach to immigration. In 1991 Americans were instructed as follows: "For Americans to understand the psychological underpinnings of the current debate among Germans on how to deal with immigration, it is necessary to realize that, unlike the multi-ethnic tapestry of the United States, the nation-states of Europe have traditionally been ethnically homogeneous" (Kanstroom 1993, p. 159). This is indeed an apt explanation of Germany's official ideology regarding "foreigner policy." It is also worthwhile to note that this is a definition *ex negativo*. Germany is "unlike" the United States. Beginning with the debates about citizenship law at the start of this century, one always finds the attempt to define German identity as a counterpoint to the United States: homogeneity versus cultural pluralism and *Volk* nation versus nation of immigrants.

Though today it is a well-known fact that Germany is an immigration country without an immigration policy, it is also worth looking at its "national" historiography. Until the 1980s migration and minorities were never major subjects for historical research. History written under the dictum of "national identity" disregarded plurality in order to construct continuity and homogeneity (Oberndörfer 1993, p. 30). It is only very recently that major works on migration history have been published in Germany (Dohse 1981; Herbert 1986; Lehmann 1991; Bade 1992a). A remarkable event has been the newly published *Encyclopedia of Ethnic Groups* (Schmalz-Jacobsen and Hansen 1995). In fact, for most European countries, immigrants have been absent from the collective memory.[9] However slowly, the awareness of the history of migration and the reality of cultural pluralism is spreading.

The different political traditions of the United States and Germany are usually regarded as being embodied in their respective citizenship laws (Brubaker 1989a). In Germany the attribution of citizenship at birth is based on descent (*ius sanguinis*). In the United States it is based on the principle of birth place (*ius soli*). In Germany naturalization is considered exceptional and is only available when the applicant is thoroughly integrated in German society—and then only when there is a public interest in his or her naturalization. In contrast, the United States expects immigrants to become U.S. citizens soon after entry. In fact, the prerequisite is only five years of residency. Immigrants who do not apply for naturalization after this period are viewed with disappointment.

A statement by the main legal adviser of the German government on citizenship, Law Professor Kay Hailbronner, shows very clearly what ideology (paradigm) is driving the German policy.

> The rationale of German naturalization law can be understood only in historical context....The German idea of nationhood is basically not a political one but a cultural, linguistic, and ethnic one...."Moral" claims to citizenship ... are generally inappropriate. There are no moral and therefore generally applicable criteria in judging a nation's citizenship policy apart from the principle forbidding a state to deprive a citizen arbitrarily of his citizenship....The United States and Canada, basically nations composed of immigrants from a variety of cultures, have conceptions of citizenship differing sharply from those prevailing on the Continent. This difference is explainable not in moral terms, but in terms of differing conceptions of the national interest....A claim to citizenship cannot be based on the democratic principle as such. Democracy, rather, presupposes membership in a political community....Dual citizenship can be exploited by the country of origin as a means of influencing the policy—particularly the foreign policy—of the country in which its expatriated reside (Hailbronner 1989).

This quote includes rather nicely all the elements of the ruling immigration paradigm allegedly rooted in a special German tradition. The romantic notions of *Volk* and *Kultur*, of state loyalty and state interests as well as indifference for individual rights have deeply penetrated the legal thinking in Germany. Citizenship is not a political concept understood as the membership in a political community, but a legal concept, which is based on apolitical ethnocultural homogeneity criteria. The legal thinking in Germany has been strongly influenced by Carl Schmitt's antiliberal racial state concept. "The racial similarity," he wrote in 1933, "of the united German people...is, therefore, the indispensable precondition and foundation for the concept of the political leadership of the German people."[10]

Those defenders of the current citizenship law in Germany still base their arguments on a predemocratic thinking of state interests and loyalty of the subjects. Lawyers claim a special inertial weight and normative dignity for this concept since it represents the "national tradition" (Brubaker 1992, pp. 186-187). However this "tradition" has been seriously challenged and exposed as incompatible with the universalistic principles of constitutional democracy (Oberndörfer 1991; Rittstieg 1991; Habermas 1992).

It is true that these ideas about a *Volk* nation have been the dominant paradigm determining German immigration—or more exactly—non-immigration policy. But what makes it a national tradition? Who determines what is national and what is "foreign" or non-German? Just a superficial look at the European history of ideas makes this claim of *the* one German tradition invalid. The concept of *Volk* nation has indeed been the dominant tradition but it is not *the* German tradition. The tradition of *Volk* nation and today's notion of a "non-immigration country" rest on an ethnicized conception of nationhood as a community of descent. Such conceptions are not empirical descriptions, but mythic constructs that are subject to manipulation in myriad ways (Klusmeyer 1995). These traditions are—to use Eric Hobsbawm's apt term—nothing but invented (Hobsbawm 1983). National history writers and lawyers have always cultivated and promoted these inventions. By stressing "national traditions" it falls into oblivion that there has also always been a strong liberal, cosmopolitan tradition in Germany beginning with the philosopher Immanuel Kant and his conception of a cosmopolitan law. During the German *Vormärz* before 1848 the liberal, republican political conceptions were dominant, and these liberal ideas continued on with the socialist movement and its conception of international solidarity.

These cosmopolitan principles inspired the Social Democrats when the citizenship law was discussed in the German Reichstag in 1913. They pointed out that the German Reich had already become an immigration country. As an SPD deputy put it: "Through the railroad, through electricity, through the mobility of our modern economic life we have today long expanded beyond our particularistic boundaries."[11] Eduard Bernstein ridiculed racial theories that preached against mixing blood of different peoples in the name of "racial purity." Instead he demanded equal rights for foreigners and pointed to the example of the United States, where, within a framework of equal rights, peoples "from every possible nation have assembled and where nevertheless an exceptionally much stronger idea of affiliation to this great polity has been formed by all...."[12]

Finally, and perhaps most importantly, there is not only a strong liberal tradition, but also the most liberal constitution that Germany ever had. It guarantees fundamental, individual rights as well as cultural freedom.[13] Dieter Oberndörfer has argued that a policy legitimized by the concept of *Volk* nation contradicts the universalism of the constitution

(Oberndörfer 1993, pp. 52-53). In this sense it could be said that those politicians and lawyers who defend the current concept of citizenship in Germany and accordingly proclaim the dogma of "non-immigration country" are referring to a constructed German tradition but contradict its constitution.

So far, I have argued that the German "non-immigration" paradigm is rooted in a predemocratic concept of citizenship. This concept finds its justification solely by referring to an allegedly exceptional political and legal tradition in Germany. However, as I mentioned at the beginning, national ideas about immigration are not static. They change, and the immigration paradigm has already changed. It is policy that has lagged behind.

Even though voices against immigration are loud and shrill, they should not mislead us. The immigration paradigm has profoundly changed within the last decade. Not only are immigration history and the current situation of immigration increasingly acknowledged, but the old ideas of nationhood are losing their prevalence. In today's immigration debate the liberal concept of citizenship, recognition of the long history of immigration, current immigration and the demand for an immigration policy dominate the debate. Government officials in power still defend the dogma that Germany is "not a country of immigration," but they are already on the defensive. Their position is simply untenable. The major newspapers—with the important exception of the *Frankfurter Allgemeine Zeitung*—now support the demand for an immigration policy.[14] The Social Democrats demand it, the Liberal Party (always fighting for survival) let it be known that it will be the reform party of the future, and that immigration policy and foreigner policy will be one of the top issues to tackle.[15] The Green party has always made immigration policy one of its top priorities. And there is also a strong group in the CDU, led by Heiner Geißler, that has always demanded a new policy. The immigration policy paradigm, I would argue, has already changed, and it, is just a question of time before the policy changes as well. And it should be noted that the citizenship law, the nucleus of national self-understanding, has already been partially reformed. The new foreigner law of 1990 makes it easier for young persons between the ages of sixteen and twenty-three from second- and third-generation-resident families to acquire citizenship. This is a timid beginning, as Helmut Rittstieg commented, for the legal recognition of a multicultural society (Rittstieg 1993, p. 11). These changes can be seen as the entry into an era of a new republican concept of citizenship and the implementation of an immigration policy.

There are, however, some social and political prerequisites for an immigration policy in Germany. First, economic integration with the

East has to be successful. Second, the perception that the "asylum crisis" has been solved must persist. Realistically, one cannot expect a sensible political discussion on an immigration policy that is associated with the notion of a controlled opening of the border, when there is still the perception that Germany is overrun. Thirdly, prudent political leadership is certainly a necessity for such a reform and needs to be based on a broad consensus of the major parties. In the current constellation of party politics, no dramatic policy initiatives will be taken soon. The CSU, as long as it is part of a coalition government, will always veto any serious immigration policy.

Finally, it will be of some importance which directions U.S. immigration policy will take, since proponents and opponents alike use the American mode—for its successes and failures—to support their arguments.

THE UNITED STATES: AN AMBIVALENT WELCOME

The year 1965 represents in many ways a watershed in U.S. immigration policy. For the first time a truly liberal immigration law was introduced (Daniels 1990; Zolberg 1990; Calavita 1995; Dittgen 1995). Although the United States is described as a traditional "country of immigration," it is frequently forgotten that it was also a pioneer in the development of systematic restrictions on immigration. In contrast to the specific American cosmopolitan and democratic tradition symbolized by the phrase, *E pluribus unum*, the United States developed an immigration policy based on racist theories.[16] Restrictionist policies began in 1882 with the Chinese Exclusion Act and peaked in the 1920s with the Immigration Act of 1924. The "golden door" was shut for all Asians, and entry curtailed for most Europeans. Until 1952 Japanese, Koreans, and Southeast and Southwest Asians were still ineligible for citizenship and thus denied admission as immigrants. The McCarran-Walter Act of 1952, passed over President Harry S Truman's veto, finally made the naturalization laws color-blind. The liberalization was, as Roger Daniels writes in his immigration history, a fruit of the cold war: "Engaged in a struggle for the hearts and minds of what it liked to call the Free World, the United States could no longer afford a policy that so blatantly excluded so many" (Daniels 1990, p. 329). However, most of the discriminatory policies of the 1924 act, in particular the national origins quota, were preserved.

During the heyday of the civil rights movement in the 1960s, both the Republican and Democratic platforms urged that more immigrants should be admitted on an equitable basis. The Republicans called for doubling the number of immigrants and for a major overhaul of the national origins quota system. The Democrats urged the end of the national origins quota system altogether as "inconsistent with our belief in the rights of man" (Fuchs 1990, p. 233). The language of democracy and universal rights and not nationhood carried the day. With Johnson's landslide election and a Democratic pro-immigration majority in Congress, the national origins quota system (including the strict numerical limits on immigrants from Asia) was abolished. Priority was now given to people with family members already in the United States or to people with skills needed in the U.S. labor market. While signing the law, Johnson expressed the driving liberal credo of immigration reform and denounced as un-American the restrictive era with its quotas based on racial theories:

> From this day forth, those wishing to emigrate into America shall be admitted on the basis of their skills and their close relationship to those already here. The fairness of this standard is so self-evident...yet the fact is that for over four decades the immigration policy has been distorted like a harsh injustice of the national origins quota system...families were kept apart because a husband or a wife or a child has been born in the wrong place. Men of needed skill and talent were denied entrance because they came from southern and eastern Europe or from one of the developing continents. The system violated the basic principle of American democracy—the principle that values and rewards each man on the basis of his merit...it has been un-American (Aleinikoff and Martin 1995, p. 57).

It should be noted that in 1965 the public was clearly opposed to letting more people in.[17] But it simply did not matter politically, because there was a considerable broad liberal consensus within the political elite that immigration law needed reform. The Civil Rights Act of 1964, the Voting Rights Act, and the Immigration Act of 1965 represented the high-water mark in a national consensus of egalitarianism (Daniels 1990, p. 338).

The new immigration law, coupled with prosperity in Europe, changed the composition of U.S. immigration dramatically—a consequence that was not foreseen when the law was signed. The law would never have passed if the radical change in immigration it was to effect had been realized at the time. During the 1970s Europe contributed less than 20 percent of U.S. immigrants; Mexico contributed nearly the same share. Since the early 1980s Europeans represented about 10 percent of legal immigrants, while Asians made up about one-third and Hispanics nearly half of all immigrants (Passel and Edmonston 1994).

Until the 1980s U.S. immigration law could have been described as a complex system that changed once each generation. This is no longer the case. Congress enacted three major reforms in the 1980s. First came the Refugee Act of 1980, which ended the year-to-year improvisation of refugee admissions by requiring the president to consult with Congress on the annual number of refugees to be admitted. The act also brought the U.S. definition of "refugee" into conformity with the United Nations standard (the Geneva convention of refugees), thus changing the previous U.S. practice of granting refugee status primarily to persons leaving Communist countries.

The Immigration Reform and Control Act of 1986 (IRCA) was the second major piece of legislation enacted during the decade. IRCA was designed to slow illegal immigration, which flowed primarily from Mexico and Central American countries. IRCA attempted to close the U.S. labor market to unauthorized workers by imposing penalties on U.S. employers who knowingly hired illegal aliens ("employer sanctions") and to grant legal immigrant status ("amnesty") to illegal aliens who had established roots in the United States. This legislation reflected the recommendations of a series of government commissions set up by Presidents Ford, Carter, and Reagan to examine the dimensions and consequences of the surge in legal and illegal immigration. The most prominent of these was the *Select Commission on Immigration and Refugee Policy*, created in 1979 and composed of members of Congress, the Cabinet, and the public. The Select Commission and previous commissions reached similar conclusions:

1. The United States must reduce "back-door" illegal immigration to prevent an anti-immigrant backlash from halting "front-door" legal immigration; and
2. Illegal immigration adversely affects unskilled American workers and should be stopped.

The commission, however, somewhat refocused the debate away from its economic impacts to an examination of the relationship of illegal immigration to the civic culture. It took the view that the presence of a substantial number of illegal aliens undercut the principle that all who live and work in the United States, regardless of ethnicity, should have fundamental, equal rights (Fuchs 1990, pp. 250-252).

The resulting legislation was a historic compromise among agricultural employers, ethnic lobbies, human rights groups, and others who wanted liberal regulations on the admission of immigrants and foreign workers, and the U.S. government, labor unions, and other groups that wanted to halt illegal immigration (Zolberg 1990; Schuck 1992). Then-Senator Pete Wilson, as an economic liberal, held the fragile legislative compromise hostage until he won approval of programs increasing the number of "temporary" farm workers available to California's growers. With his demand for guest-workers he made clear how much California's economy, in particular its agricultural sector, depends on cheap Mexican labor. Governor Pete Wilson, as a populist politician, complained a couple of years later how costly the "loss of control of our borders" was for the state of California. He was reelected to a second term, even though it was he who enabled hundreds of thousands of undocumented workers to enter and work in the state. Most of them are now legalized, but their spouses and children are and will probably remain illegal for some time, and they are, as Peter Schuck points out, major consumers of the public services that Wilson sought to limit under Proposition 187 (Schuck 1995, p. 92).

Only half of the historic compromise of the 1986 immigration law (IRCA) worked as intended. The amnesty and legalization provisions of IRCA allowed 2.7 million undocumented aliens to obtain permanent resident status. However, illegal immigration has continued, facilitated by the widespread use of fraudulent documents (Martin 1995a).

Four years after IRCA was enacted, Congress passed the third, and potentially most far-reaching, reform of immigration law. The Immigration Act of 1990 reflects the fear that previous immigration laws hampered U.S. competitiveness by assigning the highest preference for visas to relatives of U.S. citizens rather than to people with needed job skills. Some economists had predicted a shortage of skilled labor in coming decades. The influential Workforce 2000 report, released in 1987, concluded that "more, better-educated immigrants would be needed to help staff a growing economy." American business complained that "antiquated immigration laws severely hamper the ability of U.S. firms to compete in an increasingly global economy" (Papademetriou 1996).

The Immigration Act of 1990 increased the number of immigrants and their families permitted to enter under the employment-preference category from 54,000 under previous legislation to 140,000. Most of this increase consists of family members; the number of "employment-preference" workers rose from about 18,000 to 47,000. Currently, 20 percent of immigrants to the United States (excluding refugees) are admitted on the basis of their skills.

The new immigration legislation of the 1980s did not represent an incremental policy change but, rather, a genuine change of policy paradigm. The change was possible, as Schuck observes, because of a "new cultural consensus favoring expanded immigration" (Schuck 1992, p. 61). The idea of universal humanitarian principles, the principles of the American Constitution, and the prevailing economic liberalism helped to form coalitions of otherwise very different interests and political outlook. That is not to say that there were no voices against immigration. On the contrary, in the late 1970s anti-immigration groups sprang up among environmentalists and some labor interests, such as the Federation of American Immigration Reform (FAIR). The Haitian and Cuban migration in the early 1980s produced considerable anti-immigrant sentiment, but public debate never became dominated by it. In congressional and presidential election debates the issue of immigration was notably absent. That changed only when Patrick Buchanan entered the race for the Republican presidential nomination in 1992. At the 1992 Republican National Convention Buchanan announced that the time had come to "take back our culture."

Rita Simon and Susan H. Alexander reviewed editorials from the *New York Times* and found that the vast majority were pro-immigrant (Simon and Alexander 1993, pp. 221-229). In the 1980s there was not yet a market for academics and journalists to make a case against immigration because the *Zeitgeist* did not make room for enterprises like this. That immigration did not stir much interest is the fact that *U.S. News and World Report* carried just two stories on immigration in 1989, the year of immigration reform (Simon and Alexander 1993, p. 194). Therefore, when the new immigration law was enacted by Congress in 1990, most observers believed that a long-term political consensus had been reached on a relatively open-door policy (Schuck 1991). But they were all wrong.

Soon after the new immigration law of 1990 went into force, debates evolved about illegal immigration and, later, immigration in general.[18] The starting point for this political development was, as in so many other cases of new legislation to restrict immigration, the state of California.

Voter referenda in California—not only with regard to immigration but also in other policy fields—have set the agenda for national policy changes. Proposition 13 in 1978 was in many respects a predecessor of Proposition 187. Proposition 13 targeted lowering property taxes and set the stage for Reagan's fiscal policy in the early 1980s. In 1986 California approved Proposition 63, which called for the preservation of English as the state's "common language."

In California the network organizing for Proposition 187 took its organizational resources from the movement to reduce government and the long-established movement to reduce immigration. The Proposition 187 initiative, which triggered national debate about immigration, targets public assistance for illegal immigrants. Proposition 187 primarily creates a state-mandated screening system for persons seeking tax-supported benefits. In the language of Proposition 187, no citizen, legal immigrant, or illegal immigrant "shall receive any public social services to which he or she may otherwise be entitled until the legal status of that person has been verified" (Martin 1995b; Cain, MacDonald, and McCue 1996).

In 1994 Governor Pete Wilson made his support for Proposition 187, the "save our state" initiative, a cornerstone of his reelection campaign. This politically smart move saved his faltering campaign: prior to his announcement he had lagged 17 points behind challenger Kathleen Brown. Very characteristic of the hypocrisy of the whole debate were the closing days of the 1994 campaign season which were marked by charges between U.S. Senate candidates Feinstein and Huffington. Both took tough stands against illegal immigration, and both charged that the other employed an illegal alien housemaid. Indeed, much of the comfortable Californian way of life that the middle class enjoys depends on cheap and frequently "undocumented" workers.

Wilson was reelected with 55 percent of the vote. Prop. 187 was approved by California voters, 59 to 41 percent. Brown and President Clinton had taken positions against Proposition 187. By making Proposition 187 an election campaign issue Clinton helped to propel the debate into the national arena.

Following the election of November 1994 the new Republican majority was swift to introduce bills for a new immigration law. Senator Alan Simpson (Republican from Wyoming), chairman of the Senate Subcommittee on Immigration, said that an overall reduction of quotas was necessary to give Americans "breathing space" from the current historically high level of immigration. Furthermore, he stated that it was very important to respond to public concern by making it as clear as possible that illegal aliens would not be able to access the welfare system, and that immigrants who do need assistance must obtain it from the relative who sponsored them, as they promised at the time of entry.

That Congress took action in 1995 is also due to the fact that the U.S. Commission on Immigration Reform, which was created under the 1990 immigration law and chaired by former Congresswoman Barbara Jordan, submitted its interim report (U.S. Commission on Immigration Reform 1994). The report represents current mainstream thinking about immigration reform very well. In particular, it recommends reductions in the overall number of immigrant visas by one-third: 400,000 visas for nuclear family admission, elimination of certain family-based admission categories, and 100,000 visas for skill-based admission, whereby offers of employment to foreign workers would usually be conditioned on an appropriate test of the domestic labor market to ensure that qualified American workers would not be displaced. There is an exception for this requirement with regard to aliens with extraordinary abilities. 50,000 visas—half of the current number—would be provided for refugee resettlement. The Clinton administration endorsed the Jordan Commission recommendation that legal immigration be reduced.

As it turned out, reducing the amount of legal immigration was not a priority for Congress. In March 1996 the House voted to split the bill into separate legal and illegal components as the Senate Judiciary Committee had done before. The Clinton administration, while on record supporting some reductions in legal immigration, joined the effort to separate the legislation on legal and illegal immigration. An unusual coalition of liberals and ethnic advocates, high-tech businesses, libertarians, and religious groups made this legislative move possible, which makes any changes in the legal immigration system in the near future very unlikely.[19]

The original proposal of the commission and Senator Simpson to reduce the number of visas found no majority. However, the social rights of legal immigrants are severely affected by the welfare reform legislation.[20] For the first time the new welfare legislation will draw a sharp difference between citizens and immigrants. Immigrants who have not worked for 10 years or served in the military cannot get food stamps or Supplemental Security Income (SSI) and will now be denied health benefits under Medicaid, while legal immigrants with children will lose benefits from the Aid to Families with Dependent Children program (AFDC). All social service programs will have to verify the immigration status of applicants for benefits. New York City Mayor Rudolph Giuliani called the "reporting provision" inhumane and indecent. He did sue the federal government to block this provision of the welfare bill. The new immigration law holds sponsoring relatives accountable for keeping family immigrants from becoming burdens on the American taxpayers. For the first time this responsibility will become enforceable. One consequence of the new laws restricting the rights of immigrants is a dramatic surge in naturalization. In 1996 more than one million new citizens were sworn in.

It is a highly problematic feature for a liberal democracy that legal immigrants end up with reduced social rights compared to citizens, even though they pay their regular taxes. But this distinction is in many ways characteristic of the new immigration policy paradigm. Liberal principles no longer find many advocates. The discussion in Congress never focused on the question of rights. The main concern was rather whether immigrants place a burden on the social and economic system. In general the debate in Congress was driven by two questions: Do immigrants displace Americans in the job market, and do immigrants receive more in public assistance than American citizens? Both sides could marshal well-known academics and plenty of statistics to prove their positions (Clark et al. 1994; Borjas 1994; Simon 1996).

How dramatically the immigration paradigm shifted in the 1990s is evident in President Clinton's 1995 State of the Union address. After having spoken about the growing concerns about crime he said about immigration:

> All Americans are rightly disturbed by the large numbers of illegal immigrants enter-
> ing this country. The jobs they hold might otherwise be held by our citizens or legal
> immigrants, and the public services they use impose burdens on our taxpayers.
> That's why our administration has moved aggressively to secure our borders by hir-
> ing a record number of new border guards, by deporting twice as many criminal
> aliens as ever before, by cracking down on illegal aliens, who try to take American
> jobs, and by barring welfare benefits to illegal aliens.

Later the President adds: "This is a nation of immigrants. But it is also a nation of law. And it is wrong, and ultimately self-defeating, for a nation of immigrants to permit the kind of abuse of our immigration laws we have seen in recent years."[21] Any difference from the rhetoric of Governor Pete Wilson was hardly recognizable.

The usual explanation by political scientists for such a sharp change in outlook and language is an economic one. In economically good times immigration is unproblematic and welcome. However, in hard times restrictionist policies flourish. But in the case of the United States this economic explanation is problematic. Immigration policy is, in my opin-ion, doubtless reacting to external and internal economic needs, the glo-bal economy, and the national labor market. But to explain restrictionist movements one always has to search in the realm of the ideological, too. The current immigration debate as well as previous ones always centered around the question of American identity. The real question was and is, "Who are we?" or sometimes even very openly nativist, "Whose country is this, anyway?"

The call for restricting immigration always appeared in times of crisis in the wake of a new nationalism. The intellectual elite—or at least those who consider themselves part of it—have always been the upholders and promoters of nationalism. It is instructive to just mention two popular book titles of the "tribal twenties." Lothrop Stoddard, a lawyer in Brookline, Massachusetts, with a Ph.D. in history, wrote a book on the menace of the Under Man—the racially impoverished opponent of all elites; his title: *The Revolt against Civilization*. Madison Grant wrote a book with the title: *The Rising Tide of Color Against White World Supremacy*, and got sympathetic comments in the editorials of such influential publi-cations as the *New York Times* and the *Saturday Evening Post* (Higham 1955, p. 271).

The restrictionist movement of today is also the expression of a new nationalism. As in the 1920s, intellectuals are warning against unassail-able immigrants and coming cultural conflicts, as three very different titles make clear: Peter Brimelow's *Alien Nation*, Michael Lind's *The Next*

American Nation: The New Nationalism and the Fourth American Revolution, and Samuel P. Huntington's *The Clash of Civilizations and the Remaking of World Order.* These authors were not picked at random; these books were well received, and all three authors are important figures in the ongoing public discussion. They participate in many talk shows on immigration, write op-ed pieces for the major newspapers, or contribute to academic journals. They are treated by the media as people of expertise. Peter Brimelow is senior editor of *Forbes* and *National Review.* Michael Lind has been a senior editor of *Harper's* and executive editor of *The National Interest.* He is currently a senior editor of *The New Republic.* Samuel P. Huntington is a prominent political scientist at Harvard University.

The intellectual caliber of Peter Brimelow and the main message of his book becomes apparent with the very first sentences:

> There is a sense in which current immigration policy is Adolf Hitler's posthumous revenge on America. The U.S. political elite emerged from the war passionately concerned to cleanse itself from all taints of racism or xenophobia. Eventually, it enacted the epochal Immigration Act of 1965. And this, quite accidentally, triggered a renewed mass immigration, so huge and so systematically different from anything that had gone before as to transform—and ultimately, perhaps, even to destroy—the one unquestioned victor of World War II: the American nation, as it had evolved by the middle of the twentieth century. Today, U.S. government policy is literally dissolving the people and electing a new one (Brimelow 1995, p. XV).

The dreadful tone of his opening is characteristic of the entire book. Brimelow writes that the American nation has always had a specific ethnic core. And that core has been white (Brimelow 1995, p. 10). The author calls for repealing all the legislation enacted in the past 30 years, sealing the border by instituting national identity cards, as well as imprisoning and deporting all unauthorized immigrants and eliminating humanitarian categories (refugees and asylum-seekers) altogether. His model for the United States is Switzerland, which has a large foreign population of guest workers without rights to stay (p. 266).

His understanding of a nation is very close to the traditional German understanding of it. That becomes clear when he complains about the ignorance of the *New York Times,* when it very reasonably recommended that the political establishment in Bonn would do better to set a quota on immigrants and nurture a more pluralist society by adopting a formula for citizenship based on residence rather than blood ties. Peter Brimelow disagrees: "What we have here is a total absence of any understanding of the nation as a family, to which outsiders may be admitted indeed, but only under very special circumstances and with great care" (p. 225).

After all that, it is surprising what the *New York Times* had to say about Brimelow's book. Richard Bernstein characterizes the book in a rather long review as "a highly cogent presentation of what is going to be the benchmark case against immigration" and proclaims that "those who think that the system needs no fixing cannot responsibly hold that position any longer" (Bernstein 1995).[22] Moreover, he praises Brimelow, the revisionist historian: "Mr. Brimelow also shows that America is not so much a country of immigration as it is one of "intermittent immigration." The periods where there was almost no immigration are more characteristic of our history than the briefer periods when the door was open." Bernstein's review reveals to what extent the book was able to hit a raw nerve—the feeling of alienation in the United States. In the 1980s a similar review of Brimelow's book would have been simply inconceivable.

Michael Lind advocates liberal nationalism as a political movement with the goal of dismantling multicultural America and replacing it with a Fourth Republic of the United States, which he calls "Trans-America." Trans-America has nothing in common with Randolph Bournes's "Trans-national America." Randolph Bournes and Horace Kallen represent for Lind old-fashioned cultural pluralists who deny the existence of an American nation-state (Lind 1995, pp. 80-81). Lind rejects all universalistic notions of national identity as well as any nativist national concept. The very notion of a country based on an idea, he writes, is absurd.[23] Lind sees himself in the tradition of Johann Gottfried von Herder. He dismisses without much effort those who blame Herder for the illiberal tendencies of German nationalism. On the contrary, he praises Herder for championing the value of German culture against the false universalism of the then hegemonic French culture (p. 262).

How does the fact of immigration match with the concept of the American *Kulturnation?* Immigration is not only, as could be expected, very problematic but it never happened as most people probably think. In fact he writes, the United States is not a nation of immigrants and never has been: "At no point in American history have people born abroad constituted more than a minority of the U.S. population" (p. 286). This observation is, of course, true but does not permit the conclusion that all immigrants immediately identify themselves with an "American culture," however it may be defined. The definition of a country of immigration as one in which the foreign-born population has the majority is nonsense, because it has never existed.

In Trans-America, Lind's liberal-nationalistic construct, immigration should be reduced in order to create a tight labor market, boost American wages, and increase opportunities for upward mobility. The best policy might be one of "zero net immigration"—limiting the number of legal immigrants to the number of people who voluntarily emigrate from the United States each year (pp. 321-322).

In 1993 Samuel P. Huntington wrote in *Foreign Affairs* an article entitled "The Clash of Civilizations?" which generated a major international
debate. Three years later he published a book where he develops his
arguments in more detail. The hot spots in world politics are, explains
Huntington, on the "fault lines" between civilizations. Since the clash of
civilizations—"the rest against the west"—represents the character of the
new world order, it is only consistent to assume that this clash will also
be the main characteristic for societies with a plurality of cultures. In
particular those with large numbers of immigrants from non-Western
cultures will be affected.

Huntington observes that U.S. immigration policy is following Europe:

> The United States is following Europe in moving to cut back substantially the entry of
> non-Westerners into its society. Can either Europe or the United States stem the
> migrant tide?...The issue is not whether Europe will be Islamicized or the United
> States Hispanicized. It is whether Europe and America will become cleft societies
> encompassing two distinct and largely separate communities from two different civili-
> zations, which in turn depends on the number of immigrants and the extent to which
> they are assimilated into the Western cultures prevailing in Europe and America
> (Huntington 1996, pp. 203-204).

But there is not just the prospect of "Islamization" in Europe and
"Hispanization" in the United States but a real threat:

> While Muslims pose the immediate problem to Europe, Mexicans pose the problem
> for the United States....Some evidence suggests that resistance to assimilation is
> stronger among Mexican migrants than it was with other immigrant groups and that
> Mexicans tend to retain their Mexican identity, as was evident in the struggle over
> Proposition 187 in California in 1994....Mexican economic development will almost
> certainly generate Mexican revanchist sentiments. In due course, the results of Amer-
> ican military expansion in the nineteenth century could be threatened and possibly
> reversed by Mexican demographic expansion in the twenty-first century (Huntington
> 1996, p. 206).[24]

What could be the cause of this new nationalism that suddenly sheds
such a critical light on immigration? One of the most important reasons
is the end of the East-West confrontation. The disappearance of America's ideological enemy has led to great confusion about its own identity.
Without an enemy American liberalism seems to be without a power supply.[25] A liberal immigration policy contrasted particularly well with the
closed borders of the communist regimes during the East-West-confron-
tation. Back in 1953 Oscar Handlin, the author of *The Uprooted*, wrote in
the *Atlantic Monthly* that he was pro-immigrant, because immigrants have
always helped to raise the standards of native labor, and because a liberal and fair policy on immigration helped the image of the United
States in the world. "It strengthens our struggle against communism...it

is human and decent for people who live in fear of communism and want to emigrate," he asserted (Handlin 1953). With the disappearance of the communist challenge a liberal immigration policy has lost an important source for its legitimization.

The mobilization of the ideology of nationhood is also a result of the destructive forces of globalization. *"L'horreur économique,"* the economic horror, as the French call it, leads to a search for a strengthening of the nation's cultural identity. A new internal bipolarity surfaces, as Theodore Lowi has observed, "wherein each country is struggling to make its own hard policy choices of how to maintain a balance between the cultural particularities of nationhood (sometimes called community) and the economic universalism of the market" (Lowi 1996). In an era where the traditional orientations (we and them, good and bad) have vanished, not only the United States is experiencing a rekindling of nationhood as ideology. This ideology is irreconcilable with a liberal immigration policy that makes no differentiation with regard to the origin of the newcomers (cultural and ethnical neutrality) and aims at integration of these newcomers.

That the slogan "we must regain control of our borders" has resonated so well with the public in the 1990s but not in the 1980s indicates that the country has lost the optimism of the previous decade. President Clinton sensed the spirit of the country said: "I'm also trying to get people to get out of their funk." And he explained further: "What makes people insecure is when they feel like they're lost in the funhouse. They're in a room where something can hit them from any direction any time." Even though the metaphors were well taken to explain the feeling that people and their government have lost the control over their destiny, he had to put an end to the "Funk Monster," as David Broder called it. With a more Reaganesque outlook he explained, "I feel very optimistic about the country."[26] An observation by Michael Walzer in *Spheres of Justice* explains the relation between one's own feeling of security and closed borders. "The same fence that keeps most people out," writes Walzer, "is necessary to enable those within to feel safe, to think of themselves as co-ventures, and to flourish as a social, moral and political community" (Walzer 1983, p. 35).[27]

The new nationalism incorporates exactly this mechanism of gaining community and security by exclusion. The diagnosis of loss of community is omnipresent also in the writings of social scientists these days. The communitarians castigate liberalism (Sandel depreciatively calls it a procedural liberalism) for undermining the very moral resources necessary for self-government and to inspire the sense of community and civic engagement.[28] Putnam finds indications for a loss of social capital leading to the disappearance of "civic America" (Putnam 1996; Dittgen

1996a). One finds despair and longing for community wherever one looks. The East-West confrontation has for 40 years absorbed much of the political attention. Now with its end, attention has become directed at the inner life of the country, and the result is despair about the condition of American society and pessimism with regard to its future.[29] Given this state of public and academic spirit it is no wonder that trust in the country's ability to integrate many more new immigrants is low, and that, the dark forces of nativism flourish.[30]

CONCLUSIONS: THE INVENTION OF TRADITION—GERMAN-AMERICAN DIFFERENCE OR CONVERGENCE?

The intention of this chapter was to show that the politics of immigration can be sufficiently explained neither by a political economy model nor by the structural features of liberal democratic states, suggesting that this type of regime—*eo ipso* and without much difference—favor broadly expansionist and inclusive policies. In the United States immigration policy making is taking place in the political arena of interest groups by way of coalition building. In Germany immigration policy is mostly party politics. Both arenas of policy making are determined by a policy paradigm that "shapes and boundaries the discursive field" (Brubaker 1995, p. 905). The policy paradigm shaping the immigration debates is closely connected to national identity in containing ideas about the meaning of citizenship as well as about the history and future of the country. These ideas, however, are changing, and the reference to national traditions is a highly ambiguous (ideological) one, since these traditions are constructed and interpreted according to the specific cultural and political outlook of the time.

The histories of both countries have multiple traditions (Smith 1993). The only valid and formative tradition in the United States is not limited to a "nation of immigrants" nor to only a *Volk* nation in the Federal Republic of Germany. As Roger Daniels pointed out, "the nativist tradition is almost as old as the immigrant tradition in America, and notions about its demise are, as Mark Twain observed about a false report of his death, greatly exaggerated" (Daniels 1990, p. 408). In a similar way one can say that in Germany the republican tradition is as old as the ethnocultural tradition viewing the nation exclusively as a homogeneous *Volk* community. The tradition of *Volk* nation is still discernible in the German legal thinking about citizenship. But the republican tradition has manifested itself in the German constitution, the Basic Law (*Grundgesetz*). In the United States the belief in being an immigration society has provided a powerful normative tradition through which immigration is understood as a positive affirmation of the character of American life and immigration is perceived as beneficial to the nation. This tradition has promoted the acceptance of free migrants and reinforced the republican ideal of citizenship. But American national self-understanding as an immigration society has never precluded strong exclusive membership policies based on ethnicity, race, and national origin. In fact it lasted until the immigration reforms of 1965, when the national origins-quota system, with its racial selection criteria, was abolished.

Eric Hobsbawm has noted that the criteria for defining a nation, like language or ethnicity, "are fuzzy, shifting and ambiguous, and as useless...as cloud-shapes are compared to landmarks. This, of course, makes them unusually convenient for propagandists and programmatic, as distinct from descriptive purposes" (Hobsbawm 1991, p. 6). Because the criteria are shifting and ambiguous, the politics of immigration can also shift and frequently do.

In national debates on immigration one can also find an element of continuity. Both the United States and Germany have constitutions that are based on universalistic principles, and individualistic and human rights, which serve as a irremovable normative yardstick. It was the discrepancy with the principles of the constitution and the practice of discrimination that led to civil rights legislation, immigration reform, and the abandonment of the "national origins-quotas." In Germany the ethnocultural conception of citizenship is equally incompatible with the fundamental rights of the constitution. The special provisions for people of German descent have lost their justification after the unification of Germany and the end of the division of Europe. After World War II political thinking in Germany has become irreversibly integrated into the Western democratic tradition. A new citizenship law and the acceptance of multicultural reality will be the natural outcome of this modernization process. The old thinking in terms of *Volk* and homogeneity will lose its attraction since it will become less and less compatible with the process of European integration, the global marketplace, and a world where international regulations have increasing importance. In the United States as well as in Germany the ideas of democracy and human rights are, as Habermas formulated, the hard material on which the beams of national tradition refract.[31] Since unification, all German exceptionalisms (*Sonderwege*) have ended (Winkler 1994, p. 124). The open republic is therefore the only realistic option (Oberndörfer 1991). The reaction of the new right will not reverse this development (Kurthen and Minkenberg 1995).[32] But setbacks, triggered by political and economic crisis can and will always happen. This is also something to be learned from the United States.

The immigration paradigm in the United States developed independently of the requirements of the labor market. The basic features of immigration laws were instead profoundly shaped by the development of American civil society. It was the civil rights movement—the quest for realization of the constitutional principles of equal rights—that finally ended the ethnocentric character of the old immigration laws. In the 1980s the laws were further liberalized, in that an amnesty program for undocumented immigrants was instituted, and in 1990 the number of available visas was considerably raised. A liberal consensus about the value of immigration seemed to have been established.

But just at the moment when the triumph of liberal democracy was being celebrated by the end of the cold war, the liberal immigration paradigm became increasingly challenged by an anti-immigrant sentiment and a new nativism. Again this change stood in the context of a more general shift in the political climate. A new nationalism became widely acceptable and borrowed many ethnocultural features from old European thinking. While a dramatic change in immigration policy is unlikely, anti-immigration attitudes have already left their mark by reducing the social rights of immigrants. The combination of fears of cultural alienation after a high volume of immigration and general crisis resembles the situation of the 1920s. But a relapse into tribal thinking and a corresponding immigration policy are unlikely, since constitutional principles of human rights have become deeply entrenched in politics and cannot be turned back.

The present German Commissioner for Foreigners, Cornelia Schmalz-Jacobsen, recently wrote that Germany and Europe need legal regulation of immigration for two reasons—pressure of immigration and the need for immigration. She added, "Germany, too, like America, will have to find a compromise between our humanitarian responsibility and our national interest" (Schmalz-Jacobsen 1995, p. 175).[33] Indeed, if this perspective finds broad acceptance, namely that the political challenges Germany is facing and the appropriate policies are *like* those of the United States, it could be considered tremendous progress not only with regard to immigration policy but with regard to the self-understanding of the German Republic as a whole. This is exactly the answer from the government that liberal deputies of the German Reichstag were looking for more than eighty years ago.

ACKNOWLEDGMENT

An earlier version of this paper was presented at the research seminar of the Center for U.S.-Mexican Studies at the University of California, San Diego. I wish to thank the participants of the seminar, in particular, Wayne A. Cornelius and Peter Andreas, for their helpful comments.

NOTES

1. Douglas Klusmeyer at Stanford University has written a thorough historical analysis on the immigration and citizenship law reforms in Germany and the United States before the First World War and has pointed out how the American "model" as the "country of immigration" has always served as a point of reference in the German debate and historiography (Klusmeyer 1995).

2. "Die Gründe, warum man in den Vereinigten Staaten dazu übergegangen ist, die Einwanderungsbestimmungen wesentlich zu erschweren, liegen auf einem ganz anderen Gebiet. Dieselben datieren aus der Zeit der ersten Präsidentschaft Roosevelts. Damals fing die Einwanderung aus denselben europäischen Staaten an, die auch für uns in Betracht kommen, aus den europäischen südslawischen Staaten. Diese Einwanderung hat man auch in den Vereinigten Staaten nicht gern gesehen, und infolgedessen ist Präsident Roosevelt damals dagegen aufgetreten...," *Verhandlungen des Reichstages* (XIII. Legislaturperiode, Stenographische Berichte, May 29, 1991, p. 5311, quoted in Klusmeyer 1995).

3. "Das kann man gerade in den Vereinigten Staaten verfolgen, wie in denjenigen Städten, die zum großen Teil, viel mehr als in Deutschland, mit Leuten aus jenen Nationen aus dem Osten bevölkert sind, die freieren Einrichtungen und die besseren Lebensbedingungen auch eine kulturelle Hebung der Betreffenden zur Folge haben," *Verhandlungen des Reichstages*, XIII. Legislaturperiode, 29, May 1991, p. 5308, quoted in Klusmeyer 1995).

4. "Germany slows flow of illegal immigrants. Though new policy's merit debated, but not its success," *The San Diego Union Tribune* (September 27, 1994). Robert Kuttner, "Illegal Immigration: Would a National ID Card Help?" (quoted in Mills 1994, pp. 81-84).

5. Ralf Dahrendorf, very aptly wrote about the "pathology of political and civil equality" in Germany (Dahrendorf 1965, p. 93).

6. Public opinion surveys show that anti-immigrant attitudes are not correlated to intensive contact with "foreigners." For Germany and Europe see Küchler (1996, p. 253). In a national poll conducted by *Scripps Howard News Service* and *Ohio University* in 1995, people were asked, nationwide, "Are there any immigrants living in your neighborhood?" Forty-five percent answered with "no," and 11 percent were uncertain. *Scripps Howard News Service/Ohio University Poll*, February 24, 1995 (available at Roper Center).

7. See Timothy Christenfeld, "Alien Expressions. Wretched Refuse Is Just the Start," *New York Times* (March 10, 1996).

8. She writes: "Immigration policy is now shaped by forces ranging from economic globalization to international agreements on human rights, and it is made and implemented within settings ranging from national and local legislatures and judiciaries to supranational organizations" (Sassen 1996, p. 98). For a comparative political-economic approach see also Hollifield (1992).

9. For France see the excellent study by Gérard Noiriel (1996).

10. Carl Schmitt: *Staat, Bewegung, Volk* 1933 (quoted in Kanstroom 1993: 176).

11. SPD deputy Max Quarck (See *Verhandlungen des Reichstages*, XIII. Legislaturperiode, Stenographische Berichte, May 29, 1913, pp. 5296-5297, quoted in Klusmeyer 1995).

12. *Verhandlungen des Reichstages*, XIII. Legislaturperiode, Stenographische Berichte, 29. Mai 1913: 5301, quoted in Klusmeyer 1995).

13. Article 1: "Die Würde *des Menschen* ist unantastbar. Sie zu achten und zu schützen ist Verpflichtung aller staatlichen Gewalt"; Article 2: "*Jeder* hat das Recht auf die freie Entfaltung seiner Persönlichkeit"; Article 3 (1): "*Alle Menschen* sind vor dem Gesetz gleich"; Article 3(3): "*Niemand* darf wegen seines Geschlechts, seiner Abstammung, seiner Rasse, seiner Sprache, seiner Heimat und Herkunft, seines Glaubens, seiner religiösen oder politischen Anschauungen benachteiligt oder bevorzugt werden" (emphasis by author).

14. For the position of the *Frankfurter Allgemeine Zeitung* on multiculturalism, see Eckhard Fuhr's (19892) almost programmatic editorial.

15. Rudolf Scharping: "Die Einbürgerung ist nicht der krönende Abschluß der Integration," in: "Zwischen Heimat und offener Republik: Herausforderungen der Einwanderungspolitik," *Frankfurter Rundschau* (June 25, 1993, p. 16). Claus Gennrich in: "Das Spektrum verbreitern, ohne das Patent auf das Hauptthema Standort zu verlieren," *Frankfurter Allgemeine Zeitung* (October 7, 1996).

16. John Higham (1955) has written the classic analysis of American nativism.

17. In May 1965 *Louis Harris and Associates* (May 31, 1965, available by Roper Center) asked respondents: "President (Lyndon) Johnson has proposed that the immigration laws of this country be changed to allow more people into the United States as immigrants. From what you know or have heard, do you favor or oppose letting more people come to the United States as immigrants? In "favor" were 24 percent, "opposed" 58 percent, and "not sure" 18 percent.

18. For a good collection of opinions characterizing the immigration debate of the 1990s, see Mills (1994).

19. "An Unusual Immigration Alliance," *Congressional Quarterly* (March 16, 1996, p. 700), and "Senate Rejects Two Attempts to Cut Legal Immigration," *Congressional Quarterly* (April 27, 1996, pp. 1173-1174).

20. Jeffrey L. Katz, "After 60 Years, Most Control Is Passing to States," *Congressional Quarterly* (August 3, 1996: 2190-2196).

21. "Clinton says U.S. Security Depends on World Leadership Role" (Text: State of the Union address), *U.S. Policy & Texts* (January 25, 1995, p. 4).

22. See also Miles (1995).

23. Miles (1995, pp. 4f.). See also Brimelow who refutes in the same brisk manner the republican tradition of the Founding Fathers and explicitly says that the nation-state is based on a particular ethnicity (Brimelow 1995, pp. 208,225).

24. The danger of a *Reconquista* is also conjured up by David Kennedy, who wrote: "No previous immigrant group had the size and concentration and easy access to its original culture that the Mexican immigrant group in the Southwest has today. If we seek historical guidance, the closest example we have to hand is in the diagonally opposite corner of the North American Continent, in Quebec. The possibility looms that in the next generation or so we will see a kind of Chicano Quebec take shape in the American Southwest, as a group emerges with strong cultural cohesiveness and sufficient economic and political strength to insist on changes in the overall society's way of organizing itself and conducting its affairs." He closes his observations with a quote by Lincoln: "We must disenthrall ourselves, and then we shall save our country" (Kennedy 1996, p. 68).

25. For a comprehensive discussion of what impact the end of the Cold War has on the American polity, politics, and policy see Minkenberg and Dittgen (1996).

26. William Safire, "Funkmanship," *The New York Times Magazine* (October 22, 1995, pp. 30-32).

27. This fundamental social mechanism of gaining security by excluding foreigners is brilliantly described in T. Coraghessan Boyle's novel *The Tortilla Curtain*.

28. The most recent example of this communitarian critique of liberalism is Sandel (1996).

29. A comprehensive survey on the national mood taken in May 1996 by Chilton Research for ABC's *World News Tonight*, found 67 percent of respondents saying that the country "is in a long-term moral decline" (see Ladd 1996).

30. However, there is strong evidence that immigrants are assimilating as fast as ever (see Cornelius 1996a).

31. Jürgen Habermas, "Geschichtsbewußtsein und posttraditionale Identität. Die Westorientierung der Bundesrepublik," in Habermas (1987, p. 174).

32. For a more alarmist American view, see Heilbrunn (1996).

33. CDU party general secretary Heiner Geißler put it this way: "Wir sind inzwischen ein Einwanderungsland geworden... Der Unterschied zwischen den Vereinigten Staaten und uns besteht lediglich darin, daß die Amerikaner ein Konzept haben, und wir haben keines," Geißler (1993, pp. 329-330).

REFERENCEES

Aleinikoff, T. A., and D. A. Martin. 1995. *Immigration Process and Policy.* 3rd ed. St. Paul, MN: West Publishing.

Bade, K., ed. 1992a. *Deutsche im Ausland—Fremde in Deutschland. Migration in Geschichte und Gegenwart.* Munich: Beck.

Bade, K. 1992b. "Politik in der Einwanderungssituation. Migration- Integration-Minderheiten." Pp. 442-455 in *Deutsche im Ausland—Fremde in Deutschland. Migration in Geschichte und Gegenwart,* edited by K. Bade. Munich: Beck.

Bade, K., ed. 1994. *Das Manifest der 60. Deutschland und die Einwanderung.* Munich: Beck.

Bernstein, R. 1995. "The Immigration Wave: A Plea to Hold it Back." *The New York Times,* April 4, p. C17.

Bertram, E., M. Blachman, K. Sharpe, and P. Andreas. 1996. *Drug War Politics: The Price of Denial.* Berkeley: University of California Press.

Borjas, G. J. 1994. "The Economics of Immigration." *Journal of Economic Literature* 32(4): 1667-1717.

Brimelow, P. 1995. *Alien Nation: Common Sense About America's Immigration Disaster.* New York: Random House.

Brubaker, R. 1989a. "Introduction." Pp. 1-27 in *Immigration and the Politics of Citizenship in Europe and North America,* edited by R. Brubaker. Lanham, MD: University Press of America.

Brubaker, R. 1989b. "Membership Without Citizenship: The Economic and Social Rights of Non-Citizens." Pp. 145-162 in *Immigration and the Politics of Citizenship in Europe and North America,* edited by W. R. Brubaker. Lanham, MD: University Press of America.

Brubaker, R. 1992. *Citizenship and Nationhood in France and Germany.* Cambridge: Harvard University Press.

Brubaker, R. 1995a. "Are Immigration Control Efforts Really Failing?" Pp. 227-231 in *Controlling Immigration: A Global Perspective,* edited by W. A. Cornelius, P. L. Martin, and J. A. Hollifield. Stanford: Stanford University Press.

Brubaker, R. 1995b. "Comments on 'Modes of Immigration Politics in Liberal Democratic States'." *International Migration Review* 29: 903-908.

Cain, B. E., K. MacDonald, and K. F. McCue. 1996. "Nativism, Partisanship and Immigration: An Analysis of Prop. 187." Paper delivered at the 1996 annual meeting of the American Political Science Association, San Francisco, August 29-September 1.

Calavita, K. 1995. "U.S. Immigration and Policy Responses: The Limits of Legislation." Pp. 55-82 in *Controlling Immigration: A Global Perspective,* edited by W.A. Cornelius, P.L. Martin, and J.A. Hollifield. Stanford: Stanford University Press.

Clark, R. L., J. S. Passel, W. N. Zimmermann, and M. E. Fix. 1994. *Fiscal Impacts of Undocumented Immigrants. Selected Estimates for Seven States.* Washington, DC: The Urban Institute.

Cornelius, W. A. 1996a. "Playing Politics Over People." *Los Angeles Times,* August 5, p. B5.

Cornelius, W. A. 1996b. "Economics, Culture, and the Politics of Restricting Immigration." *The Chronicle of Higher Education* 43(2): B4-B5.

Cornelius, W. A., P. L. Martin, and J. A. Hollifield, eds. 1995. *Controlling Immigration: A Global Perspective*. Stanford: Stanford University Press.

Dahrendorf, R. 1965. *Gesellschaft und Demokratie in Deutschland*. Munich: Piper.

Daniels, R. 1991. *Coming to America: A History of Immigration and Ethnicity in American Life*. New York: HarperCollins.

Dittgen, H. 1995. "Die Reformen in der Einwanderungs- und Flüchtlingspolitik in den achtziger Jahren." *Amerikastudien/American Studies* 40: 345-366.

Dittgen, H. 1996a. "Vaterlandslose Gesellschaft. Die zunehmende Bindungsschwäche der Gesellschaft der Vereinigten Staaten." *Frankfurter Allgemeine Zeitung*, June 12, p. N6.

Dittgen, H. 1996b. "The Foreign Policy Impasse: In Search of a New Doctrine." Pp. 238-263 in *The American Impasse: U.S. Domestic and Foreign Policy after the Cold War*, edited by M. Minkenberg and H. Dittgen. Pittsburgh: University of Pittsburgh Press.

Dohse, K. 1981. *Ausländische Arbeiter und bürgerlicher Staat: Genese und Funktion von staatlicher Ausländerpolitik und Ausländerrecht*. Königstein/Taunus: Hain Verlag.

Freeman, G. P. 1995. "Modes of Immigration Politics in Liberal Democratic States." *International Migration Review* 29 (4): 881-902.

Fuchs, L. H. 1990. *The American Kaleidoscope: Race, Ethnicity, and the Civic Culture*. Hanover, NH: Wesleyan University and the University Press of New England.

Fuhr, E. 1992. "Keine Vielvölkerrepublik." *Frankfurter Allgemeine Zeitung*, February 13, p. 1.

Geißler, H. 1993. *Heiner Geißler im Gespräch mit Gunter Hoffmann und Werner A. Perger*. Frankfurt: Eichborn.

Habermas, J. 1987. *Eine Art Schadensabwicklung--Kleine Politische Schriften IV*. Frankfurt: Suhrkamp.

Habermas, J. 1992. "Citizenship and National Identity: Some Reflections on the Future of Europe." *Praxis International* 12: 1-19.

Hailbronner, K. 1989. "Citizenship and Nationhood in Germany." Pp. 67-79 in *Immigration and the Politics of Citizenship in Europe and North America*, edited by W. R. Brubaker. Lanham, MD: University Press of America.

Hall, P. A. 1993. "Policy Paradigms, Social Learning, and the State: The Case of Economic Policymaking in Britain." *Comparative Politics* 25: 275-296.

Handlin, O. 1953. "We Need More Immigrants." *Atlantic Monthly*, May.

Heilbrunn, J. 1996. "Germany's New Right." *Foreign Affairs* 75(6): 80-98.

Herbert, U. 1986. *Geschichte der Ausländerbeschäftigung in Deutschland 1880 bis 1980. Saisonarbeiter, Zwangsarbeiter, Gastarbeiter*. Bonn: Dietz.

Higham, J. 1955. *Strangers in the Land: Patterns of American Nativism, 1860-1925*. New Brunswick, NJ: Rutgers University Press.

Hobsbawm, E. 1983. "Introduction: Inventing Traditions." Pp. 1-14 in *The Invention of Tradition*, edited by E. Hobsbawm and T. Ranger. Cambridge: Cambridge University Press.

Hobsbawm, E. 1991. *Nations and Nationalism since 1780: Programme, Myth, Reality*. Cambridge: Cambridge University Press.

Hoffmann, L. 1990. *Die unvollendete Republik. Zwischen Einwanderungsland und deutschem Nationalstaat*. Köln: PapyRossa.

Hollifield, J. F. 1992. *Immigrants, Markets and States: The Political Economy of Postwar Europe*. Cambridge: Harvard University Press.

Huntington, S. P. 1996. *The Clash of Civilizations and the Remaking of World Order*. New York. Simon&Schuster.

Jacobson, D. 1996. *Rights across Borders: Immigration and the Decline of Citizenship*. Baltimore and London: Johns Hopkins University Press.

Kanstroom, D. 1993. "Wer Sind Wir Wieder? Laws of Asylum, Immigration, and Citizenship in the Struggle for the Soul of the New Germany." *Yale Journal of International Law* 18: 155-211.

Kennedy, D. M. 1996. "Can We Still Afford to Be a Nation of Immigrants?" *The Atlantic Monthly* (November): 51-68.

Klusmeyer, D. B. 1995. "Race, Nation, and Labor: Immigration and Citizenship Law Reforms in Imperial Germany and the United States before the First World War." Unpublished paper.

Küchler, M. 1996. "Xenophobie im internationalen Vergleich." Pp. 248-262 in *Rechtsextremismus. Ergebnisse und Perspektiven der Forschung*, edited by J. Falter, H-G. Jaschke, and J. R. Winkler (PVS Sonderheft 27).

Kurthen, H., and M. Minkenberg. 1995. Germany in Transition: Immigration, Racism and the Extreme Right." *Nations and Nationalism* 1: 175-196.

Ladd, E. 1996. "Electoral Setting: The Public's Views of National Performance." *The Public Perspective* (October/November): 15-25.

Lehmann, A. 1991. *Im Fremden ungewollt zuhause. Flüchtlinge und Vertriebene in Westdeutschland 1945-1990*. Munich: Beck.

Lind, M. 1995. *The Next American Nation: The New Nationalism and the Fourth American Revolution*. New York: The Free Press.

Lowi, T. J. 1996. "American Impasse: The Ideological Dimension at Era's End." Pp. 1-12 in *The American Impasse: U.S. Domestic and Foreign Policy after the Cold War*, edited by M. Minkenberg and H. Dittgen. Pittsburgh: University of Pittsburgh Press.

Martin, P. L. 1995a. "Germany: Reluctant Land of Immigration." Pp. 189-225 in *Controlling Immigration: A Global Perspective*, edited by W. A. Cornelius, P. L. Martin, and J. F. Hollifield, Stanford: Stanford University Press.

Martin, P. L. 1995b. "Proposition 187 in California." *International Migration Review* 29: 255-263.

Miles, J. 1995. "The Coming Immigration Debate." *The Atlantic Monthly* 275 (4): 130-140.

Mills, N., ed. 1994. *Arguing Immigration: The Debate over the Changing Face of America*. New York: Touchstone.

Minkenberg, M., and H. Dittgen, eds. 1996. *The American Impasse: U.S. Domestic and Foreign Policy after the Cold War*. Pittsburgh: University of Pittsburgh Press.

Noiriel, G. 1996. *The French Melting Pot: Immigration, Citizenship, and National Identity*. Minneapolis, MN: University of Minnesota Press.

Oberndörfer, D. 1991. *Die offene Republik. Zur Zukunft Deutschlands und Europas*. Freiburg: Herder.

Oberndörfer, D. 1993. *Der Wahn des Nationalen. Die Alternative der offenen Republik*. Freiburg: Herder.

Papademetriou, D. G. 1996. "U.S. Immigration Policy after the Cold War." Pp. 298-321 in *The American Impasse: U.S. Domestic and Foreign Policy after the Cold War*, edited by M. Minkenberg and H. Dittgen. Pittsburgh: University of Pittsburgh Press.

Passel, J. S., and B. Edmonston. 1994. "Immigration and Race: Recent Trends in Immigration to the United States." Pp. 31-58 in *Immigration and Ethnicity: The Integration of America's Newest Arrivals*, edited by B. Edmonston and J. S. Passel. Washington, DC: The Urban Institute Press.

Putnam, R. D. 1996. "The Strange Disappearance of Civic America." *The American Prospect* 24: 34-48.

Rittstieg, H. 1991. "Staatsangehörigkeit und Minderheiten in der transnationalen Industriegesellschaft." *Neue Juristische Wochenschrift* 22: 1383-1390.

Rittstieg, H. 1993. "Einführung." Pp. 1-20 in *Deutsches Ausländerrecht. Die wesentlichen Vorschriften des deutschen Fremdenrechts*. Munich: Deutscher Taschenbuchverlag.

Sandel, M. J. 1996. *Democracy's Discontent: America in Search of a Public Philosophy.* Cambridge, MA: Harvard University Press.

Sassen, S. 1996. *Losing Control? Sovereignty in an Age of Globalization.* New York: Columbia University Press.

Schmalz-Jacobsen, C. 1995. "Ten Points Concerning German Immigration Policy." Pp. 173-179 in *Migration Policies: A Comparative Perspective,* edited by F. Heckmann and W. Bosswick. Stuttgart: Enke.

Schmalz-Jacobsen, C., and G. Hansen, eds. 1995. *Ethnische Minderheiten in der Bundesrepublik Deutschland. Ein Lexikon.* Munich: Beck.

Schnapper, D. 1991. *La France de l'intégration: sociologie de la nation en 1990.* Paris: Gallimard.

Schuck, P. H. 1991. "The Emerging Political Consensus on Immigration Law." *Georgetown Immigration Law Journal* 5: 1-33.

Schuck, P. H. 1992. "The Politics of Rapid Legal Change: Immigration Policy in the 1980s." *Studies in American Political Development* 6: 37-92.

Schuck, P. H. 1995. "The Message of 187." *The American Prospect* 21: 85-92.

Simon, J. L. 1996. "Public Expenditures on Immigrants to the United States, Past and Present." *Population and Development Review* 22: 99-109.

Simon, R. J., and S. H. Alexander. 1993. *The Ambivalent Welcome: Print Media, Public Opinion and Immigration.* Westport, CT: Praeger.

Smith, R. M. 1993. "Beyond Tocqueville, Myrdal, and Hartz: The Multiple Traditions in America." *American Political Science Review* 87 (3): 549-566.

Soysal, Y. N. 1994. *Limits of Citizenship: Migrants and Postnational Membership in Europe.* Chicago: University of Chicago Press.

U.S. Commission on Immigration Reform. 1994. *U.S. Immigration Policy: Restoring Credibility.* Washington, DC.

Walzer, M. 1983. *Spheres of Justice: A Defense of Pluralism and Equality.* New York: Basic Books.

Weiner, M. 1993. "Security, Stability, and International Migration." *International Security* 17: 91-126.

Winkler, H-A. 1994. "Rebuilding of a Nation: The Germans Before and After Unification." *Daedalus* 123(1): 107-127.

Zolberg, A. R. 1990. "Reforming the Back Door: The Immigration Reform and Control Act of 1986 in Historical Perspective." Pp. 315-339 in *Immigration Reconsidered: History, Sociology, and Politics,* edited by V. Yans-McLaughlin. Oxford: Oxford University Press.

MEMBERSHIP WITHOUT POLITICS?
THE SOCIAL AND POLITICAL RIGHTS OF FOREIGNERS IN GERMANY

Gregg O. Kvistad

In the late 1990s it is conceivable to argue that the differences between the experiences of membership in different nation-states may be more formal than real. If membership is understood to entail more than the legal right to vote and include incorporation into a modern welfare state broadly defined, then the concrete experience of membership in communities with vastly different legal attributions of formal citizenship may, for practical purposes, be negligible. This kind of reconceptualization of membership is consistent with a postnational or postmodern understanding of belonging as essentially the consumption of an attributed status. In these accounts, the legal attribution of membership as a "political" citizen, with active and passive political rights and duties within a national-state context, carries no singular overarching significance for either states or individuals relative to the attribution of "civil" or "social" rights of membership. As one recent study concludes, guest-workers in Europe, by means of integration in welfare regimes, labor markets, and other social institutions, have acquired significant statuses of membership in states that legally and politically are not "their own" (Soysal 1994, pp. 2f.).

This chapter will first address the value of political citizenship relative to other forms of membership in the modern nation-state. It will consider how these forms of membership variously contribute to the relationship of democratic legitimization both objectively, from the perspective of the community, and subjectively, from the perspective of the individual member. We will then turn to a specific discussion of the modern German case and argue that social incorporation is today and has been historically fundamentally different from political incorporation in Germany; that successful political incorporation in Germany is necessary for secure social incorporation; and that understanding membership in Germany without political citizenship rests on a normatively impoverished and, in light of political transformations in Germany in the last 30 years, empirically problematic foundation.

POLITICAL AND SOCIAL CITIZENSHIP IN THE MODERN STATE

In "Citizenship and Social Class," written in 1949, the sociologist T. H. Marshall addresses the question, "Is it...true that basic equality, when enriched in substance and embodied in the formal rights of citizenship, is consistent with the inequality of social class?" Investigating the nature of modern citizenship, Marshall answers, yes, "citizenship has itself become, in certain respects, the architect of legitimate social inequality." By "citizenship," Marshall means "the concept of full membership in a community" constructed on a "kind of basic human equality" (Marshall 1950, pp. 8-10ff.). Marshall's main finding—that social welfare can compensate for the inequalities of capitalism—has not gone unchallenged in modern social theory (Offe 1984, pp. 131-161). The concern of this paper, however, is not the relationship between citizenship and capitalism, but the interrelations among what Marshall calls the various "aspects" of modern citizenship and the acquisition of full membership in a community.

Marshall posits that "the evolution of citizenship...has been in continuous progress for some 250 years" (Marshall 1950, p. 10). This process occurs in societies which "create an image of an ideal citizenship against which achievement can be measured and towards which aspirations can be directed" (p. 28). By the twentieth century, he argues, citizenship had developed in Britain to include a civil aspect, denoting individual rights and their legal protections, a political aspect, entailing passive and active political rights, and a social aspect, referring to rights to welfare and education. The social aspect involves "the right to share to the full in the social heritage and to live the life of a civilized being according to the standards prevailing in the society" (pp. 10-14). It developed in the late nineteenth century and posited "a universal right to real income which is not proportionate to the market value of the claimant" (pp. 46f.). This produced, according to Marshall, "a general enrichment of the concrete substance of civilized life," within a "superstructure of legitimate expectations" (p. 58). But the evolution of modern citizenship is not, for Marshall, an inevitable process. "Its growth," he writes, "is stimulated both by the struggle to win those rights and by their enjoyment when won," and that involves decades of conflict and reform. The outcome of this process is a "direct sense of community membership based on loyalty to a civilization which is a common possession. It is a loyalty of free men endowed with rights and protected by a common law" (pp. 40f.).

Marshall's categories and periodization have come under scrutiny in recent work on citizenship and immigration. His triadic and sequential conceptualization of the aspects of citizenship and reliance on the nation-state have been questioned. Soysal (1994, pp. 1-3) argues that a "new and more universal concept of citizenship has unfolded in the post-war era, one whose organizing and legitimating principles are based on universal personhood rather than national belonging." The "postnational" model whereby "entitlements are legitimized on the basis of personhood" rests on a normative framework that "derive[s] from transnational discourse and structures celebrating human rights as a world-level organizing principle." This conclusion, consistent with the unwillingness of postwar European regimes to send guest-workers home in periods of economic downturn and with the willingness to make welfare services available to them, points to the steady accretion of rights and privileges of foreigners in these states. Soysal suggests that the "scope and inventory of non-citizens' rights do not differ significantly from those of citizens" (1994, p. 119). She further contends that,

> the order in which rights are extended to guestworkers reverses T. H. Marshall's way of organizing rights historically...in fact...economic and social rights were the first ones to be fully granted to migrant workers in European host countries. Political rights became part of the agenda much later (p. 120).

She argues that the postnational context of late twentieth-century Europe has considerably reduced the significance of citizenship as a political capacity, though, she adds, "the right to vote still carries a symbolic meaning in terms of national sovereignty" (pp. 120, 128, 130-131). Noncitizen and citizen rights do not differ "significantly" from each other because the transnational discourse of human rights has not expanded, but profoundly "transformed the institution of citizenship." In the model of postnational membership, "the individual transcends the citizen" (pp. 139-142).

Postnational membership is also addressed by Hollifield (1992, pp. 170f.), who points to the development of "a new brand of liberalism" in industrial states that, coupled with an "erosion of the classical, realist conceptions of the sovereignty and autonomy of the nation-state," makes it "difficult for states to exercise sweeping, exclusionary powers with respect to aliens." This liberalism, most pronounced in the United States, has increasingly informed the postwar political cultures and juris-prudence of France and Germany. The United States has "moved fur-ther" than European states, which have nonetheless "shown signs of adapting to the realities of social and cultural pluralism" (pp. 204, 211, and 213). Hollifield's analysis suggests that Marshall's civil and social "aspects" of citizenship have increasingly spread to these communities' residents, including noncitizens, without the political struggle that, in Marshall's view, produces citizenship as an organic community identity. Somers (1993) also critically addressed Marshall's thesis in a finely tex-tured historical reconsideration of Marshall's own case, eighteenth-cen-tury England. Though the temporal context of Somers's case study is different from Soysal's, she concludes, like Soysal, that the nation-state is an incorrect level of analysis for understanding citizenship development. Unlike Soysal, however, Somers recommends a deconstruction of the nation-state and the capitalist economy into smaller units of analysis, not their transcendence to a transnational human rights regime. She argues that efforts to understand citizenship development "should not be cen-tered only on states and economies, but should include family, commu-nity, and associational life (civil society) and political public spheres." That holds not only for eighteenth-century England, but for Western states in the late twentieth century as well (Somers 1993, pp. 612f.). Only then can citizenship be understood properly, as an evolving "insti-tuted process" involving the pushes and pulls of multiple agents and institutions.

THE VALUE OF POLITICAL CITIZENSHIP

These critiques do not render Marshall's classic analysis of citizenship development irrelevant for understanding the nature of membership in a community in the late twentieth century. His emphasis on the process of citizenship development, on the political and social struggle to win the extension of full membership in a community, is a powerful reminder of the importance of a protected individual political agency. Being treated as an equal by a welfare institution is not the same as act-ing as an equal. Petitioning courts for equal treatment, or having courts petitioned for you, is not the same as electing governments that appoint court judges.

The idea that political citizenship is practically meaningless in the presence of substantial civil and social rights rests on a normatively impoverished notion of politics—both subjectively, in terms of the non-citizen's status and perception of self, and objectively, in terms of a community's democratic legitimacy. That impoverishment, or "devaluation," is encouraged, Schuck (1989) argues, by the primacy of the consent principle in modern liberal ideology. In a system that allows substantial "social" and "civil" membership to noncitizens, what may be gained by naturalization may appear to noncitizens to be marginally insignificant or even threatening—to property claims, for example, in a person's home country (pp. 51-58). The "choice" to remain a noncitizen even in the face of a relatively liberal naturalization policy reduces both the noncitizen and the community to role-players in a system of material exchange. Membership becomes the right to get and have; governing becomes the duty to distribute entitlements. Lost is what Schuck calls:

> the ethos that legitimates certain process values and nourishes particular ways of thinking about the means and ends of politics. Its success depends upon the discipline of self-restraint; a willingness to sacrifice advantages and share burdens; a concern for the public interest; the capacity to inspire and accept leadership; a reverence for law; and pride in one's political community (p. 61).

In a modern multiethnic and multicultural community, he concludes, these classical democratic values might be emotionally nurturable only via the status of political citizenship (p. 62).

There is a long tradition of understanding citizenship in Western political thought on which Schuck's argument draws. In that tradition, active political participation in a community, or at least the right to participate politically, is regarded not only as instrumental for securing civil and social rights, but also as necessary for being human and creating a good community (Aristotle 1958; Rousseau 1983; Marx 1975; Arendt 1955). Even one of the least participatory understandings of political citizenship, found in the United States, points to the vulnerability and degradation of residents without political rights (Shklar 1992). Vulnerability is a threat to those "members" of modern states who enjoy social rights but not the political rights of citizenship. The twice- or thrice-mediated power of a human rights agenda in existing national-state or regional (EU) communities is, for the foreseeable future, considerably less significant than the willful ability of national-state parliaments and bureaucracies to determine the content of an alien's social membership status. The highly vaunted and now tattered postwar "social contract" between owners and workers in Western industrial states suggesting that social rights would be protected as long as workers eschewed radicalism was at best a tacit agreement, the structural precariousness of which was no better illustrated than by the Thatcher regime in Britain in the early 1980s (Krieger 1986). Thatcher's "revolution" revealed the fundamental particularity—and thus vulnerability—of the social aspect of citizenship even for full political members of Western industrial states. Barbalet (1988, p. 71) argues, "The provision of social services as a right is necessarily conditional on the capacity of the fiscal basis of the state to pay for such services." Such conditionality simply does not inhere in the status of political citizenship, and the structural vulnerability of aliens enjoying social rights in a community is obviously greater than that of full political members (Brochmann 1993, p. 18).

Unlike political rights, social rights are matters of conditional social policies; social policies providing social rights are expensive—both economically, in terms of what is delivered and the bureaucratic apparatus necessary to deliver it, and possibly politically, in terms of threats to a governing coalition; and social policies can be changed dramatically to lower their economic and political costs (Gieseck, Heilemann, and Loeffelholz 1995, p. 705, 715; Faist 1994, pp. 58f.). As Barbalet (1988, p. 20) puts it, "For persons to *act* as citizens there must be freedoms the state cannot invade and therefore actions which the state cannot perform; for persons to *consume* as citizens the state must provide and is therefore obliged to perform certain specific actions." If a state no longer accepts that obligation, for whatever reason, social rights disappear, especially if those social rights did not appear in the first place as the product of political struggle, as Marshall suggests. Governments will be less inclined to accept that obligation in times of stress—fiscal and/or political—when the population it affects most directly cannot vote, or better, may be deported (Blanke 1993, p. 19). Indeed, one of the prime functions of the spread of social citizenship in the postwar era has been to keep the social peace; one function of *removing* social citizenship from non-holders of political citizenship may also be to keep the social peace—which characterized the intention and effect of the recent tightening of asylum in the Federal Republic (Kurthen 1995, pp. 927-928; Freeman 1995, p. 893; Büssow 1994, p. 314; Blay and Zimmermann 1994, p. 363).

To note the presence of social rights and the absence of political rights in some states is not to demonstrate that this development is "insignificant"—for either the individuals concerned or the community's democratic legitimacy. Western political theory has consistently and with considerable reflection elevated the status of the "active" political above that of the "consuming" social. Marshall's own discussion rests on the progressive incorporation of the different aspects of citizenship and not their compensatory exchange. The development from civil to political to social citizenship is the movement of a particular "civilization," as he terms it, engaged in struggle, and involving the "general enrichment" of membership in a community. It is born of conflictual political action, not the passive experience of the social services of a "housekeeping" welfare state.

SOCIAL CITIZENSHIP FOR FOREIGNERS IN THE FEDERAL REPUBLIC

The provision of welfare benefits to foreigners in modern states has not turned significantly on legal citizenship status. Access to welfare state benefits for foreigners in six industrialized states is influenced by nine different factors, and foreigner status was found to be the least significant among them (Brubaker 1989, pp. 155-159). This is consistent with practice in the Federal Republic. Contributory social welfare schemes in the Federal Republic generally do not discriminate between citizen and noncitizen. Sickness, accident, retirement, unemployment, and training benefits provided in social insurance programs by means of employee and employer contributions are available to legal foreigners in the Federal Republic (Ausländer-Sozialrecht 1992, p. 382). Noncontributory schemes, however, including children allowances, housing allowances, and "social assistance" are somewhat more restricted for this population: while legal residents and their family members with limited residence permits have a right to equal receipt of social assistance, they are deportable if found to have entered the Federal Republic with the intent of seeking such assistance (Gesetz zur Neuregelung des Ausländerrechts 1990, pp. 1359-1360, 1365-1366).

Foreigners' relationship to the state in the Federal Republic can have four dimensions: passive, negative, positive, and active (Heinelt 1993). "Passive" refers to the subjection of the individual to the state, while the other three relationships entail rights. Negative status roughly corresponds to Marshall's civil rights, positive to social rights, and active to political rights. Heinelt argues that foreigners in Germany—broken down according to asylum-seekers, successful asylees, foreign workers, and *Aussiedler* (ethnic Germans)—"enter a selection corridor" to determine their assigned status. For state provision of welfare, positive status is differentiated according to these different categories of foreigner (Heinelt 1993, p. 87). Asylum-seekers have the lowest positive status in terms of rights. Their rights to special social assistance provide them with modest housing and a small living stipend. Successful asylees have rights to more generous benefits, including housing allowances, children allowances, and educational allowances. Foreign workers have a similar right to more this more generous social assistance, but with some restrictions, reflecting the original principle that their presence in Germany is to provide needed labor power and not to settle in the country. Contributory social insurance in the form or unemployment or sickness insurance is provided to foreign workers relative to their contributions. *Aussiedler* are the most privileged among the holders of positive status. Some temporary restrictions on housing apply, but they are eligible to receive, like German nationals, general noncontributory social assistance, all forms of contributory insurance and some special compensations. Once in the Federal Republic, *Aussiedler*—who are attributed German citizenship according to *ius sanguinis*—are the only holders of active status, that is, full rights of political participation equivalent to those held by German citizens (Heinelt 1993, pp. 87-93). In short, these provisions and other social rights make the Federal Republic one of the most generous welfare states in the world (Katzenstein 1987p. 186).

The generosity and tight weave of the Federal Republic's welfare state derive, in part, from Germany's role in the 1880s, under Bismarck, of initiating the first systematic program of social insurance in an industrial state. The genesis of this program was eminently political in nature. According to Rimlinger (1971),

> The social insurance legislation of the 1880s made social and economic relations among individuals an object of statecraft. It was a conscious attempt at cementing the social fabric of the industrial order, with the interests of the state instead of the welfare of the worker as the prime objective (p. 93).

Germany's late and intense industrialization at the end of the nineteenth century produced extreme social and economic dislocations within the nascent German working class that were successfully exploited by the German Social Democratic Party. Bismarck believed that it was crucial to wed the German working class to the German state, if not to destroy the SPD, then at least to preserve the traditional patriarchal relationship between the authoritative state and German subjects. As Bismarck stated, "whoever has a pension for his old age is far more content and far easier to handle than one who has no such prospect" (Eyck 1950, p. 239). Contrary to Marshall's understanding of citizenship as a developmental acquisition of membership,

> Bismarck's ideological justification of these rights ... came from above, from the patriarchal conception of the duties of the state. His central political consideration was not the creation of new rights, consistent with a new interpretation of the rights of citizenship, but the preservation of the traditional relationship of the individual to the state. In a sense, social rights were granted to prevent having to grant enlarged political rights (Rimlinger 1971, p. 112).

This interpretation suggests the application of "passive status" to Bismarck's social insurance recipients and not the "positive status" associated with the acquisition of Marshall's social rights (Heinelt 1993, pp. 87). Contrary to Marshall's schema, the appearance of the welfare state in Germany was less a political victory than an attempt at political buy-off. These roots of the welfare state in Germany must give pause to any suggestion that the absence of political rights in contemporary Germany might adequately be compensated for by the presence of generous social rights.

POLITICAL CITIZENSHIP AND NATURALIZATION IN GERMANY

The formal region of equality constituting the "natural" (as opposed to "naturalized") status of German citizenship has been delineated since 1913 by the principle of *ius sanguinis* (*Reichs- und Staatsangehörigkeitsgesetz* 1913, pp. 583-584). This principle holds that citizenship status is transmitted genealogically; location of birth, the fact relevant for the principle of *ius soli*, is in itself meaningless for natural German citizenship. Prior to 1913 a "state-national" understanding of citizenship assumed that a genealogical transmission of citizenship provided a deeper and more reliable bond to the German nation-state than the accidental physical location of birth (Brubaker 1992, pp. 115, 123). After 1913 an ethnonational adjustment to that understanding meant that loyalty lost its legal relevance for the retention though not attribution or acquisition of German citizenship. With the removal of all traces of residence consideration from the law, "ethnic Germans" joined "ethnic non-Germans" in having natural citizenship attribution and retention be controlled solely by descent. This formal "de-statification" of German citizenship meant that political loyalty was no longer regarded as variable for "ethnic Germans" regardless of residence. For "ethnic non-Germans," the assumption of non-loyalty—regardless of residence, place of birth, or political belief and actions—remained unchanged (Brubaker 1992, p. 115).

Since the Second World War "ethnic Germans" have included not only Germans inhabiting the Federal Republic, but also Germans carrying a GDR passport, who were legally treated as citizens of the Federal Republic, and "ethnic Germans" outside of the combined territory of the FRG and the GDR. Officially, this last group included only those who qualified as postwar expellees (*Vertriebene*) from Eastern Europe and the former USSR because of their German "ethnicity." A combination of cold war policy and the political clout of the organization of expellees in the Federal Republic, however, led authorities to "consider virtually all ethnic German immigrants from Eastern Europe and the Soviet Union as *Vertriebene*, without inquiring into the actual circumstances of their emigration" (Katzenstein 1987, pp. 212f.). The political loyalty assumptions that underlay *ius sanguinis* thus labeled "ethnic Germans" who had never set foot in the Federal Republic, knew nothing of its political and social system, and spoke no German as categorically "loyal" to the free democratic basic order. The volume of "ethnic German" migrants to the Federal Republic (nearly 1,200,000 between 1988 and 1991) after the collapse of communism combined with the absurdity of this assumption to lead to a slight tightening of the treatment of "ethnic German" *Aussiedler* in 1991, including more stringent application procedures, some demonstration of connection to German "culture," and limitations on freedom of settlement once in the Federal Republic (Marshall 1992, pp. 256f.).

"Ethnic non-German" naturalization applicants have had a rather high wall to scale in the Federal Republic. Part of that height was constructed, until the reforms of 1991 and 1993, by the rigorous formal demands made by the German state on the political beliefs and actions of naturalization applicants. Because the principle of pure *ius sanguinis* makes irrelevant a person's country of birth or residence, long-term residents in the Federal Republic, including even second- and third-generation, "ethnic non-German" guest-workers who had never visited the country of their formal citizenship, were forced positively to demonstrate a number of extraordinary characteristics to qualify for German citizenship—characteristics not legally required of lifetime "ethnic Germans" of the Federal Republic, ex-East-German *Übersiedler*, or "ethnic German" *Aussiedler* from Eastern Europe and the ex-USSR at least until 1991 (Fijalkowski 1993, p. 19). Most generally, these characteristics were captured in what was referred to as a "positive attitude toward German culture." Specifically, these included a long period of permanent residence and adequate accommodation in the Federal Republic; a good reputation; the capability to make a living for self and dependents without reliance on welfare; spoken and written German-language fluency; a "voluntary attachment" to Germany; a basic knowledge of Germany's political and social structures; no criminal record; and a positive commitment to the Federal Republic's "free democratic basic order" (Hailbronner 1989, pp. 68f.). The loyal political ties to the ethnonational community that were assumed to be in place among "ethnic Germans" had to be positively demonstrated by "ethnic non-Germans" seeking naturalized membership in the Federal Republic. Naturalization remained discretionary, controlled by state authorities whose job it was to determine the public interest in naturalizing any particular applicant.

In the 1990s reformers in the Federal Republic argued that xenophobia and ethnocultural discrimination could be diminished if citizenship status were made less difficult to obtain via natural attribution and naturalized acquisition: fewer "foreigners" would exist in Germany, an officially sanctioned definition of "otherness" would end, and political membership in the Federal Republic would become more universalized (Fijalkowski 1993, pp. 26f.). The new Aliens Law that took effect in January 1991 did not alter *ius sanguinis* for attributing "natural" citizenship, but it did significantly change some of the necessary criteria that an applicant had to meet to acquire naturalized status (Marshall 1992, pp. 251f.). Most important, the 1991 reform granted a *Regelanspruch auf Einbürgerung*, or a typical eligibility for naturalization, to foreigners who had renounced their previous citizenship and met a number of formal, mainly domicile-based, conditions (*Gesetz zur Neuregelung des Ausländerrechts* 1990, p. 1375). Gone was the explicit demand to demonstrate an extraordinary (at least relative to "ethnic Germans") attachment and "positive attitude toward German culture." Remaining in the 1991 law was, however, a continued reliance on bureaucratic discretion, or *Ermessen der zuständigen Behörden*, for determining the public interest in granting German citizenship to any particular naturalization applicant.

The Aliens Law of 1991 did not affect the definition of the Federal Republic as "not an immigrant country," and it did not reverse federal government policy, in force since October 1982, to strive for "integration" and the "peaceful coexistence between people of different origins," but not their "assimilation" (Schröder and Horstkotte 1993, pp. 2f.). By 1991 peaceful coexistence among adult foreigners and Germans for 15 years produced an eligibility for naturalization *in der Regel*. The odd juxtaposition of peaceful coexistence and eligibility for naturalization was an artifact of a government willing to liberalize the determinants of naturalized German membership status, but not its natural attribution, which still occurred according to the principle of *ius sanguinis*. By the end of 1992, however, policymakers in the Federal Republic had agreed to amend the 1991 provision of a typical legal eligibility, or *Regelanspruch*, for naturalization, to a legal right, or *Rechtsanspruch*, to naturalization for persons meeting the formal, mainly domicile-related, requirements (*Gesetz zur Änderung Asylverfahrens-, Ausländer- und Staatsangehörigkeitsrechtlicher Vorschriften* 1993, pp. 1062f.). This amendment was not trivial: politically, it removed the need to positively demonstrate a deep loyal attachment to "German culture" and its institutionalization; bureaucratic discretion disappeared; and long-term foreign residents of Germany acquired the legal right to naturalize relatively unproblematically. That status would not flow automatically, but it could legally be claimed by persons meeting formal and universalistic requirements.

THE HISTORICAL CONTEXT OF MEMBERSHIP IN GERMANY

It is thus clear that foreigners in the Federal Republic of Germany in the 1990s enjoy substantial rights of social membership. It is also the case that foreigners have historically faced substantial impediments—now diminished, but still significant—to acquiring naturalized citizenship in Germany. Yet a postnational or postmodern understanding of member-ship in a community might suggest that the current state of affairs is not problematic: legal foreigners in Germany are protected from material hardship with a substantial catalogue of protected social and human rights, and even according to foreigners' own perceptions of self-inter-est (frequently involving property rights in their home countries), social membership may be preferable to, if not just compensatory for a lack of, full rights of political membership (Bauböck and Cinar 1994, p. 194). This paper has suggested, however, that political citizenship is required for meaningful full membership in a community in the late twentieth century, both objectively, for democratic legitimacy, and subjectively, for safeguarding the individuals involved. This is not only a normative posi-tion. It is also consistent with the expansion of what Marshall calls citi-zenship's "superstructure of legitimate expectations" in the Federal Republic in the last 30 years—a process entailing political struggle, insti-tutional response, and policy reform, not bureaucratic largesse.

Since the late 1960s a logic of political membership with very deep historical roots in German political thought and practice has steadily diminished in meaningfulness in the Federal Republic. That logic, or what Kielmansegg (1989) has called the "above-parties ideology of the authoritarian state" dichotomized the realms of state and society and posited the state as a site of hortatory political agency in which a public interest could be discerned and implemented. Only in the state realm, protected from the vicissitudes of the market for the satisfaction of needs, could the universal good of the entire community and not the partial good of individuals or groups be articulated and properly pur-sued. State actors, who were mainly professional civil servants, were understood as experts skilled at the maintenance of public order and civil life in the face of the threat of an economically motivated, conflict-ual, untrustworthy, and proto-anarchic civil society of ordinary citizens organized in particularistic interest groups and political parties (Dyson 1980, pp. 25-78).

While the institutional artifacts of that ideology mainly disappeared with the Federal Republic's founding, its political-cultural elements survived but began irrevocably to unravel in the 1960s as part of protracted Marshallian struggle over the nature of membership. In this period a political-cultural "revolution" demanding "more democracy" produced substantial growth in the subjective "citizen" competence attitudes among ordinary German citizens (Baring 1982, pp. 39f.; Hildebrand 1984, p. 369; Baker, Dalton, and Hildebrandt 1981). That continued in the 1970s with the proliferation of citizen initiatives and the appearance of the participatory-democratic Greens at the end of the decade. The period also saw one of the most divisive policy battles ever experienced in the Federal Republic. The so-called Radicals Decree demanded that German public employees loyally demonstrate a willingness to uphold the "free democratic basic order" at all times (Kvistad 1987; Braunthal 1990). By the early 1990s, and explicitly in the unification treaty of 1990, the decree's most restrictive measures had disappeared at the federal and *Land* (state) levels (Kvistad 1994). Political loyalty that was positively demanded and monitored from above for membership in a segmented political community was ultimately rejected.

As the West German state was concerned about the political reliability of civil servants in the 1970s and 1980s, it was also concerned about the political reliability of foreigners, including those wishing to naturalize before the reforms of 1991 and 1993. The political stakes of West German naturalization reform in the 1980s turned directly on the concern for political loyalty in the Federal Republic's "militant democracy." In the early 1980s concerns for the "undivided loyalty" of German citizens and the "German nation's right to protect its own culture" drove the CDU/CSU to reject a liberalization of German naturalization policy (Murray 1994, p. 28). The SPD stressed the need for foreigners in the Federal Republic to be provided assimilationist opportunities like education that would allow them to "earn" the "trust to respect democratic politics and eschew extremism;" the CDU/CSU argued for integration and posited the desire of many foreigners to return to their countries of origin.

In naturalization policy in this period, as well as with civil service policy, the old German logic of political membership was being invoked. That logic registered a deep concern for the reliable political protection of German society from "above." The concern in the 1980s to protect German democracy "militantly" from the political threat of foreigners on German soil replicated West German civil service policy's concern to protect the "free democratic basic order," also "militantly," from the Federal Republic's dangerous citizens. An Administrative Appeals Court judge in Baden-Württemberg argued:

Political activities in emigrant organizations are usually taken as evidence against a
permanent attachment to Germany. Activities in extremist or radical organizations
justify, in general, the conclusion that the applicant is not committed to the democratic order of the Federal Republic (Hailbronner 1989, pp. 68f.).

The requirement to demonstrate a heightened positive political loyalty
and not mere political legality was language nearly identical to that used
in the 1970s to rationalize the exclusion of certain applicants, especially
members of the communist party, from the West German civil service. If
an "ethnic non-German" desired naturalization, he or she had to demonstrate to a state official an extraordinarily positive tie to Germany and
its political institutions in order to remove a definitionally non-loyal status, regardless of possible domicile in the Federal Republic for decades.

The introduction of *ius domicilii* for naturalized political membership
in the Federal Republic in 1993 did not alter pure *ius sanguinis* for
attributing "natural" membership, but it marked a clear liberalization
and universalization of German citizenship law. It also marked—as did
the repudiation of the Radicals Decree for the civil service—the increasing anachronism of German statism, with its central role of political loyalty, as a logic of political membership in the Federal Republic. These
policy shifts occurred as the ideology of German statism was being politically rejected, on the streets and elsewhere, as inappropriate for inform-
ing German political membership. The expansion of substantive
citizenship in the form of a "politics of the first person" in the Federal
Republic was not provided by a bureaucratic state but was won through
political struggle beginning in the 1960s—precisely the process, according to Marshall, for expanding meaningful membership in a community.

All political parties in the early 1990s, including the most reluctant
CDU/CSU, recognized the undesirability of having vast numbers of legal
foreign residents without citizenship living in the Federal Republic. After
the murderous violence against foreigners, especially in 1991 and 1992,
hundreds of thousands of Germans from all parties, interest groups, and
religious denominations protested in candlelight marches against intolerance and the mistreatment of foreigners on German soil. Though the
1993 law still required 15 years of "integration" before the status of citizenship became a legal right, its passage marked a considerable shift
away from the historical politicization and segmentation of political
membership in Germany. That is not to say that all concern for political
loyalty and attachment to "Germanness" disappeared with the recent
reform, but rather to suggest that the statist practice of measuring these
bureaucratically from above was replaced by an assumption and trust
that such phenomena would develop and grow naturally, much as Marshall suggests, and in an adequate amount, from the experience of
long-term residence in and integration and assimilation into German

society. As such, recent naturalization reform in the Federal Republic cannot but pose a challenge to citizenship law: the domicile modification of naturalization law suggests a parallel domicile modification of citizenship law (Funk 1995, p. 317; Kurthen 1995, p. 933). Indeed, in 1996 German policymakers from across the political spectrum began to entertain possible *ius soli* amendments to *ius sanguinis* in the Federal Republic (Buchsteiner 1996; Schmalz-Jacobsen 1996; Lafontaine 1996). Only by making political citizenship easier to obtain in the Federal Republic will the millions of persons who are fortunate beneficiaries of the German welfare state (through no doing of their own) become full members of the German community and be able not only fully to experience the "superstructure of legitimate expectations" that goes with that, but also—like German citizens did in the last 30 years—democratically expand and develop those expectations.

ACKNOWLEDGMENT

The author would like to thank Paul Colomy, Susan Sterett, and Hermann Kurthen for comments on earlier drafts, and the University of Denver's Office of Internationalization for research support.

REFERENCES

Arendt, H. 1959. *The Human Condition*. Garden City, NY: Doubleday.
Aristotle. 1958. *The Politics*, edited and translated by E. Barker. London: Oxford University Press.
Ausländer-Sozialrecht. 1992. In *Deutsches Rechts-Lexikon*, vol. 1, edited by H. Tilch. Munich: C.H. Beck.
Baker, K., R. Dalton, and K. Hildebrandt. 1981. *Germany Transformed: Political Culture and the New Politics*. Cambridge: Harvard University Press.
Barbalet, J. M. 1988. *Citizenship, Rights, Struggle, and Class Inequality*. Minneapolis: University of Minnesota Press.
Baring, A. 1982. *Machtwechsel: Die Ära Brandt-Scheel*. Stuttgart: Deutsche Verlagsanstalt.
Bauböck, R., and D. Cinar. 1994. "Briefing Paper: Naturalisation Policies in Western Europe." *West European Politics* 17(2): 192-196.
Blanke, B. 1993. "Zuwanderung und Asyl: Zur Kommunikationsstruktur der Asyldebatte." *Leviathan* 21(1): 13-23.
Blay, S., and A. Zimmermann. 1994. "Recent Changes in German Refugee Law: A Critical Assessment." *The American Journal of International Law* 88(2): 361-378.
Braunthal, G. 1990. *Political Loyalty and Public Service in West Germany*. Amherst: University of Massachusetts Press.
Brochmann, G. 1993. "Immigration Control, the Welfare State and Xenophobia Towards an Integrated Europe." *Migration* 18(2): 5-23.
Brubaker, R. 1989. "Membership Without Citizenship: The Economic and Social Rights of Non-Citizens." Pp. 145-162 in *Immigration and the Politics of Citizenship in Europe and North America*, edited by W. R. Brubaker. Lanham, MD: University Press of America.

Brubaker, R. 1992. *Citizenship and Nationhood in France and Germany*. Cambridge: Harvard University Press.

Buchsteiner, J. 1996. "Unter Blutsbrüdern: Wie die CSU ein neues Staatsbürgerrecht verhindert." *Die Zeit* 27.

Büssow, J. 1994. "Für eine neue Flüchtlingspolitik." *Die neue Gesellschaft* 37: 307-316.

Dyson, K. H. F. 1980. *The State Tradition in Western Europe: A Study of an Idea and Institution*. New York: Oxford University Press.

Eyck, E. 1950. *Bismarck and the German Empire*. London: Unwin.

Reichs- und Staatsangehörigkeitsgesetz. 1913. *Reichs-Gesetzblatt* 46: 583-593.

Faist, T. 1994. "How to Define a Foreigner? The Symbolic Politics of Immigration in German Partisan Discourse, 1978-1992." *West European Politics* 17(2): 50-71.

Fijalkowski, J. 1993. *Aggressive Nationalism, Immigration Pressure, and Asylum Policy Disputes in Contemporary German*. Washington, DC: German Historical Institute.

Freeman, G. P. 1995. "Modes of Immigration Politics in Liberal Democratic States." *International Migration Review* 29 (4): 881- 902.

Funk, A. 1995. "Wer ist Deutscher, wer ist Deutsche?" *Leviathan* 23(3): 307-320.

Gieseck, A., U. Heilemann, and H. D. von Loeffelholz. 1995. "Economic Implications of Migration into the Federal Republic of Germany, 1988-1992." *International Migration Review* 29(3): 693-721.

Hailbronner, K. 1989. "Citizenship and Nationhood in Germany." Pp. 67-79 in *Immigration and the Politics of Citizenship in Europe and North America*, edited by W. R. Brubaker. Lanham, MD: University Press of America.

Heinelt, H. 1993. "Immigration and the Welfare State in Germany." *German Politics* 2(1): 78-96.

Hildebrand, K. 1984. *Geschichte der Bundesrepublik Deutschland, vol. 4: Von Erhard zur Großen Koalition*. Stuttgart: Deutsche Verlagsanstalt.

Hollifield, J. F. 1992. *Immigrants, Markets and States: The Political Economy of Postwar Europe*. Cambridge: Harvard University Press.

Katzenstein, P. J. 1987. *Policy and Politics in West Germany—The Growth of a Semisovereign State*. Philadelphia: Temple University Press.

Kielmannsegg, P. G. 1989. "The Basic Law—Response to the Past or Design for the Future?" *Forty Years of the Grundgesetz*. Washington, DC: German Historical Institute.

Krieger, J. 1986. *Reagan, Thatcher, and the Politics of Decline*. New York: Oxford University Press.

Kurthen, H. 1995. "Germany at the Crossroads: National Identity and the Challenges of Immigration." *International Migration Review* 29 (4): 914-938.

Kvistad, G. O. 1987. "Between State and Society: Green Political Ideology in the Mid-1980s." *West European Politics* 10(2): 211-228.

Kvistad, Gregg O. 1994. "Accommodation or 'Cleansing': Germany's State Employees from the Old Regime." *West European Politics* 17(4): 52-73.

Lafontaine, O. 1996. "Integration verbessern und Zuwanderung von Aussiedlern begrenzen." *SPD- Bundestagsfraktion Pressemitteilung*. March 16, 1996.

Marshall, T. H. 1950. *Class, Citizenship, and Social Development*. Cambridge: Cambridge University Press/Garden City, NY: Anchor Books.

Marx, K. 1975. "On the Jewish Question." Pp. 146-174 in *Collected Works*, vol. 3, K. Marx and F. Engels. New York: International Publishers.

Murray, L. M. 1994. "Einwanderungsland Bundesrepublik Deutschland? Explaining the Evolving Positions of German Political Parties on Citizenship Policy." *German Politics and Society* 33: 23-56.

Offe, C. 1984. *Contradictions of the Welfare State*. Cambridge: The MIT Press.

Rimlinger, G. 1971. *Welfare Policy and Industrialization in Europe, America, and Russia*. New York: John Wiley.

Rousseau, J-J. 1983. *On the Social Contract*, edited and translated by D. A. Cress. Indianapolis: Hackett Publishers.

Schmalz-Jacobsen, C. 1996. "Koalition wird Einbürgerung erleichtern." *F.D.P.-Bundestagsfraktion Pressemitteilung*. April 15, 1996.

Schröder, K., and H. Horstkotte. 1993. "Foreigners in Germany." *Sozial-Report* 2: 1-5.

Somers, M. R. 1993. "Citizenship and the Place of the Public Sphere: Law, Community, and Political Culture in the Transition to Democracy." *American Sociological Review* 58: 587-620.

Soysal, Y. N. 1994. *Limits of Citizenship. Migrants and Postnational Membership in Europe*. Chicago: University of Chicago Press.

INCORPORATING IMMIGRANTS AND EXPANDING CITIZENSHIP

Jürgen Fijalkowski

The following paper is a contribution to the discourse on the reform of German citizenship regulations within the wider context of European integration. In the agreements of Schengen and Dublin many European Union member states resolved to abolish passport controls of persons crossing internal EU borders; they also defined the necessary prerequisites for this change. After the agreements were signed, however, reservations were raised, in Germany and elsewhere. Critics argued that the issue of integrating non-EU citizens into the EU framework had been neglected. Freedom of mobility would also make it necessary to consider recognition of dual or multiple citizenship. The question is whether this assessment can be justified.

CONCEPTS OF CITIZENSHIP

In almost all Western European countries a trend currently exists to slow down immigration that would require full incorporation of the immigrants. Some countries already feel burdened by difficulties in accommodating native-born inhabitants who—for whatever reason—have to fear social marginalization. In addition, governments face the challenge of integrating former guest-workers' families who have acquired legal resi-

159

dency and to accommodate legally recognized refugees or a backlog of asylum-seekers whose cases are pending. Some countries are also having difficulty coping with problems arising from increasing intra-European competition in local labor markets (construction work, for instance). Finally, some countries are confronted with new or revitalized interethnic conflicts which have increased as a result of social polarization in recent years. Native-born and established-resident populations have expressed fears of "foreign infiltration" and cultural alienation. In some instances open hostility against resident aliens and foreigners has even flared up.

These developments have to be seen against a background in which national economies and political cultures of the respective EU member states as well as non-EU "third" states differ significantly. Differences of national origin have gained importance per se, depending on whether a country belongs to the wealthy and politically stable democracies or to rather poor and politically unstable "crisis" states. Unequal socioeconomic, political, and cultural development give rise to a tug-of-war situation, causing a person's change of residence no longer to be a question of the individual's whim and "free will" but, rather, determined by differentials of wealth, welfare, health, and security between nations. Depending on the domestic social and political order and degree of conflict management, nations restrict or regulate admission and integration of foreigners, define nationality laws, and develop policies to confront, avoid, or prevent immigration-related problems. Those favoring dual citizenship argue that opponents perpetuate an artificial distinction between human and citizen rights, and indirectly assign entire countries a "second-class" status. Supporters reject such distinctions, because they believe them to be incompatible with the normative value of equal human rights. Can this assessment be justified?

In political debate and academic literature, a broad spectrum of opinion exists on the meaning of citizenship. All of these views presuppose the distinction between, on the one hand, economic and sociocultural membership of a person or group to a surrounding society and, on the other hand, political and legal membership to a political community, the latter being defined as the legally sovereign member of the international system of state societies. All interpretations of citizenship also acknowledge a tension between these two elements of citizens' state membership. The two elements must be made mutually congruent through means that belong to the realm of international politics as well as domestic (public welfare) incorporation policies.

A detailed order of how organized state societies deal with accommodating citizenship requirements can be distinguished (Fijalkowski 1991). On a scale from Left to Right, these state strategies vary from rigorous human rights egalitarianism to liberal pluriculturalism, nation-state conservatism, and regressive ethnonationalism, or, as Bauböck (1995) has demonstrated, from "thin positivism" and "thin liberalism" to "dense republicanism" and "dense nationalism." Different historical developments have contributed to the formation of these models, which serve as an orientation in shaping regulations for admission and incorporation of immigrants. Consequently, national regulations vary. The extent to which public welfare commitments are defined and practiced is of particular importance.

Basically, the following has to be kept in mind. Belonging to a nation, in the sense of citizenship, always means that a state and its individual members each have assumed duties and rights in their mutual relationship that are more extensive than those subsumed under the universal human rights code. No matter what contractual citizen-state relationship is chosen in a particular case, it always includes a distinction between universal human rights and specific citizen rights. This construction allows for the exclusion of noncitizens from participating in (equal) rights granted only to citizens of a particular state. Each individual political community has to define the special status of immigrants or resident aliens in contrast to full-fledged citizens, taking into account a country's specific history and traditions. For the purpose of this paper, the principles of orientation shall be described along two axes. Placed in order of priority, the goals of civil freedom (rule of law), political participation (democracy), and claims to public benefits (social welfare) comprise one axis. Also prioritized, on the other axis, are the values of an individual's freedom of decision, current interests (individualism), and inclusion in a system encompassing group solidarity, collective cultural identities, and historically founded responsibilities (communitarianism). The scheme can be derived as follows: According to Jellinek (1892, pp. 39-50) one can distinguish four dimensions to define the status of individuals, insofar as they are holders of subjective public rights. The way Marshall (1949, 1965) defined the historical development of status rights, which are related to an individual's membership in a state society, can be seen as following a sort of teleologically directed development through Jellinek's four dimensions, proceeding from *status passivus* to *status negativus*, then to *status activus*, and ultimately, to *status positivus*. The application of these distinctions in international comparison will demonstrate that the degree to which specific countries have implemented this hypothetical teleological sequence varies greatly. There have also been retrograde developments due to unexpected side effects. In defining the ranking of *status negativus*, *status activus*, and *status positivus*, the various state societies are either oriented toward a preference for *status activus* plus *status positivus* (i.e., characterized as active democracies with people sharing the benefits of the welfare state), or toward a preference for *status activus*

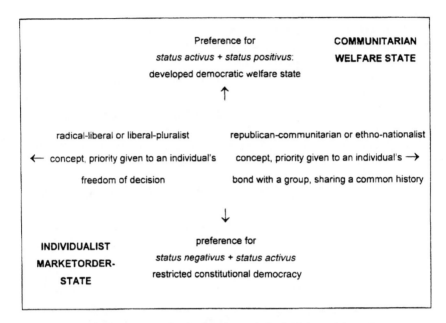

Figure 1.   Idealtypical Model of Citizenship

plus *status negativus* (i.e., characterized as active democracies in which sole priority is placed on the defense of individual liberties). It is significant whether a state society open to immigrants views itself officially as a system solely dedicated to the protection of civil freedoms and participatory democracy, or, in addition, as a community of organized solidarity and welfare, which uses its *status activus* to promote the *status positivus* of its citizens.

Following Bauböck one can further distinguish a liberal from a communitarian model of defining the meaning of citizenship (1994). As mentioned earlier, defining the essentials of citizenship and recognizing them in public law depends on assessments about the importance of historical and cultural traditions, the relative significance accorded to the capacity of individuals to act for themselves, and the degree of responsibilities of the collective toward its individual members. Therefore we can identify radical, or liberal, pluralist models of citizenship in contrast to republican, communitarian, or even ethnonationalist types. Thus one can outline the two-axis scheme shown in Figure 1.

The predominant feature of a so-called "communitarian welfare state" is a community whose members are mobilized to form the populace of a state society, share a common history and common responsibilities.

According to this model the state's public tasks and responsibilities are to demonstrate communitarian solidarity. Social unity constitutes more than living in a territorial neighborhood and being connected by economic market relations. According to the "communitarian welfare state" model, membership in a nation-state community functions as the primary source and medium of collective identity and solidarity, bridging interest conflicts between economic classes, genders, and generations. It is the task of the state to observe social outcomes of economic market relations and intervene if necessary. Thus the state has collective liability with regard to its citizens which is put into practice by a highly developed system of direct and indirect public services in support of the citizens' social security and general welfare. Membership requirements according to this model are based on the notion of a common history and culture which binds people together irrespective of their place of residence, their neighborhood relations, or contrasting class positions. The "republican version" of the communitarian model aims at an open community of people united by a common conviction in the principles of a constitutional order as well as by a strong common interest in the future; the "ethnonationalist version," on the other hand, involves a closed community with a common cultural, if not ethnic, background, and a strong interest in common history, dominating even the private sphere.

On the other hand, the most characteristic feature of the "individualist market order state" is its provision for maximum freedom for the individual citizen. This goal enjoys higher priority than all other goals, as far as the legitimization of political power is concerned. State actions are by no means permitted to interfere in market relations between individuals, who protect their interests by exploiting chances and warding off disadvantages. Right-wing libertarian liberals such as Nozick (1974) emphasize individual freedoms and property rights, and, accordingly, want to restrict state power to the maintenance of public order and security, absolutely rejecting any intervention whatsoever in market relations. Left-wing egalitarian liberals such as John Rawls and R.M. Dworkin, on the other hand, aim to furnish citizenship with additional social rights, which improve the situation of the worst-situated citizens (Rawls 1971) or are meant to recompense them for the unequal distribution of resources (Dworkin 1981). Welfare-state activities in the interest of a territory's population are not totally absent. However, in the ranking of the state's public obligations, welfare-state activities are distinctly subordinate to activities guaranteeing individual protection and freedom.

The "individualist market-order state," which is restricted to guaranteeing equal rights of citizens to civic defense and political participation, thus may be described as having derived its raison d'être from the preeminence of the market order. A community displaying a common history and mutual solidarity which mobilizes its members to use political participation in the interest of their claims to welfare benefits—which are so central to the communitarian model—is only of minor, subordinate importance for the market model. According to the individualist market model, the central notion of membership is that people, regardless of differences in their home cultures and class situations, are bound together because they reside in the same territory and are associated through a contingent but real neighborhood. In the "radical liberal" and the "liberal pluralist" models, a member's current neighborhood is accorded high priority, regardless of whether it was formed arbitrarily.

The models described above have implications, each with its respective logic with regard to foreigners. According to the different interpretations of the meaning of citizenship, the scope of access by foreigners depends on the degree to which the state is prepared and organized to commit itself in favor of the country's citizens. If the welfare state is highly developed, and if a society offers relatively many public benefits, restrictions on immigration will increase along with unresolved problems facing the host society with respect to the granting of welfare. Public opinion will easily be convinced to demand that priority be given to the historically corporate community instead of the actual, present, territorial neighborhood; a sharp distinction can also be expected to be made between members and nonmembers. Accordingly, admission regulations, at least, will be shaped rather restrictively, and the number of immigrants admitted after application and agreement will be kept relatively low. Arguments holding that it is necessary to exclude aliens from welfare benefits will then be employed, especially if they can be derived from dominant nationalist and "ethnonationalist" sentiments in collective identification.

On the other hand, a country with a less-developed welfare state and relatively few public benefits is better prepared to support liberal admission regulations, that is, to grant a rather high share of final admission to those who have de facto managed to enter and stay. This seems plausible because, according to this model, the established residents are less affected by measures of redistribution, and new immigrants place only a minimum of new burdens on them. Like the established citizens, the immigrants have to protect their own interests and take advantage of what the market offers. From these conditions it follows that the welfare state implies neither absolute openness to immigrants, nor the opposite. The welfare state might reduce social inequality by means of redistribution among citizens or those accepted as legal residents. At the same time, however, it tends to protect the privileges of its resident population from nonprivileged populations through harsher immigration legislation. This is a consequence of the model.

The most important decision is made prior to migrants' entering the territory, not after they have become residents. With respect to incorporation or naturalization prerequisites, however, the level of welfare state development is of minor, if any, significance. Social welfare benefits are extended to all persons present on the territory, irrespective of their citizenship. They include a priori foreigners and resident aliens. This exclusive territoriality of claims to the welfare state's benefits is protected by human rights conventions and specifically by the European civil and social rights conventions. A country without an extended system of public social security might be able to afford to show considerable generosity. However, every country in the world would be restrictive regarding naturalization of persons who would be permanently dependent on public assistance. Furthermore, based on human rights demands, there is considerable flexibility in shaping admission and incorporation regulations. Regulations become inadmissible only if they violate restrictions on deportation, or if they attempt to institutionalize *perioikoi*, that is, a system with different classes of members, whether by attempting to determine a legal distinction of the established residents into first- and second-class citizens on the basis of origin, race, religion, cultural heritage, and so on, or by attempting to lay down a permanent relationship of dominance and dependence with respect to those categories for state societies as a whole.

THE REFORM OF GERMAN CITIZENSHIP LAW IN COMPARATIVE PERSPECTIVE

What follows from my discussion of models shaping citizenship with regard to the discourse about a reform of citizenship law in Germany? If one applies the model's distinctions to Germany from a comparative perspective (e.g., the United States), it becomes obvious that many of the difficulties in adapting the German citizenship regulations to the exigencies of increasing international migration and growing domestic heterogeneity result from Germany's option for the welfare state model.

According to internationally valid regulations for citizenship, individuals usually acquire upon birth the nationality of the territory on which they are born, since their parents hold this nationality and reside in this country. Individuals obtain full citizenship (encompassing all status dimensions) as soon as they attain legal age, that is, after having acquired all cognitive and evaluative patterns of communication and living that characterize the dominant culture in a given country. However, increasing transnational migration has meanwhile caused the domestic situation in Western countries to be characterized by an increasing heterogeneity of the resident population. The question arises, how will countries cope with this situation in the long run? Currently, individual states react differently to these developments by either restricting or expanding access to and by changing the regulations for incorporation and naturalization. In addition, political cultures have to be recognized as important factors that determine concepts of citizenship in single countries. Any assessment of present and future immigration policies has to recognize that the degree of exclusion/inclusion of new members depends not only on differing attitudes about demands of (labor) markets and a community's compensatory welfare responsibilities; it is also based on different concepts of what is meant by *demos* (people) and *natio* (nation), since it develops from a nation's and people's history as well as collective identities that have evolved historically.

Concepts range from pluricultural to monocultural. Pluriculturality is more likely if the composition of a population is polyethnic or plurinational, and if groups of comparable size and strength are involved in defining citizenship from the very beginning of a nation-state. Nation, in such cases, is not understood primarily as a population whose members have a similar ethnic background, that is, as a "nation by origin" according to contexts viewed as ethnic kinship relations. Rather, nation is understood primarily as a nation by will, which follows a common set of beliefs in certain basic political principles, serving to unite the people. Consequently, citizenship is based a priori on pluriculturality, and not on monoculturalism.[1] This, however, does not rule out the domination of one member group over another.

In the case of Germany, with its strong welfare state and communitarian orientation, the interpretation of being a "nation by origin" dominates citizenship discourses. Ordinary German citizens are generally not aware that the regulations to which they owe their citizenship could, in principle, take a form other than the familiar one.[2] However, the most important reason why citizenship regulations in Germany have become problematic has to do with the country's increasing diversity as a result of becoming an immigration society. According to Castles (1995), the response of a nation-state to immigration and ethnic diversity can take a variety of forms:

- total exclusion,
- differential exclusion,
- obligatory assimilation to a dominant culture, or
- a form of pluralism that interprets the dominant culture as one among several cultures, all of which possess the same right to be acknowledged.

Germany falls into the "differential exclusion" category, according to Castles, where later-arriving immigrants are excluded from collective solidarity and treated as minorities separate from the earlier established native-born population. Castles maintains that, to the extent that both the expanding diversity of the population and intensified transnational mobility have become permanent elements of social reality, current German citizenship and incorporation policies run the risk of engendering segregation, if not outright open antagonism between majority and minority populations. This would be exacerbated further if immigrants have the chance to become integrated to only a limited degree and into only certain sectors of society, but are otherwise kept isolated from the native-born population because of their different ethnocultural origins and status as temporary residents, and if foreigners have only restricted access to welfare benefits and political participation, that is the advantages of *status positivus* and *status activus*.

From this viewpoint the "communitarian welfare state" concept of citizenship and incorporation appears to risk even greater conflicts than the individualist "market and rights" orientation. Radical liberal individualism fails, on the other hand, by simply ignoring existing primary bonds and the individual's need for solidarity. The ethnonationalist version of communitarianism feeds conflict by treating foreigners and aliens with what Castles calls "total" or "differential exclusion." And even what Bauböck refers to as the "republican version of communitarianism," although concentrating on the association of individuals and groups by common consensus, may encourage conflict by pressing heterogeneous minorities into assimilation toward a dominant culture, which has not been accepted consensually.

What would be an appropriate response, considering these assumptions, with respect to Germany? Above all, current regulations for immigrant incorporation need to be rid of those last remnants of ethnonationalist elements that allow ethnic Germans from Eastern European countries to receive virtually automatic admittance into Germany as fully recognized citizens. This immigration procedure is distinctly biased in favor of so-called ethnic Germans from Eastern Europe as compared with non-Germans from non-EU countries, who are subject to a very different procedure before being permitted to become incorporated permanently, even if they have been living in Germany for many years.

With respect to immigration and naturalization, the German Basic Law grants privileged status to those citizens of former East bloc countries who can prove they are ethnic Germans. Annually, hundreds of thousands of people have taken advantage of this privilege since the dissolution of the Soviet system, and it is still used to the present day, although some procedural restrictions have been established in the last years. With regard to citizens of the Mediterranean countries, from which millions of guest-workers had been recruited via official invitation during the 1960s and early 1970s, and who have since settled in Germany in great numbers with their families, the German government has been falling back on the principle that Germany is not a country of immigration and does not wish to become one. This principle has been applied to an even greater extent with respect to the many hundreds of thousands of asylum-seekers and refugees who have come to Germany over the last few decades.

Consider the socialization of descendants of ethnic Germans who had settled in Eastern Europe and Russia after being recruited by Czarist invitation during the eighteenth century. Irrespective of the grievous fate suffered by many under the Soviet regime, it has to be acknowledged that ethnic German "resettlers" are often more "alien" to German society and culture than children of former guest-worker families, who often are very well adapted to a modern German lifestyle. A nationality law that allows such discretion is no longer convincing, nor is it justifiable.

I conclude, therefore, the need to introduce elements of *ius soli* in order to guarantee children of guest-worker families, who were born and raised in Germany, an indisputable legal claim to naturalization, even if the countries of their parents' citizenship continue to resist releasing the so-called second generation from their citizenship. Additionally, adjustments of the German nationality law should be based in policies that foster more liberal public attitudes and a new collective identification in Germany, since such a change is fundamental in legitimizing the polity and authority of the state. A reform should provide assurances that the declaration of one's belief in the principles of constitutional democracy takes unconditional priority over legal or even constitutional attention given to ethnocultural characteristics of the population. Naturalization of persons legally residing in Germany for a certain length of time should require, primarily, identification with the principles of constitutional democracy and a sufficient ability to communicate in the German language, instead of preceding and declared identification with German culture and customs.

Although, without doubt, some steps have been taken in this direction already, the following reforms are important in order to bring German citizenship laws and incorporation procedures closer to the pluralist model: Abolishing the immigration privileges of recent ethnic Germans (*Spätaussiedler*) and facilitating the naturalization of long-term resident guest-workers and their children. At the same time those requirements need to be eliminated that demand to "demonstrate a will to assimilate," which—in addition to the requirements of loyalty to Germany's democratic constitutional order—expects from immigrants an identification with the German national culture and customs at cost of the immigrants' resignation from their own culture. On the other hand, the often-heard arguments demanding general recognition of dual citizenship are not based on a precise, thorough criticism of existing regulations. The need for amendments as outlined here does not justify automatic acceptance of dual citizenship. On the contrary, the more extensive a country's efforts are to protect the cultural autonomy of minorities, the less is the need for expanding citizenship as a precaution against undue intervention into minority affairs. In fact, a country following the pluralist model may be less confronted with irredentist movements than countries following a non-pluralist model. The pluralist country can more legitimately object to demands for dual citizenship because such demands cannot be justified by exigencies of protecting the autonomy of heterogeneous cultures. But what alternatives to dual citizenship exist?

REFORM PRIORITIES AND DUAL CITIZENSHIP IN A EUROPEAN CONTEXT

Advocates of dual citizenship ultimately intend to establish equal rights between residents of the wealthier regions of the world and people who live in the poorer peripheries. Persons in the latter have good reasons to migrate, even if, in the end, most of them lack the means to move. Although legal recognition of dual citizenship might appear to be a good means of fostering equality, there are two main arguments against the institutionalization of dual citizenship for non-EU residents in EU countries: EU member states have agreed to require applicants to renounce their former citizenship as a prerequisite to becoming naturalized. A plurality of citizenship has been considered undesirable.[3] This argument, however, seems to be less important insofar as most of the concerned states enjoy stable, friendly relations with each other without danger of hostility and warfare. In addition, legal uncertainties stemming from double or multiple loyalties could be overcome by international agreements designed to avoid or compensate for cumulative obligations.

The main argument against a strategy of expanding dual citizenship, which deserves support, is that dual citizenship for non-EU citizens residing within the EU would not help to solve the problem of inequality and discrimination. It would not eliminate the causes of mass migration which only bring about the need to regulate admission and border protection. Also, dual citizenship does not create sufficient loyalty to adhere to existing republican citizenship requirements, and it underestimates the persisting difference between universal human rights and specific citizen rights. Finally, it fails to consider the interests of non-EU countries and the populations remaining in those countries.

The nation-state order established in the nineteenth century and in the inter-war period of the twentieth century has been more or less ethnonationalist in character and, in any case, has proven susceptible to chauvinism. However, neither now nor in the near future can one reasonably expect that a global order under the auspices of the United Nations will develop and replace the existing nation-state system. Given the present course of history, it remains a difficult path indeed to find consensus on procedures of conflict resolution and political decision making, that is, on those conditions that represent a common respect for a common judiciary which could constitute a worldwide confederation with a unified, central authority enjoying sovereign rule over a global territory inhabited by a universally pluricultural citizenry. War still remains a serious threat of being the last resort for conflict resolution. Reality has shown that war and civil war continue to be waged, despite the renunciation of war as political instrument by major world powers. Especially many younger nations and developing societies on all continents, including the European Union's own neighborhood, have proven susceptible to ethnonational conflicts.

State membership with full civil and political citizenship rights remains a serious matter as long as societies are organized as nation-states. Deliberations about the nature of citizenship have to recognize obligations of citizens toward the state they belong to that result from the state's monopoly to use legitimate force in and outside their territory—according to Max Weber's famous dictum. In exceptional cases individuals have to prove their loyalty and obligations by going to war and possibly paying with their health, property, and life. Such obligations do not exist for association among states preparing for a future (con)federation. However, the fact is that the governing power of the nation-states is obviously decreasing. This is demonstrated particularly in the fields of labor market as well as refugee movements and transnational migrations, the latter of which have increased immensely in size and pace over the last few decades. These phenomena have magnified tasks and problems of social integration, not least as a result of continued globalization of economic and social interdependence. In comparing Germany with the United States, many experts have, therefore, come to the conclusion that Germany should explicitly acknowledge its status as an immigration country instead of officially denying this reality. Observers also feel that Germany should change its policy regarding the incorporation of foreigners and resident aliens. This contribution intends to demonstrate that all these arguments suffer from a basic flaw, in that they refer to dimensions of political regulation that are narrower in scope than would be required by the practical social and economic problems they aim to solve. Instead, we need more detailed strategies, designed for a higher level of actors and action.

CONCLUSIONS

If it is true, first of all, that transnational migration is unavoidable and, at best, can be slowed down by political intervention and, second, that nation-states have a decreasing capacity to govern, then, basically, three political options exist:

1. Renewed attempts to reinforce the nation-state's powers of government. Most governments are tempted to choose this course, limited only by international public opinion. The United Arab Emirates, for example, rigorously controls all migratory movements.
2. Adaptation to globalizing market forces, acceptance of migratory movements as unavoidable, and support for the extension of human rights. This includes what Soysal (1994) and Jacobsen (1996) call the extension of "postnational membership" for de facto migrants, superseding traditional nation-state citizenship, and what Hollifield (1992, p. 220) means by the "confluence of markets and rights." But migration as a consequence of socioeconomic inequality is essentially linked with differences in welfare standards. Therefore, the strategy of equal inclusion of immigrants into the framework of rights and welfare benefits in the host country will inevitably cause conflicts of distribution. Thus, instead of reducing the risk of interethnic conflict, the "market and rights strategy" could unintentionally provoke particularist and xenophobic countermovements by the native population.
3. A loss of governing powers could also be responded to by developing higher and new levels of policy making in the context of international relations and politics. Governments and citizens could establish "large global regions," or post-nation-state political orders that encompass extended welfare state elements and elements of pluriculturality.

This third option, in comparison with the other two, appears to offer the best alternatives. The real test for each of the different incorporation schemes lies in the reestablishment of government capacities on a higher level: it is European integration that needs to continue and be extended, so that single nation-state incorporation, irrespective of their special modes, will gradually lose relevance. It is no coincidence that dual nation-state citizenship is of much less interest for citizens of EU member states than for non-EU citizens residing in an EU country. Citizens of EU member states already have postnational membership and freedom of movement and settlement throughout the EU, which the non-EU citizens would like to have as well. Citizens of non-EU countries need full incorporation into the host country's polity in order to be able to make full use of their *status activus* and *status positivus*. Citizens of EU member states have this status in all member states simply by being citizens of an EU member state. The status gap is between citizens of EU member states and citizens of non-EU member states; resident immigrant populations in EU countries are already well aware of this. The immigrants from specific non-EU countries, such as Turkey, the former Yugoslavia, the countries of northern Africa, as well as some East European nations are in a position to demand preferential treatment for recognition of dual citizenship. Their interests are becoming stronger the more they realize that full membership in an expanded European Union or even association status with future EU-membership will not happen in the foreseeable future. Under these conditions there seems to be no better, realistic solution than to take the "lesser path" of incorporation.

The "greater path" of incorporation means introducing procedures and starting a process which leads to the creation of associations of nation states that are incorporated in a subsequent phase as full members of an intergovernmental system of cooperation and institutionalized confederation, or even into a federal system encompassing a global region. At the end of this process, freedom of movement and settlement could be offered to all citizens of the member states. Increasing access to dual or plural citizenship is only recommended within the developing union of European member states. The precondition for pluriculturalism is, at the least, a confederate system of state societies that intends to become an extended political community and not merely acknowledge dual or plural citizenship of individuals under conditions where sovereign nation-states still maintain reservations about mutual recognition of each others' citizens.

The less ambitious form of incorporation, the so-called "lesser path," consists of the liberalization of regulations dealing with issues of citizenship and naturalization; the more ambitious form—the "greater path"—involves the creation and establishment of prerequisites for a common EU citizenship in the future. Bi- and multilateral interstate cooperation is necessary to serve the interests of those remaining outside the EU, that is, design and implementation of foreign aid policies and association status, even if this might seem far-fetched utopianism at present.

Since all nation-states are faced with problems of transnational migration, the only forward-looking policy would be one that integrates these states into a transnational and postnational framework, aiming, at the end of a gradual integration process, to grant general freedom of movement and common citizenship. With respect to both the more distant peripheries of the EU and the closer periphery of the EU associates, one of the most important goals must be to minimize undocumented migration by arranging bi- and multilateral "migration regimes" between the countries of emigration and immigration. "Regimes" in this context refers to internationally agreed-upon and contracted cooperation networks of coordinated policies of several nation-states regarding problems of mutual concern. The official controls of movements across the outer borders of the EU must be effective and efficient. The processes of broadening acceptance of ethnoculturally diverse immigrants must not come to a standstill or, worse yet, suffer a reversal. Acceptance of foreigners within the EU countries requires that EU expansion does not progress faster toward the south and the east than the common advantage of the member countries allows. "International migration regimes," however, are precursors to the association of out-migration countries with the union: Greece, Spain, and Portugal also had to satisfy prerequisites before being granted full membership in the EU, and before their citizens could enjoy freedom of movement and settlement.

NOTES

1. In the legal definition of nationality or citizenship, this understanding of the principles tends to stress elements of *ius soli* or at least bring with it increased tolerance with regard to plurinationality or parallel citizenship in more than one nation-state. This is illustrated by the Flemings and Walloons in Belgium, or Swiss-Germans, -French, -Italians, and -Rhaetians in Switzerland, or by the large immigration countries of Australia and North and South America. Under such conditions, the *demos*, that is, the populace of a nation-state, is from the beginning not identified with only one historically "first" and ethnocultural predominant group. Only the totality of all groups can claim to form the *natio*.

2. In Germany a tradition of pluricultural tolerance also existed from the late seventeenth to the nineteenth centuries in Prussia, when Huguenot immigrants from France, Bohemian Brethren, Dutch, Danes, and Poles were received with openness, if not welcomed outright (this includes, with some reservations, even Jews). This tradition, however, was eclipsed by horrid nationalist developments in the late nineteenth century and, finally, the ethnonationalist genocide of the twentieth century. This history had a strong impact on attitudes of postwar Germans toward their history and "inherited" collective responsibility. But one has to differentiate between the native "ethnic" Germans' responsibility toward the historical legacy of the Holocaust and that of new German citizens of Turkish descent. Would it be legitimate to expect a Turkish-German who acquires German citizenship today, to identify fully with the German community and its responsibility for past events and to participate in bearing the burdens and legal responsibilities stemming from Germany's national and international obligations to compensate for the crimes of the Nazi period?

3. Multiple citizenship, for single persons as well as families, has been criticized since the Hague Convention of 1930 ("Konvention über gewisse Fragen beim Konflikt von Staatsangehörigkeitsfragen vom 12. April 1930," The Hague, in Hecker 1970, pp. 15-20) and especially since the agreement of the Council of Europe in Strasbourg of May 6, 1963 ("Konvention zur Verminderung von Fällen mehrfacher Staatsangehörigkeit und betreffend Wehrpflicht bei mehrfacher Staatsangehörigkeit," *Law Gazette of the Federal Republic of Germany* (BGBL) 1969 II, pp. 1953). In view of the increasing numbers of dual citizenship, one must ask whether this would increase the number of conflict cases having negative consequences for individuals and authorities alike.

REFERENCES

Bauböck, R., ed. 1994. *From Aliens to Citizens: Redefining the Status of Immigrants in Europe.* Aldershot: Avebury.

Bauböck, R. 1995. "Nation, Migration und Staatsbürgerschaft." Pp. 325–348 in *Politische Theorien in der Ära der Transformation*, edited by K. von Beyme and C. Offe. Politische Vierteljahrsschrift Sonderheft 26/1995. Opladen: Westdeutscher Verlag.

Castles, S. 1995. "How Nation-states respond to Immigration and Ethnic Diversity." *New Community* 21 (3): 293-308.

Dworkin, R. 1981. "What is Equality? Part I: Equality of Welfare. Part 2: Equality of Ressources. In *Philosophy and Public Affairs* 3 and 4.

Fijalkowski, J. 1991. "Nationale Identität versus multikulturelle Gesellschaft—Entwicklungen der Problemlage und Alternativen der Orientierung in der politischen Kultur der Bundesrepublik in den 80er Jahren." Pp. 235-250 in *Die Bundesrepublik in den achtziger Jahren. Innenpolitik, Politische Kultur, Außenpolitik*, edited by W. Süß. Opladen: Leske+Budrich.

Hecker, H. 1970. *Mehrseitige völkerrechtliche Verträge zum Staatsangehörigkeitsrecht.* Frankfurt/Main and Berlin.

Hollifield, J. F. 1992. *Immigrants, Markets and States: The Political Economy of Postwar Europe.* Cambridge: Harvard University Press.

Jacobsen, D. 1996. *Rights across Borders: Immigration and the Decline of Citizenship.* Baltimore and London: Johns Hopkins University Press.

Jellinek, G. 1892. *System der subjektiven öffentlichen Rechte.* Freiburg: Mohr.

Marshall, T. H. 1949. "Citizenship and Social Class." reprinted in *Class, Citizenship, and Social Development*, edited by T. H. Marshall. New York: Doubleday.

Marshall, T. H. 1950/1965. *Class, Citizenship, and Social Development.* Cambridge: Cambridge University Press/Garden City, NY: Anchor Books.

Nozick, R. 1974. *Anarchy, State, and Utopia.* Oxford: Blackwell.

Rawls, J. 1971. *A Theory of Justice.* Cambridge, MA: Harvard University Press.

Soysal, Y. N. 1994. *Limits of Citizenship: Migrants and Postnational Membership in Europe.* Chicago: University of Chicago Press.

CONCLUDING REMARKS:
CHALLENGES OF IMMIGRATION
POLICY AND WELFARE REFORM IN
COMPARATIVE PERSPECTIVE

Hermann Kurthen, Jürgen Fijalkowski,
and Gert G. Wagner

In addition to Part A of this volume edited by Hermann Kurthen, Jürgen Fijalkowski, and Gert G. Wagner, titled *Immigrant Incorporation*, which deals with issues of education, labor markets, and welfare expenditures, the focus of Part B was on a comparative examination of German and U.S. citizenship policies and their significance for immigrant incorporation. We asked how does the market-oriented U.S. economy affect the character and degree of incorporation of large immigrant minorities in comparison with the welfare-oriented German market economy? And what citizenship policies are best suited to counteract both the social and political marginalization of immigrants and prevent ethnonational tensions? Now that these questions have been investigated, what answers can this part provide?

After WWII almost all industrialized Western countries experienced unprecedented mass immigration and large-scale refugee movements which changed their demographic compositions and ethnocultural maps. High levels of immigration have increased diversity and pluralism as well as productive interactions between the native born and immigrants. Processes of ethnic community formation have led to the establishment of economic, cultural, and political bridgeheads of immigrants in the host society. But mass migration has also contributed to tensions and triggered a debate about border controls, multicultural citizenship rights, and obligations. In addition, migration has led to the refinement or development of policies that deal with issues of immigrant incorporation into the legal system, labor markets, education, or public order. Budgetary restraints and the struggle for scarcer resources have more recently created a partially real, partially imagined competition between natives and immigrants. Hostile, anti-immigrant attitudes question the participation of newcomers in the social system of the host country resulting in the retrenchment of the welfare state. Demands for a limitation of immigration or even the return of immigrants have also gained ground. Ethnic polarization and socioeconomic inequality have put into question the capacity of government to control migration and immigrant incorporation.

Our German-American comparison indicates that although each country has its own historical and country-specific characteristics, concepts, attitudes, and policies determining the degree of immigrant inclusion or exclusion, we also can find striking similarities, for example, a rising demand for more border controls to protect the erosion of living standards and welfare entitlements, coupled with ethnocentrist exclusion, nativist fears, and anti-immigrant resentment. In other words, the United States and Germany are confronted with similar problems.

Both societies, of course, can also point to some success in their endeavors to mediate the effects of mass migration on both host society and newcomers. Governments have intervened through a multitude of direct or indirect policy instruments in education, labor markets, and communication to cope with tensions and adverse attitudes between immigrants and natives. Unions, ethnic businesses, local politics, religious and ethnic communities, neighborhood initiatives, and other networks are various institutions that represent and advance immigrant interests, avoid the development of persisting ethnic inequality and stratification, and help immigrants to become peacefully integrated into the host society. The question of the compatibility of immigration and the welfare state depends largely on the success or failure of these initiatives, institutions, and efforts. The issues addressed in Part B concern the question of how to regulate citizenship and naturalization, how to define the nature of national identity, and how to reform public welfare, education, and labor market access.

Contributions in both parts confirm that the *differentia specifica* of a political culture and the uncertainties of contemporary developments (such as the problems created by unresolved fiscal crises and global economic pressures) influence public and elite opinion, political priorities, and instruments of integration. Analyzing policy levels in the context of immigrant incorporation, *Schmitter-Heisler* rejects simplistic models. In her view the incorporation of immigrants and their descendants is neither a process of gradual, yet inevitable, assimilation, nor is it determined only by racist-discriminatory exclusion or segregation. Instead, policies remain more multidimensional and complex than these two idealtypical models (modeled after the U.S. and European experiences) presuppose. *Schmitter-Heisler* argues that one may learn much from Portes's matrix of immigrant incorporation which distinguishes the level of government policy toward different immigrant groups, the level of civic society and public opinion, and the characteristics of ethnic communities.

With the exception of ethnic German resettlers from Eastern Europe, the Federal Republic remains more restrictive and at the same time less formally regulated by admission quotas and waiting lists (e.g., for family unification) than the United States in its immigration and naturalization policy. This is irrespective of improvements in Germany's 1991 legislation, which facilitated more discretion and greater tolerance of dual and multiple citizenship, a concept that has been increasingly practiced by naturalization administrations, although it remains unpopular with the public. The United States, on the other hand, has become more restrictive in its admission and deportation policy with the 1996 "Illegal Immigration Reform and Immigrant Responsibility Act" and the "Anti-Terrorism and Effective Death Penalty Act." And it has become less hospitable in terms of welfare rights than Germany, although some of the harsher provisions of the original "Personal Responsibility and Work Opportunity Reconciliation Act" have been modified since then. The United States now places an additional premium on citizenship, which induced a significant increase in applications for naturalization after the so-called welfare reform was passed by Congress on August 22, 1996. Even resident "commuters" from neighboring countries, such as the Dominican Republic and Mexico, who originally intended not to apply, now bring in their relatives for naturalization to safeguard their welfare rights, because full-fledged citizenship in America is relatively easy to obtain and denizenship is less attractive. In contrast, privileges and rights (including voting rights) of permanent residents (denizens), and, in particular, EU-member-state citizens are more advanced in Germany, and, consequently, naturalization levels are comparatively low. That tendency is exacerbated by the more cumbersome process of acquiring citizenship in Germany despite recent improvements and the expected extension of *ius soli* and dual nationality rights to German-born offspring of immigrants. From a liberal point of view the German ethnocultural concept of citizenship or the requirement for national identification cards seems problematic. However, in comparison with the United States, it also has, so far, reduced incentives of undocumented migration because immigrant children are not automatically naturalized by birth, and because employers using illegal and underpaid labor are more easily tracked down.

Whereas an ethnically segmented pluralism prevails in the United States, a class-oriented corporatism dominates in Germany on the level of the societal reception of immigrants. In an ethnically segmented, pluralist society like the United States, access to strong ethnic communities clearly affords members of low-status ethnic groups social and economic advantages which are not available to those in societies with weak communities. The United States offers better opportunities for the establishment of strong ethnic communities because of the low level of state penetration in the areas of business and labor activities. In Germany laws have discouraged rather than encouraged associations of immigrants and citizens and, therefore, restricted the development of strong ethnic communities. In addition, the level of immigrant self-employment and entrepreneurship is lower in Germany too. German policymakers can learn from the United States that ethnic communities and their growth are not necessarily in conflict with the goal of an increasing interaction between majority and minority groups. In fact, immigrant self-associations may be a necessary condition for incorporating diverse ethnocultural groups into a multicultural society.

Another finding of Part B is the strong influence of historically generated, national, political cultures on immigrant and immigration policies. *Kvistad, Fijalkowski, Dittgen*, and *Schmitter-Heisler* demonstrate that deep-rooted ideological concepts about the purpose and meaning of citizenship and national identity help shape immigration and incorporation policy. In this regard *Parrillo* and *Dittgen* criticize with good reason the ideological myths of a cultural threat posed by heterogeneous immigration to the allegedly more or less "homogeneous" heritage, customs, and attitudes of a society. Strikingly, prior generations considered the very elements as "heterogeneous" that their descendants today regard as "homogeneous." This phenomenon can be explained by the complex and long-term process of ethnogenesis.

Fijalkowski demonstrates that if a society defines itself from an individual, formal, liberal and equal rights viewpoint this will have different consequences in comparison with a nation that refers to collective responsibilities on behalf of its individual members. The preferences given either to social welfare rights (*status positivus*) or to protection from state intervention (*status negativus*), and the direction in which political participation (*status activus*) is used to support either of these alternatives, is also relevant. Using the *"status activus"* to improve the *"status positivus"* may, consequently, lead to a policy of improved border controls interpreted by some as undue state intervention.

As mentioned earlier, maintenance of comprehensive welfare state coverage and, at the same time, preserving an open immigration policy remains not just a question of political priorities but is dependent to a large degree on "structural" economic, institutional, fiscal, and ideological constraints. From this perspective it is useful to ask how much the American, market-oriented and the German, corporatist welfare states are capable of effectively managing diversity and ethnocultural pluralism, reforming their laws and institutions, changing public attitudes and behavior, and practicing tolerance and understanding to avoid immigrants' marginalization and ethnic tension. Several papers in Part B point to the effects of cuts in social services on patterns of immigration and naturalization. Many immigrants to the United States, who initially only intended to stay for a short time to earn money rather than to seek permanent residency and naturalization, now file applications for naturalization to be eligible for continuing health and retirement benefits. In Germany we can observe similar patterns to secure denizen rights but on a much lower scale because, for most purposes, only residence status and not citizenship are crucial for defining the socioeconomic status of immigrants.

As other research has pointed out, the extension of social denizen rights paradoxically facilitates the (self) exclusion of migrants from the political community because it diminishes the incentive to naturalize. However, the lively debate in Germany and other European countries about immigrants' voting rights on the local and state levels disproves this view. Naturally, the extension of denizen political rights and the easing of naturalization neither guarantee the effective exercise of political rights, nor will it necessarily lead to dramatic changes in the real economic position of long-term residents, particularly by groups that are poorly endowed with organizational and financial resources. Central problems of social and cultural incorporation will remain at large, although more political rights could be a very useful instrument to counter present welfare retrenchments and anti-immigrant measures.

In the European case the issue of extending political rights is particularly complicated, because membership in the European Union offers individual, resident EU members basic social and political guarantees while it increases exclusive tendencies toward non-EU residents. In addition, naturalization retains a different significance in Europe than in the United States. Accession of a neighboring state into the European Union ensures freedom of movement and legal security for its citizens without sacrificing any national citizenship privileges. The United States seems to deal with this issue through a relatively liberal approach toward dual citizenship, whereas most European countries remain more restrictive in their naturalization of non-EU immigrants following agreements of Schengen and Dublin.

In the American case *Hollifield* and *Zuk* point at the strong impact of political constellations, the so-called market-rights coalition, on changes not only in immigrants' welfare rights (unless slowed by Supreme Court interventions on behalf of constitutional equal protection guarantees and due process rights) but also in the tenets of traditional U.S. immigration policy. In fact, advocates of exclusion have even begun to dilute the American legal principle of *ius soli*. At the same time, they have distracted attention from the issue of immigrant minorities' domestic exclusion, exploitation, and discrimination to issues of (ineffective) border control. By denying immigrants their constitutional equal protection guarantees and due process rights and making naturalization and welfare participation more cumbersome, these nativist forces embark on a course that supports de facto self-deportation of immigrants, particularly those from unwanted "third world" countries.

In a political system such as the United States where individuals and groups in vulnerable socioeconomic positions, with weak political ties, and a legal status that excludes them from the formal political decision-making process are easily controlled by special and powerful interest groups and elites who dominate mass opinion and policy making, an anti-immigration roll-back policy seems to be much more effective than in a corporatist environment, such as Germany, where denizens are more comprehensively protected from marginalization, and where unions, churches, self-associations, bureaucracies, and other institutions are firmly entrenched in policy negotiations that determine outcomes.

Parrillo more optimistically argues that in the end most immigrants have "always pulled their own weight" and overcome the common prejudice that mass immigration is responsible for the current fiscal crisis of public and welfare budgets. And although he points out that most economists agree that immigration helps rather than harms the growth of wealth in a host society, it is not self-evident that policy trends and public attitudes can easily be reversed in the short or mid term. Rather, policymakers (often against their own allegiances to the well-being of society as a whole) tend to simply mirror popular fears and resentment, particularly in times of crisis and extraordinary change. But it is clear from most contributions to this volume that a policy that is only defensively trying to keep immigrants out misses the point of integrating those who are already in the country and the global push-and-pull forces that lead inadvertently to immigration pressures in present Western economies.

Clark and *Schultz* illustrate the dialectical relationship between external border control policies and the degree of internal immigrant incorporation. Certainly, a minimum of effective border control remains crucial for keeping domestic spill-over effects of immigration at bay. In the same vein, *Espenshade* and *Huber* argue that extensive welfare state policies and an open immigration policy are not compatible if fiscal problems and allegations of welfare abuse cloud public perception. Governments, regardless of the party in power, will most likely react by limiting social services, excluding noncitizens, and restraining immigration, even in traditional immigrant societies and irrespective of the economists' assessments of positive impacts of immigration on growth, jobs, tax receipt, and so on. Therefore it is necessary to build not only national alliances and to politically empower denizen immigrants as *Hollifield* and *Zuk*, *Demleitner*, and *Kvistad* suggest, but also to develop an international covenant on migration or even an international migration regime, as some experts have already suggested.

Putting the issues into a longer historical perspective, *Fijalkowski* differentiates between what he calls the "smaller" nation-state level and the transcending "larger" supra-national-level incorporation policy. In the latter case citizenship rights become more than just arbitrary privileges granted by single nations; rather, they become a tool for creating a system of interstate confederations based on the freedom of movement of all member-state citizens and potentially of all denizens, as in the case of the European Union.

What effects have the present crisis in public finance and related welfare "reform" attempts in the United States and Germany had on the relationship between host society and immigrant minorities, and how has it affected actual migration processes? *Parrillo* asserts that recent attempts to cut back social services in the United States effectively changed a long-standing American tradition to welcome newcomers regardless of their prior economic and occupational status, age, health, and other criteria. In Germany the recent liberalization of naturalization, in contrast, has effectively questioned the dominant ideology that Germany is not an immigration society.

Ongoing attempts at European integration offer the possibility to solve some of the normatively unpalatable dichotomies between the desire to maintain the welfare state and at the same time to retain an open immigration policy. The German experience illustrates that the capacity of single nation-states (in the European context, even large ones like Germany) to deal appropriately with the problems at hand is too narrow. On the other hand, the American case reveals that problems associated with continuing mass immigration and increasing diversity need to be dealt with by long-term strategies, not short-term policies that mirror public resentment. To be sure, problems may neither be solved comprehensively, conclusively, and satisfactorily at any given moment, nor may only one feasible policy option exist. Some tensions and contradictions cannot be solved at all, since they are of such a nature that only a succession of generations can hope to work at them. Immigration and incorporation are issues that are never definitely solved but, instead, require permanent effort.

ABOUT THE CONTRIBUTORS

Nora V. Demleitner was born in Schwabach, Bavaria, Germany, where she received her *Abitur*. She graduated *summa cum laude* from Bates College (Lewiston, ME) and received her J.D. from Yale Law School in 1992, where she served on the board of the *Yale Law Journal*. After clerking for the Honorable Samuel A. Alito, Jr., of the U.S. Court of Appeals for the Third Circuit, she was awarded an LL.M. degree in international and comparative law, with distinction, from the Georgetown University Law Center. Currently, she is an associate professor of law at St. Mary's University in San Antonio, TX. She publishes and teaches in the areas of immigration law, comparative law, criminal law, and gender issues, with a focus on the United States and Europe. Demleitner is the recipient of a Max Planck research fellowship. She is also one of the editors of and a frequent contributor to the *Federal Sentencing Reporter*. Her articles are included in *Georgetown Immigration Law Journal*, *Federal Sentencing Reporter*, and the *Fordham International Law Journal*. Demleitner also has authored a chapter in a forthcoming three-volume series on women's international human rights. In addition, she recently gave presentations at the Free University of Berlin, the University of Utah, the University of Michigan, and the University of Colorado.

Herbert Dittgen was born in Dinslaken (North Rhine-Westphalia). He studied political science, philosophy, German literature, and economics at the Albert-Ludwigs-Universität Freiburg and at Georgetown University. In 1988 he received his Ph.D. at the University of Freiburg, where he also taught as an assistant professor. In 1997, he held a Heisenberg-Fellowship and was a senior associate member at St. Antony's College in Oxford. Prior to that he was a visiting scholar at the Center for U.S.-Mexican Studies, University of California, San Diego and at the Center for International Affairs, Harvard University, an assistant professor at the Center for European and North American Studies at the University of Göttingen, as well as a guest scholar at the Brookings Institution and

the Carnegie Endowment for International Peace. He co-edited (with
Michael Minkenberg) *The American Impasse: U.S. Domestic and Foreign Policy after the Cold War* (University of Pittsburgh Press 1996) and authored
Politik zwischen Freiheit und Despotismus: Alexis de Tocqueville und Karl Marx
(Alber Verlag 1986), *Deutsch-amerikanische Sicherheitsbeziehungen in der Ära
Helmut Schmidt* (Munich: Fink Verlag 1991) and *Amerikanische Demokratie
und Weltpolitik: Außenpolitik in den Vereinigten Staaten* (Schöningh Verlag
1998). He has published numerous chapters and articles on German
and U.S. foreign policy and on migration issues, most recently, in *Stanford Humanities Review*.

Thomas J. Espenshade is professor of sociology and faculty associate at
the Office of Population Research, Princeton University. He was born in
Harrisburg, PA and received degrees from The College of Wooster (economics, B.A., 1965), Yale University (mathematics, M.A.T., 1966), and
Princeton University (economics, Ph.D., 1972). Prior to joining the Princeton faculty in 1988, Espenshade held teaching and research positions
at the University of California (Berkeley), Bowdoin College, Florida
State University, The Urban Institute, and Brown University. Espenshade's research interests center on contemporary immigration to the
United States and include such topics as public opinion toward immigrants, the fiscal impacts of immigration, and models of undocumented
migration to the United States. Among his recent publications are *Keys to
Successful Immigration: Implications of the New Jersey Experience* (The Urban
Institute Press 1997); *A Stone's Throw from Ellis Island: Economic Implications of Immigration to New Jersey* (University Press of America 1994); *The
Fourth Wave: California's Newest Immigrants* (with T. Muller, The Urban
Institute Press 1985); and appear in *Social Science Quarterly*; *American
Sociological Review*; *International Migration Review*; and *Population Research
and Policy Review*.

Jürgen Fijalkowski was born in 1928 in Berlin and received his Ph.D. in
1958 at the Freie Universität Berlin (FUB). From 1959 to 1970 he was
instructor of a research training program, then he chaired a section of
the Freie Universität Berlin Research Institute of Political Science. After
completing his Habilitation in 1970, Fijalkowski was professor of political education and political science at the Berlin Pädagogische Hochschule. In 1976 he became full professor of political science and political
sociology at Freie Universität Berlin until his retirement in 1992. In
1986 Fijalkowski founded and, since then, directed the Freie Universität
Research Institute on Labor Migration, Refugee Movements, and Minority Policy. Between 1979 and 1983 he chaired the FUB political science
department, held various professional positions, and received several

research grants. Among his recent book publications in the field of transnational migrations and minority policies are *Transnationale Migranten in der Arbeitswelt* (Edition Sigma 1989), *Ethnicity, Structured Inequality, and the State in Canada and the Federal Republic of Germany* (Lang 1991), and *Ausländervereine—ein Forschungsbericht* (Hitit Verlag 1997). Recent articles, among others, are found in *Die Bundesrepublik in den achtziger Jahren* (Leske & Budrich 1991), *International Migration Review,* and *Revue Européenne des Migrations Internationales.*

James F. Hollifield is professor of political science, Ora Nixon Arnold Fellow of international political economy, and director of international studies at Southern Methodist University. In addition to SMU, he has held faculty appointments at Auburn, Brandeis, and Duke universities. In 1993 he was a research fellow at the Center for U.S.-Mexican Studies of the University of California at San Diego. In 1992 he was associate director of research at the CNRS and the Centre d'Etudes et de Recherches Internationales of the FNSP in Paris. From 1986 to 1992 he was a research associate at Harvard University's Minda de Gunzburg Center for European Studies and co-chair of the French study group, and in 1991-1992 he was an associate at Harvard's Center for International Affairs. He has worked as a consultant for the U.S. government, as well as several international organizations, including the United Nations. Hollifield has been the recipient of grants from private foundations and government agencies, including the Social Science Research Council, the Sloan Foundation, and the National Science Foundation. He has written numerous articles and books, including *Immigrants, Markets, and States* (Harvard UP 1992) and *Controlling Immigration* (Stanford UP 1994). He just completed his fifth book, entitled *Immigration et l'État-Nation* (Immigration and the Nation-State), to be published in 1997 by Hachette. His most recent work looks at the rapidly evolving relationship between trade, migration, and the nation-state. His teaching interests lie primarily in the areas of international and comparative political economy.

Gregory A. Huber is a Ph.D. candidate in the department of politics, Princeton University. He was born in Evanston, IL, and received degrees from Emory University (political science, B.A. and M.A., 1995). Huber's research interests include public opinion about questions of immigration policy, research methods and design, and the behavior of bureaucratic agencies.

Hermann Kurthen was born in Stuttgart (Baden-Württemberg) and acquired two M.A.s in sociology and political economy and a B.A. in political science at the Freie Universität Berlin before he received his

Ph.D. (1984) in social science and became a researcher at the Berlin For-
schungsstelle Arbeitsmigration, Flüchtlingsbewegungen und Minder-
heitenpolitik (Research Center for Labor Migration, Refugee Movements, and Minority Politics). Kurthen has taught and conducted
research in Berlin, Canada, and the United States. He has been awarded
grants from the German National Science Foundation (Deutsche Fors-
chungsgemeinschaft) and the German Marshall Fund of the United
States. From 1991 to 1993 he held a DAAD (German Academic
Exchange Service) lectureship as associate professor of German studies
at the University of North Carolina at Chapel Hill and is currently a visiting assistant professor in Sociology at the State University of New York,
Stony Brook. His teaching and research interests are in the field of
minority politics and multiculturalism, ethnic relations and stratification,
and labor immigration and anti-discrimination. He has co-authored,
among other works, *Antisemitism and Xenophobia in Germany after Unification* (Oxford University Press 1997), *Ausländerbeschäftigung in der Krise?
Die Beschäftigungschancen und -risiken Ausländischer Arbeitnehmer am Beispiel
der West Berliner Industrie* (Sigma 1989), and published his doctoral thesis, *Politische Ökonomie und Persönlichkeitstheorie: Aneignung und Individual-
ität in der bürgerlichen Gesellschaft* (Pahl Rugenstein 1985). Recent articles
and book chapters are included in *Comparative Perspectives on Interethnic
Relations and Social Incorporation in Europe and North America, New Community, International Migration Review, Amerikastudien/American Studies,* and
Nations and Nationalism.

Gregg O. Kvistad is an associate professor and the chair of the department of political science at the University of Denver. He received his
Ph.D. at the University of California, Berkeley, in 1984, taught at Welles-
ley College, and did postdoctoral work at the Freie Universität Berlin.
He has received research grants from the Fulbright Commission, the
Social Science Research Council, and the German Academic Exchange
Service (DAAD). His research interests mainly concern the politics of
membership in German society, broadly conceived. Recent publications
are included in *German Politics, West European Politics,* and *The Invention of
Identity and the Practice of Intolerance: Nationalism, Racism, and Xenophobia
in Germany and the United States.*

Vincent N. Parrillo was born in Paterson, NJ. A graduate of Seton Hall
University with a major in business management, he earned his M.A. in
English at Montclair State University and his Ph.D. in sociology at Rutgers University. After a brief career in business and four years of high
school teaching, he joined William Paterson College of New Jersey,
where he first served in a variety of administrative positions, including

assistant dean of graduate programs and twice as acting dean. He is now professor of sociology and department chairperson. His teaching and research interests are in the field of immigration, multiculturalism, race, and ethnic relations. He has written numerous articles on these subjects, many of them appearing in one of eight different languages, including *Comparativ* (1994). Among his books are *Cities and Urban Life* (with John Macionis, Prentice-Hall, forthcoming), *Strangers to These Shores* (Allyn and Bacon 1997), *Diversity in America* (Pine Forge Press 1996), *Contemporary Social Problems* (with John and Ardyth Stimson, Allyn and Bacon 1996), and *Rethinking Today's Minorities* (Greenwood Press 1991). He served as editor and contributor to a special issue of *Sociological Forum* on multiculturalism (December 1994) and has just completed a historical novel, *Guardians of the Gate*. He is also the writer, executive producer, and narrator of two award-winning PBS television documentaries, *Ellis Island: Gateway to America* (1991), and *Smokestacks and Steeples: A Portrait of Paterson* (1992). Named Outstanding Educator of America (1975) and listed in the *International Who's Who in Education* (Cambridge 1986), he has been a keynote speaker at two international conferences (Liege, 1996, and Pulawy, Poland, 1994) and lectured at dozens of universities in Canada and Europe. He has also appeared on dozens of Canadian and U.S. radio and television talk shows.

Barbara Schmitter-Heisler was born in Heidelberg, Germany. She received a master's degree (1976) and a Ph.D. (1979) in sociology from the University of Chicago. Her dissertation, *Immigration and Citizenship in Germany and Switzerland*, was supported by a Social Science Research Council Dissertation Research Fellowship in Western Europe. From 1979 to 1980 she was a postdoctoral fellow in comparative studies in immigration and ethnicity at Duke University. In 1990 she was awarded a research fellowship from the German Marshall Fund of the United States to do comparative research on poverty and social exclusion in the United Kingdom, Germany and the Netherlands. She has taught at SUNY-Buffalo, Cleveland State University, and is currently professor of sociology in the department of sociology and anthropology at Gettysburg College in Gettysburg, PA. Her research interests have centered on the processes of social inclusion and exclusion in advanced industrial societies, and in particular, on the intersection of race/ethnicity and class in structuring these processes. She has published numerous articles on immigration, citizenship, and poverty in a comparative context. Among her recent publications are in: *Theory and Society, Journal of Urban Affairs,* and *Journal of European Public Policy*. Professor Schmitter-Heisler is one of the recipients of the Inaugural Berlin Prize of the American Academy in

Berlin for 1998-1999. She will do research on local government responses to immigration in Germany.

Gert G. Wagner was born in 1953 in Kelsterbach am Main (West Germany). He is professor of economics at Viadrina European University, Frankfurt (Oder). He studied economics, and sociology at University of Frankfurt(Main), where he aquired an MA in economics (Diplom-Volkswirt) in 1978. He received his Ph.D. (Dr. rer. oec., 1984) and his post-doctoral degree (Habilitation 1992) in Economics at the Technical University Berlin. Wagner was teaching assistant and researcher (Technische Universität Berlin) and senior researcher at different institutes in Frankfurt, Mannheim and Berlin. Since July 1989 he has been director of the German Socio-Economic Panel Study (GSOEP) at the German Institute for Economic Research (DIW) in Berlin. From 1992 to 1997 he was also full professor of public administration at the Ruhr-University of Bochum (West Germany). Wagner was visiting scholar at the Carolina Population Center of the University of North Carolina at Chapel Hill in 1993, and visiting professorship at the department of economics at Syracuse University in 1995. Since 1997 he has been research associate at the Centre for Economic Policy Research (CEPR), London. From 1995 to 1998 he served as an expert on the study commission, "Demographic Aging," of the German Parliament (*Enquete Kommission "Demographischer Wandel" des Deutschen Bundestages*). Wagner's research interests are in the fields of population economics, labor economics, and social policy analysis. Recent journal articles and contributions to readers are included in *Economic Bulletin, Journal of Conflict, Journal of Comparative Economics, Population and Development Review, Industrial and Labor Relations Review*, and *Journal of European Social Policy*. His most recent book is *Income Inequality and Poverty in Eastern and Western Europe* (Physica 1996, edited with N. Ott).

Gary Zuk is a professor of political science at Auburn University, AL. He received a master's degree (1980) and Ph.D. (1983) in political science at Florida State University. He joined the Auburn University faculty in 1988. Before that Professor Zuk was an instructor and, later, assistant professor at Virginia Tech University in Blacksburg, VA. He is currently developing a database on the federal district courts which will include tracking numbers for every judge along with personal and career information on each one. The project is funded by the National Science Foundation and it complements the recently completed and archived federal appellate court database that Professor Zuk and his colleagues constructed under a series of NSF contracts. Professor Zuk's research interests include the political economy of immigration policy in the

United States and Germany, the dynamics of minority appointments to the U.S. federal courts, and the institutional evolution of these courts. He has published numerous articles on these and other subjects in a wide variety of scholarly journals, including the *American Political Science Review*, the *American Journal of Political Science*, and the *Journal of Politics and Comparative Politics*. His most recent book, *The Federal Judiciary and Institutional Change*, was published by the University of Michigan Press in 1996.

INDEX